BLACKENING CANADA

Diaspora, Race, Multiculturalism

Focusing on the work of black, diasporic writers in Canada, particularly Dionne Brand, Austin Clarke, and Tessa McWatt, *Blackening Canada* investigates the manner in which literature can transform conceptions of nation and diaspora. Through a consideration of literary representation, public discourse, and the language of political protest, Paul Barrett argues that Canadian multiculturalism uniquely enables black diasporic writers to transform national literature and identity. These writers seize upon the ambiguities and tensions within Canadian discourses of nation to rewrite the nation from their own perspective, transforming a sense of exclusion into the impetus for their creative endeavours.

Within this context, Barrett suggests, debates over who counts as Canadian, the limits of tolerance, and the breaking points of Canadian multiculturalism serve not as signs of multiculturalism's failure but as proof of its vitality and of the unique challenges that black writing in Canada poses to politics and the nation itself.

PAUL BARRETT is a Banting postdoctoral fellow in the Department of English and Cultural Studies at McMaster University.

Blackening Canada

Diaspora, Race, Multiculturalism

PAUL BARRETT

UNIVERSITY OF TORONTO PRESS
Toronto Buffalo London

Toronto Buffalo London
www.utppublishing.com

ISBN 978-1-4426-4770-1 (cloth)
ISBN 978-1-4426-1576-2 (paper)

Library and Archives Canada Cataloguing in Publication

Barrett, Paul, 1979–, author
Blackening Canada : diaspora, race, multiculturalism / Paul Barrett.

Includes bibliographical references and index.
ISBN 978-1-4426-4770-1 (bound). ISBN 978-1-4426-1576-2 (pbk.)

1. Canadian literature – Black Canadian authors – History and criticism. 2. African diaspora in literature. 3. Race in literature. 4. Multiculturalism in literature. I. Title.

PS8089.5.B5B38 2015 C810.9'896071 C2015-900525-6

University of Toronto Press acknowledges the financial assistance to its publishing program of the Canada Council for the Arts and the Ontario Arts Council, an agency of the Government of Ontario.

Canada Council for the Arts Conseil des Arts du Canada

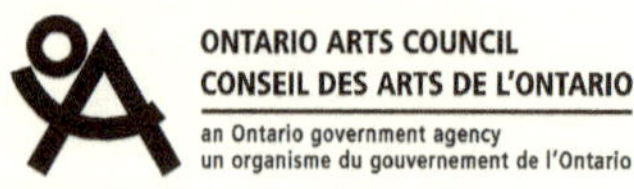

This book has been published with the help of a grant from the Canadian Federation for the Humanities and Social Sciences, through the Awards to Scholarly Publications Program, using funds provided by the Social Sciences and Humanities Research Council of Canada.

University of Toronto Press acknowledges the financial support of the Government of Canada through the Canada Book Fund for its publishing activities.

Table of Contents

Acknowledgments

I would like to acknowledge the support of the Social Sciences and Humanities Research Council in funding this project. Thanks to Katherine McKittrick for her diligent reading and criticism of this project. Thanks also to Neil ten Kortenaar for his past and continued support. Thank you to Daniel Coleman for his support and encouragement of my work. Siobhan McMenemy deserves particular thanks as she valiantly and patiently helped me develop this book and never once lost patience with this slow writer. Thank you also to my friends and colleagues in the Engineering Communication Program at the University of Toronto. My experience there has taught me the value of clear and effective writing and has left an indelible mark on this project.

I would also like to acknowledge the help of my friends and family. They have given me the necessary support, comfort, distraction, and encouragement to see me through this project. Special thanks to Asha Varadharajan for her support, friendship, encouragement, and pragmatic optimism – she never lost hope when this work was at its most baggy and monstrous! Particular thanks to Guybrush Taylor whose design work helped make this book what it is but whose real contribution comes from letting me regularly draw on his wit, intelligence, and creativity. To everyone in Heart Lake, Brampton, Toronto, Kingston, Newcastle, and lots of other places, you have all helped me in various capacities – thank you! Special thanks to Aimée, Alexis, Allan, Andrew P, Andrew S, Anne-Marie, Breanne, Brooke, Drew, Emmy, Eric, Grace, Jem, Martin, Matt, Nyron, Peter, Ryan, and Tim. I have debated parts of this book with you all at various bars, cottages, logs, forests, hockey games, trivia nights, and magic games. I often check the strength of my arguments and my logic by proposing my ideas, in their most extreme form, to one of you (after a few drinks, ideally). I couldn't ask for a better intellectual forum and better friends. Your friendship and sharp intellects are invaluable and your insights echo in my head as I write. Similarly, my family – Barretts, Dinsdales, and Keenans – in Canada and overseas have been a huge source of support for me before and throughout this project. Thanks to Tony, Rosemary, Patrick, Kathleen, Michael, Francis, and Tina for their interest in my work and keen questions and ideas that have found their way into this project. Special thanks to my Mom, Lynda, Dad, Gavin, Kirsten, Jason, Emily, and Kaitlyn for their endless love and support. There is no doubt that this work had its genesis in the discussion, debate and laughter around our family dinner table, so thank you for everything. Thank you also for the experience of moving from one culture to another, for the pleasure and difficulty of living between cultures, and for the opportunity to know the feeling of critical multiculturalism before I knew what to call it. Particular thanks to Joan Dinsdale whose spirit of compassion, decency, and critical thinking helped me write this book.

Finally, thanks to Susan for all her love and support throughout this entire process. I couldn't have asked for a better friend, troublemaker, interlocutor, and life partner, and I definitely could not have persevered without your continuous support and friendship. You helped me when I asked for it and pushed when I needed it. You have challenged, prompted, and questioned the arguments in the book during our long walks and conversations. Your combination of critical analysis and charitable optimism has proven an excellent model for me to follow in writing this book. Thanks, Susan. Finally, thank you to young Patrick who has brought so much joy and happiness into our lives. I look forward to all of our adventures together and I dedicate this book to Susan and Patrick.

Permissions

BLACKENING CANADA

Diaspora, Race, Multiculturalism

Texts and Contexts of Blackening

The 1960s marked the flowering, formalization, institutionalization, and perhaps invention, of both Canadian literature and Canadian multiculturalism. Northrop Frye's conclusion to Carl F. Klinck's *Literary History of Canada* (1965) accompanied the emergence of the New Canadian Library as two critical enterprises that attempted to survey the terrain of a Canadian literary canon. Meanwhile, Trudeau's 1963 Royal Commission on Biculturalism and Bilingualism undertook to understand Confederation as a partnership between Anglophone and Francophone communities. Of course Trudeau's commissioners, like critics working in the emergent field of Canadian literature, soon established that the old language and staid national taxonomies would not suffice. It is out of this failure of biculturalism to adequately describe the nation that the concept and language of Canadian multiculturalism emerged. Similarly, the failure of Frye's conclusion to settle the question of the existence – let alone the defining features – of a Canadian canon has provoked decades of querying, challenging, and persistent reimagining of the Canadian canon. Or, at least, that is one story.

Another story is that Canadian multiculturalism was cynically adopted by a waning Liberal Party to disenfranchise French-Canadians and capitalize on Canada's shifting demographics for electoral gain. Another is that it is a tale Canadians tell themselves, providing an inverted image of a largely segregated and racist society. Another is that Canadian multiculturalism is an inspired form of public policy and cultural practice, cutting the Gordian knot of an outdated nationalism that binds citizenship, ethnicity, and race. Yet another is that it is mere window dressing designed to make the erosion of the nation in the face of globalization and American hegemony more palatable. The point, and the argument made throughout this book, is that Canadian multiculturalism is about the stories Canadians tell themselves about their nation, and this language of Canadian multiculturalism sets out the imaginative terrain from which Canadians narrate their nation from both the centre and the margin.

The editors of the *Globe & Mail* appreciate this connection between multiculturalism, narrative, and language. As part of their official relaunch, complete with a new post-national slogan, "Time to Lead," and post-attention-span layout, the *Globe* began a special series on multiculturalism with an editorial entitled "Strike multiculturalism from the national vocabulary" (8 Oct 2010). The editorial argues that "The tired, flawed debate over the benefits of multiculturalism ... has been on a continuous loop since the 1970s," and that "the debate has become more fraught, while the terminology has ceased to have any real meaning." Rather than see this terminological failure as grounds for reinvigorating the language of multiculturalism, the *Globe* insists that "Multiculturalism should be struck from the national vocabulary." The editorial attempts to put to rest not just the "tired, flawed debate," but the very language of multiculturalism itself. Is this "multicultural fatigue" (Kamboureli, *Scandalous* 83) just the latest national narrative, or does it indicate the final throes of the so-called multiculturalism debate? In the new post-national and trans-national Canada, are these questions of race and multiculturalism merely tired holdovers of the 1970s and of little interest to Canadians?

The *Globe*'s paradoxical argument – repeatedly invoking the very language of multiculturalism it calls upon Canadians to forget – indicates the contradictions that continue to torment Canadian public discourse. Questions of race, the rights and responsibilities of immigrants, and the shifting nature of citizenship, all vaguely lumped together under the term "multiculturalism," remain vital concerns in contemporary Canada. Indeed, if multiculturalism is such a tired and exhausted concept, how does one explain the *Globe*'s contradictory, almost pathological, fascination with resurrecting the multiculturalism debate only to insist that it be laid to rest?[1] Contrary to the paper's assertion, questions of race and multiculturalism continue to haunt Canadian conscience and public consciousness. Public discourse thrives on the contradictory notions that Canadian multiculturalism is a sign of national vitality and progressiveness as well as national weakness and cultural formlessness; a vulnerability that bespeaks the fiction at the heart of the nation.

Thus, the effort to simultaneously erase and trumpet Canadian multiculturalism enacts a form of national forgetting that champions the symbolic value of the policy while jettisoning its history, ignoring its effect, and silencing further debate over its meaning. While the contours and crises of the debate may have shifted, Canadian public discourse is characterized by this chronic ambivalence over the language and meaning of multiculturalism.

I contend that the fraught nature of the debate on multiculturalism is precisely what renders it meaningful and demands that it be revisited with ever more at stake in its rearticulation. This book focuses exclusively on black diasporic writing in Canada in order to differentiate between race and ethnicity in Canada and to insist on the significance of diasporic histories in the formation of multicultural identities. For whom is multiculturalism bereft of meaning and from whose perspective does it become the means to erode rather than inflect and enrich national unity? For the black writers whose provocative and sobering corpus I examine, citizenship and community have been tenuous accomplishments at best, and unfulfilled aspirations at worst, often resulting in a hyphenated and interstitial relationship with Canada. The popular fatigue that the *Globe* expresses is often shared by the writers in this study, but with completely different connotations and implications. Their ambivalence is born of struggle and alienation, of desire and hope, in a national landscape corroded by systemic racism and deprivation. The writers who inhabit this study lay claim to the space of the multicultural nation in a bid to unsettle the Canadian imaginary that excludes them.

An exemplary moment of this ambivalence occurs in Tessa McWatt's *Out of My Skin* (1998), when the protagonist Daphne meets her biological Aunt Sheila for the first time. Sheila wonders how Daphne responds when people ask her,

> what was your hyphenation? I have a friend, a lady from home – she makes me laugh. She says, "In dis country it's important to have the propa' hyphenation." Funny, makes it sound like havin the propa' papers, but it's just what you call yourself when someone asks you where you're from. "Where are you from?" "I'm a Canadian." "No, I mean where you *from*?" "I've heard that so many times in thirty years. Now you know your hyphenation. West-Indian Canadian. What did you used to say?" … "Nothing. I'd say nothing …" (81; italics in original)

For Daphne and Sheila, the insistence in the question, "where you *from*," reveals the trap of multicultural hyphenation that marks black Canadians as belonging elsewhere. A subtle act of exclusion emerges in the repetition in and shifting emphasis between the questions, "Where are you from" to "I mean where you *from*." This barely detectable meaning indicates the virtually invisible means through which the exclusion of black people in Canada operates.

Sheila's reflection contains echoes of the first policy statement of the Canadian Multiculturalism Act (1985): the state shall "recognize and promote the understanding that multiculturalism reflects the cultural and racial diversity of Canadian society and acknowledges the freedom of all members of Canadian society to preserve, enhance and share their cultural heritage" (Preamble 1988 n. pag.). The real world effects of this policy to "recognize and promote ... cultural and racial diversity" are seen in the question "where you *from*." Yet, where the Act positions the multicultural subject as the acting, speaking subject ("freedom... preserve, enhance, and share"), the question "where you *from*" transforms Daphne and Sheila into passive respondents to an invisible interlocutor. Both Sheila's interrogator and the recognizing agent of the Multiculturalism Act are unmarked and invisible, just as whiteness and racism in Canada are equally unmarked and invisible. Furthermore, in Sheila's narration of this interpellation, the acts of recognition and hyphenation do not safeguard the "freedom of all members of Canadian society to preserve ... their cultural heritage," but rather consign black Canadians to an elsewhere beyond the nation's confines. Where the language of the act slides easily between "cultural and racial diversity," the question posed to Sheila communicates, with subtle efficacy, that race matters. This question forces Sheila to accept a hyphenated identity, rendering her membership in the diaspora involuntary; she is seen as somatically black, always diasporic, and only provisionally here.

Yet *Out of My Skin* does not merely rebuke Canadian racism but offers dual narrative responses to the forced hyphenation that bespeaks ambivalence towards Canadian multiculturalism. Sheila is resolved to answer these questions of race and nationality, later laughing about it with her friend. Daphne's utterance, "Nothing," reveals her discomfort with this interrogation and with being forced to occupy the space of the hyphen. Furthermore, Daphne's terse reply suggests that despite Sheila's willingness to express her hyphenated identity, the process of hyphenation has rendered them both "Nothing." Daphne's statement and the silence signified by the ellipses illustrate how the logic of the hyphen paradoxically recognizes, identifies, excludes, and silences black people in Canada. Sheila's laughter and Daphne's silence function as two distinct responses to this forced hyphenation while also showing the continuity between them. Their responses turn the impossible question of "where you *from*?" back on itself and the questioner. The ambivalence here reflects both the pain of this exclusion and the resilience inherent in Sheila's treatment of hyphenation as something to be dismissed and laughed about.

Out of My Skin's representation of the dual responses to this forced hyphenation is typical of the works in this study. These texts depict both the exclusionary and racist practices of the Canadian state, alongside the strategies for coping and surviving practised by black people in Canada. Similarly, Sheila's use of storytelling to transform a painful moment into something she can laugh about is typical of each author's use of narrative as a means of survival. Acts of narration, unlike public discourse, make it possible to navigate the contradictions of hyphenation and the doubled response of dismissal and resistance it produces, without making such ambivalence the mark of fatigue and futility. Black diasporic writing communicates not only the texture and affective experience of the ambivalences of alienation and assimilation, but turns ambivalence towards nation and belonging into a structural principle of narrative form.

Idora, in Austin Clarke's *More* (2008), offers her own take on Daphne's and Sheila's predicament when she recounts an encounter with a cheerful white woman riding the subway:

> "You don't talk like a Negro-Canadian!" the woman said, in a pleasant voice. "But where're you from before that?"
>
> "I like the cold!" Idora told her. "I was born here."
>
> "I know," the woman said, in a pleasant voice. "But where're you really from, before that?"
>
> "I was born here."
>
> The woman smiled. After a while the smile disappeared (154).

The hyphen constructs Canadian identity as an opposition between "Negro" and "Canadian," making it impossible for Idora to identify as both. Clarke reveals how the insistent repetition of the question "where're you from" makes it an act of disavowal rather than of exclusionary identification. Idora's account makes this question the woman's problem rather than hers even while the woman's "pleasant voice" reveals how the "cold" mechanisms of racism operate subtly, invisibly, and persistently in Canada. Idora offers an insistence of her own, claiming falsely that she was born in Canada, thus disrupting the forced hyphenation and challenging her interrogator. The white woman's identification of Idora as "Negro-Canadian" reveals how Idora's blackness trumps and undermines any possible claims to citizenship, but the eventual disappearance of her smile suggests that Idora has succeeded in penetrating her mask of pleasantness and made her occupy Daphne's erstwhile position of silent nothingness. Thus, Idora's status as a "visible minority" (128) condemns her blackness as being forever incompatible with Canadianness while strengthening her desire to belong on her own terms.

The language of Canadian multiculturalism does not capture the experience of invisible visibility, and of being rendered "Nothing," which each of these writers express in their work. While multiculturalism potentially refers to a range of federal, provincial, and municipal laws, institutions, programs, and government initiatives, the writers in this study repeatedly insist that multiculturalism, in its many forms, insufficiently addresses race and racism in Canada.[2] Banting and Kymlicka concede that "The challenges posed by racism are not fully captured in our inherited terminology of 'visible minorities' within multicultural discourse" (64). Yet this is not merely a problem of inadequate terminology; indeed, in the production of Canada's national unity, out of the "raw material...of Canadian diversity" (Day 9), Canada's national narrative is rewritten such that histories of Canadian racism and colonialism are effaced and buried. Multiculturalism thus becomes a tool for excising critical race analysis from Canadian public discourse. In a notable act of cooperation between legislation and criticism, multiculturalism scholarship has inadequately theorized differences between ethnicity and race in Canadian multiculturalism. The authors in this study intervene in the simplified and amnesiac narrative of national genesis towards multicultural harmony, revealing how the legislated claims that "No citizen or group of citizens is other than Canadian," and the promise that no "ethnic group take precedence over any other" (Trudeau) are undermined by the persistent question posed to black people in Canada of "where are you really from?"

In a strangely paradoxical twist, however, Canadian multiculturalism at once interrogates black subjects concerning their origin and seeming misplacement in the nation, while also providing a vocabulary to answer and rebuke the very questions it poses. Like their African-American counterparts, the authors in this study struggle to illuminate "that which is perceived by others as not existing at all" (Christian 35). They employ the "inherited terminology" of Canadian multiculturalism to make black presences visible such that Daphne's "Nothing" and Sheila's laughter make silence speak. Yet, they must also contend with multicultural politics that recognizes them while it renders them invisible. This simultaneously disabling and enabling quality of Canadian multiculturalism is parodied, seized upon, challenged, and celebrated within black diasporic writing in Canada. For instance, the language of Canada's "multicultural heritage" (*Multiculturalism Act* Preamble 1988 n. pag.) enables these authors to counteract national forgetting, reminding Canadians of their repressed history of racism and colonialism and insist that this history, along with the absented history of the black Atlantic, are integral components of this "multicultural heritage." While many critics have attacked multicultural policy on the grounds of its incoherence, contradictions, and incompleteness, it is precisely multiculturalism's ambiguous, conflicted, multiple, and contradictory definitions that enable the authors in this study to seize upon the language and discourse of Canadian multiculturalism; to invert the terms of their interrogation; and to rewrite Canada from a black diasporic perspective. These authors do not abandon the nation as irredeemable, but call it to task for failing to live up to its obligations. They rewrite these open, contradictory, and incoherent elements of Canadian multiculturalism in their re-articulation of the nation.

It is in their fiction and poetry, rather than in their sociological accounts or public protest, that these authors rewrite the nation from a black diasporic perspective. The first author in this study, Dionne Brand, has written extensively on this tenuous position of black people in Canada, arguing in her *A Map to the Door of No Return: Notes to Belonging* (2002) that "Multiculturalism is relative to the state of white fear" (79) and that the promises of Canadian multiculturalism "do not guarantee nation for Blacks in the Diaspora" (67). She insists that "To live in the Black Diaspora is I think to live as a fiction – a creation of empires, and also self-creation. It is to be a being living inside and outside of herself. It is to apprehend the sign one makes yet to be unable to escape it except in radiant moments of ordinariness made like art" (*Map* 18–19). While the examples from McWatt's and Clarke's fiction might seem commonplace, for Brand this ordinariness is precisely the point. For her, writing transfigures such ordinariness, and communicates how the lives of black people like Daphne and Idora become meaningful in and through such seemingly banal moments of suffering and self-realization. Indeed, the poetic qualities of Brand's and Clarke's critical essays and public polemics suggest that the plainness of prose and the mechanics of argumentation do not capture the contradictory sensation of what it means to be black and diasporic in multicultural Canada. Rather, it is in these "radiant moments of ordinariness made like art" that these writers can express this sense of contradictory doubleness, of being "inside and outside" of oneself, of being paradoxically recognized "by others as not existing at all," and of attempting to speak while being rendered "Nothing." When Brand describes black disaporic subjectivity as akin to living "as a fiction," she insists on the importance of narrative to mediating and constructing identity as well as a poetic sensibility that revels in contradiction. Brand draws attention to the distinctive quality of "fictions" – both the fictions of the nation that exclude black people and the empowering fictions of black diasporic identity. These fictions do not merely depict multicultural conflict, but also show how black diasporic fiction in Canada uniquely transforms the narrative of the multicultural nation. The contradictions of race and multiculturalism's failure to address systemic racism are represented in these poems, essays, and novels in ways that sociological reports and statistical analyses cannot duplicate.[3]

Dionne Brand, Austin Clarke, and Tessa McWatt are my chosen examples within the annals of black literary production in Canada, of what Gilroy describes as "a stereoscopic sensibility adequate to building a dialogue with the West: within and without" (*Black Atlantic* 196). However, Gilroy's notion of "dialogue" is too "seamless" for Brand (*Bread Out of Stone* 30) as it ignores the affective sense of doubleness that goes beyond being "within and without" the nation and that pervades these writers' work. Gilroy and the subjects of this project take their cue from W.E.B. Du Bois's famous exposition of double-consciousness. In *The Souls of Black Folk* (1903), Du Bois attempts to answer the question "How does it feel to be a problem" (9)? He writes,

> It is a peculiar sensation, this double-consciousness, this sense of always looking at one's self through the eyes of others, of measuring one's soul by the tape of a world that looks on in amused contempt and pity. One ever feels his twoness, – an American, a Negro; two souls, two thoughts, two unreconciled strivings; two warring ideals in one dark body, whose dogged strength alone keeps it from being torn asunder (11).

This visceral depiction of double-consciousness is at odds with Canadian multiculturalism's claim to sever the ties between race and citizenship, to work against this feeling of "twoness," and to "recognize and promote" (*Act* Preamble n. pag.) the manifold identities of all Canadians. As such, the affective experience of double-consciousness challenges staid narratives of multicultural identity. These writers give voice to the experience of simultaneous visibility and marginalization, recognized, but only as a "problem." Double-consciousness transforms the language of Canadian multiculturalism to give voice to the contradictory experience of being "perceived by others as not existing at all."

George Elliott Clarke puts Du Bois into dialogue with Canadian multiculturalism thus: "Tussling with our own 'double consciousness,' African Canadians question whether the 'Canadian' half of the epithet 'African-Canadian' … hints at an identity. Is it possible to think of the hyphen as an ampersand, or is it really a double-edged minus sign? Is an 'African Canadian' always more black than Canadian" (*Odysseys* 40)? For Clarke, the question of African-Canadian identity turns on the meaning of the hyphen; in Daphne's terms, whether it suggests a uniting of "black" and "Canada" or a sundering, a reduction of the black Canadian subject to "Nothing." He goes on to insist that "African-Canadian consciousness is not simply dualistic … African Canadians possess … not merely 'double consciousness' but … 'poly-consciousness'" (40). Clarke denies the tension Daphne discerns or even the violence Du Bois describes in favour of containing blackness within the discourses of nation and multiculturalism. He describes the evolution of his own poetic voice as moving from "Quasi-Canadian, I dreamed in the haven of the hyphen," to finding "a voice that was black – *and* Canadian – like me" (*North Star* xii; italics in original). Progressing from the "haven of the hyphen" to the suturing of "black – *and* Canadian" is the process of maturation and coming-to-voice that Clarke envisions for African-Canadians.

George Elliott Clarke's views are not reflected by the writers in this study whose voices express the pain of hyphenation, and for whom the meaning of the hyphen in black-Canadian identity is at best unresolved and at worst a threat.[4] They view the hyphen as that which isolates, segments, and atomizes black and Canadian aspects of identity, while simultaneously expressing a diasporic double-consciousness which brings "black" and "Canadian" into a troubled dialogue. Yet these writers also undermine the question "Where you from" by locating black diasporic subjectivity, in however difficult and contested a fashion, here. Rather than attempt to forcibly transform the hyphen into an ampersand, these writers dwell in and speak from that contradictory space of the hyphen, and from the position of the black Canadian subject as a problem. They transform their doubleness from a contradiction to be resolved into a resource from which to rewrite both nation and diaspora. Speaking from a place that is both diasporic and "within and without" the nation, these writers reject their fixed marginality as well as the minority-by-default prescription of official multiculturalism. Instead, they employ fiction to undermine the positions of minority and majority and render the nation itself diasporic. In their work, the exclusion of black people from the nation is transformed into a position of critique which challenges the form of the nation on its own terms. If the hyphen is a double-edged minus sign, these writers show that subtraction paradoxically adds up to a unique position of critique and agency. They reimagine the hyphen in George Elliott Clarke's expression of "black – *and* Canadian" as a minus sign expressing abjection. Clarke's move from hyphen to em-dash expresses the strange combination of abjection and inclusion, absence and presence, minus and joining, that reveals how these authors locate blackness, however uncomfortably, within the nation.

In place of Canadian multiculturalism's identification of all blackness as a priori diasporic and George Elliott Clarke's efforts to transform the negating hyphen into an ampersand, these writers employ another strategy. Brand, Austin Clarke, and McWatt engage in a practice that places nation, diaspora, race, and citizenship into a troubled and transformative exchange. Rather than desire diaspora in place of nation, they render the nation diasporic, articulating the fiction of the nation from its margins in order to imagine different conceptions of national and individual identity and belonging. This is akin to Brah's notion of articulation as "not a simple joining of two or more discrete entities. Rather, it is a transformative move of relational configurations" (110). The terminology and language of Canadian multiculturalism are transformed through this form of narrative "dissemination" involving a "constant disjoining and relinking of the chain of events that constitutes diasporic experience" (Kamboureli, *Scandalous* 38). Thus the lived experience of black diasporic life in Canada provides a narrative framework by which to transform the nation from the uneasy space of the diaspora within. These narratives accomplish what political critique and sociological analysis cannot: a linking of black diasporic and Canadian aesthetics, politics, and identities in a manner that is not a simple unification nor a violent segmentation, but an ongoing transformative practice. Double-consciousness inflects this dissemination of fictions in each writer's unwillingness to resolve the problem of the hyphen, but rather to inhabit it as the space of diasporic articulation. Such practice stresses not merely the movement of diasporic people across nations, but the recasting of the nation itself as diasporic through the struggle to establish and uncover the links between the local, the national, and the diasporic. Thus, the diasporic subject is not always-already hyphenated or diasporic without consent or confined to the diaspora as a nationless subject, but rather is engaged in producing the nation from the shifting grounds of the diaspora. These writers dwell in the space of the double-edged minus sign, employing this doubly conscious position to demonstrate not only how Canada tears them asunder, but also how they render the nation itself diasporic.

I identify two distinct threads within each author's work, both of which stress the process of diaspora as dissemination, disjoining, and transformation and are exemplified in Rinaldo Walcott's conception of "blackening" and Lily Cho's notion of "becoming diasporic". Walcott's blackening is an adaptation of double-consciousness as diasporic practice and is composed of "two important but related ideas. First, that nation-state administrators try to force what it means to be black on people through various mechanisms of domination and subordination ... On the other hand, blackening also signals the various inscriptions with which black people mark their bodies ... and the discourses and articulations that both contest and resist subordination and domination" (*Black Like Who* 125). Walcott posits two aspects of blackening: the state construction of blackness as foreign, problematic, and criminal, and the means by which black people "contest and resist" those forms of "subordination and domination," and conceive of black subjectivity beyond dominant paradigms and oppressive stereotypes. For McWatt, Clarke, and Brand, the two notions of blackening rarely occur in isolation; they struggle to engage in a "transformative move" that reimagines the "mechanisms of domination," including state multiculturalism, as containing the conditions for resistance. These authors endorse Walcott's argument that black diasporic writing in Canada employs "a deterritorialized strategy that is consciously aware of the ground of the nation from which it speaks" (*Black Like Who* 15) and they use their consciousness of location against received notions of belonging and imposed forms of abjection from the body politic. Blackening stresses the importance of race in multicultural discourse while simultaneously undermining "black" as a stable identity defined by skin or corporeality, and instead conceives of black identity in terms of process, performance, and strategy. [5]

Lily Cho echoes this sense of black identity as discursive and strategic in her argument that "diaspora must be understood as a *condition of subjectivity* and not as an object of analysis" (11; italics in original). She argues, "one *becomes* diasporic through a complex process of memory and emergence ... Black diaspora subjectivity emerges in what it means to be black and live through the displacements of slavery and to carry into the future the memory of the losses compelled by the legacy of slavery, to be torn by the ambivalence of mourning losses that are both your own and yet not quite your own" (21; italics in original). "Negro-Canadian" or "African-Canadian" suggest stable, if hyphenated, identities to be possessed and rooted in the place "where you're really from," but Cho's and Walcott's theories insist that identity is always composed of historical "displacements" and "torn by the ambivalence of mourning." Cho's expression of diasporic *becoming* as a "complex process of memory and emergence" gives meaning to blackening, particularly as these authors contend with memories of diasporic movement, displacement, loss, and absence. Narratives of blackening stress Canada's barely visible racial hierarchy and historical and ongoing racism while also inserting the aesthetic forms of the black diaspora into the nation. This is complemented by the manner in which these writers transform the signs of the nation, linking them to new international and diasporic contexts.[6] These narratives insist on the importance of race to Canadian multiculturalism and also query notions of presence and belonging in the nation for diasporic and so-called Canadian-Canadian (Mackey 157) subjects alike.

The "becoming" of diasporic practice, rather than the positive condition of "being" in the diaspora, stresses the importance of process and narrative within the ongoing project of situating oneself in the diaspora. Further, the attention to process, discourse, memory, and language involved in blackening and becoming diasporic provide a framework for interpreting the narrative forms that these authors employ. Thus, Brand's depiction of Toronto as "not a place of origins" but rather "a place of transmigrations and transmogrifications" (*Map* 62) illuminates what it means to become diasporic. She describes her literary project as the struggle to "describe this mix of utter, hopeless pain and elation leaning against the door" (*Map* 41), and in this sense, Brand's image of the Door of No Return conjures the memory of and emergence from the Middle Passage, while the leaning suggests the push and pull of "losses that are both your own and yet not quite your own." Blackening and becoming diasporic invoke a vocabulary for the articulation of black diasporic practices and imagine Canada as a space in the black diaspora. In each of these texts, the figures of crossing, moulting, emerging, lusting, wounding, and catachresis expand Walcott's "inscriptions" into a repository of imaginative diasporic practices. Whether conceiving of the nation temporally, spatially, as palimpsest, or as genealogy, these authors generate an alternative vocabulary of presence and belonging that exceeds the boundaries of the nation.

Walcott's analysis of the disciplinary and liberating aspects of blackening and Cho's depiction of the diasporic subject "torn by the ambivalences of mourning" both recall Du Bois's characterizing of the doubly-conscious black subject who is in constant danger of being "torn asunder." This link indicates not merely the shared interstitiality of African-American and black Canadian diasporic subjects but also the sense of tearing, contradiction, and division that is at the core of both subjectivities: the recurring sense of "How does it feel to be a problem." Hortense Spillers argues that Du Bois "was trying to ... posit – an *ontological* meaning in the dilemma of blackness" ("All The Things" 104; italics in original) and I believe this tearing, paradoxically enough, *is* the ontological meaning of these diasporic practices. Each of these writers occupies a position caught between nation and diaspora, and in this sense is in constant danger of being "torn asunder." Du Bois's phrase captures the violence and potential for self-annihilation that characterizes many of the depictions of double-consciousness in these texts. This possibility of violence and annihilation underwrites the creative acts of crossing in each of these texts in ways that are not captured by poly-consciousness. The ontological tearing describes the position of the black diasporic subject in Canada while also cutting apart the too easily sutured identities endorsed by Canadian multiculturalism. Brand describes her own discomfort towards any "seamless, undifferentiated" (*Bread Out of Stone* 30) identity or form of belonging, and in her writing the act of being "torn asunder" gestures towards more fluid and unsutured evocations of identity. Whereas Brand revels in this feeling of identity "torn asunder," Austin Clarke's depiction of black male subjects torn between Canada and the Caribbean is less liberating and sanguine, evident in the title of his first novel, *The Survivors of the Crossing* (1964). In McWatt's *Out of My Skin*, Daphne describes a sensation of "falling between the cracks, of stepping and missing. The same feeling that had persisted throughout most of her life" (2). Daphne links "the appearance of the crack" to the recurring question *"what are you"* (17; italics in original), suggesting that the tear of double consciousness irradiates the gestures, postures, and affects of black diasporic life and survival in Canada.

George Elliott Clarke's critique of the "haven of the hyphen" and his transformation of double-consciousness into poly-consciousness is at once an effort to unite black and Canadian identities and to insist upon the importance of region and locality in understanding articulations of blackness in Canada. He rightly critiques definitions of Canadian blackness as either American or Caribbean in nature, as they efface Clarke's own community of Africadians (his "coinage from 'African' and 'Acadian'" [*Fire* 11]) and similar communities. Clarke argues that the tendency to read all expressions of blackness as diasporic or transnational not only excludes black people from the nation but also erases the historical and cultural legacy of black communities that have been in Canada for generations.[7] His work thus offers a necessary supplement to Walcott's blackening by insisting that blackness is not always diasporic, and that not only does Canada possess a black history but also "*blackness* possesses a Canadian dimension that is recognized by engaging with black cultural works located here or that address black existence here" (*Odyssey's* 10; italics in original).

Despite Clarke's critique of Walcott, Brand, and others, however, there is a means of getting beyond the seeming impasse of Clarke's insistence on the importance of locality and Walcott's argument that black diasporic writing practices "a deterritorialized strategy." Brand, Austin Clarke, McWatt, and others give voice to the meaning of blackness within Canadian localities, yet in doing so they render those localities part of the black diaspora. Their work does reflect "black existence here," but transforms the meaning of "here" such that it is refracted by the tear of double-consciousness and is transformed by diasporic routes and absented histories. In Brah's terms, these texts place the discourses "of 'home' and 'dispersion' in creative tension, *inscribing a homing desire while simultaneously critiquing discourses of fixed origins*" (Brah 192–3; italics in original). There is a continuity between Walcott's blackening and Clarke's argument that interpretations of local expressions of blackness requires "historiographic and sociological analyses of specific national and regional cultures" (*Odyssey's Home* 202) in order to understand notions of Canadian blackness within particular geographic contexts. Thus, Brand's Toronto and McWatt's Montreal are creative rewritings of the local that transform these spaces by locating them within extranational diasporic routes.

Yet where the writers in this study attend to the tension between the local and the diasporic and also express their own position "within and without" the nation, G.E. Clarke attempts to locate black cultures *within* the nation. He argues that "it is natural that Africadians should believe that they constitute a distinct society" (*Fire* 1:15), that "African Canadians are an assembly of miniature nations," and that "African-Canadian literature…is a branch of Canadian literature" (*Odyssey's Home* 203). Clarke's arguments slide from an expression of the local to an assertion of indigenous blackness contained within the nation: "African-Canadian culture and literature have domesticated – nationalized – their influences enough to create an aboriginal *blackness*, even if this mode of being remains difficult to define" (*Odyssey's Home* 12–13; italics in original). The difference between the authors in this study and Clarke is evident in his move from "domesticated" to "nationalized." Where Clarke attempts to suture the differences between the domestic, the local, and the national, thus writing a space for "aboriginal" blackness *within* the nation, the authors in this study write "*locationality in contradiction*" (Brah 204; italics in original), and the tearing of double-consciousness is evident in the space *between* blackness "domesticated" and blackness "nationalized."

Clarke's own Africadian community resists this sliding from domesticated to nationalized blackness and exhibits elements of Du Bois's double-consciousness. For instance, in one of Frederick Ward's contributions to Clarke's anthology, the speaker describes the experience of being forcibly moved from Africville:

> just went and stood in the
> corner …
> Then shadows come'd right round me. Come'd in here without
> asking pardon fer themselves and took things from they place
> …
> Some one of them apologized for
> moving me. But they made off with me evidence. I ACCEPTS!
> But I expects they'd lease done the least, ceptin' they ain't.
> THEY MOVED ME IN GARBAGE TRUCKS!
>
> (Clarke, *Fire on the Water II* 18–19)

The speaker is indignant that her domestic space, reduced here to a "corner," is invaded by the representatives of the city. Her depiction of the "shadows" who "apologized for / moving me" recalls the "polite" racism witnessed by Idora and Daphne and the movement from "ACCEPTS" to "expects" to "ceptin'" suggest the speaker's sense of wry humour and irony in being expected to accept this treatment. Yet her true indignation arrives at the close of the dialogue when the movers transport her out of Africville "IN GARBAGE TRUCKS!" The invasion of domestic space, the speaker's indignation, and the "trashing" of Africadian people and history by the state suggests that the sliding from "domestic" to "nationalized" blackness remains difficult for Africadians. Similarly, Sylvia Hamilton's poem "In My Neighbourhood" juxtaposes two different images of home and neighbourhood to undermine any easy suturing of black and Canadian. The speaker describes, "In my neighbourhood / the wind blows in from the bay / Small purple wildflowers / idly watch from the roadside." This image of idyllic homeplace gives way to a depiction of the local as a space of violent racism: "In my neighbourhood / they sprayed KKK in black / on my mailbox." Hence, the local and the quotidian are repeatedly undercut by the racism of the state as well as subtle and explicit forms of racism. Other works collected in the second volume of Clarke's *Fire on the Water: An Anthology of Black Nova Scotian Writing* (1991), including Carrie M. Best's "That Lonesome Road" and George. A. Borden's "Plantation North" evince a distinctly Canadian form of double-consciousness that problematizes the suturing of domestic and national expressions of blackness.[8]

At the heart of Walcott's notion of blackening and Clarke's expression of black Canadians as a collection of "miniature nations" is the ongoing struggle to understand the meaning of blackness within the context of the nation. This struggle pervades black writing in Canada and turns on the questions of what is meant by "black identity," what is the relationship between nation, race, and identity, and how does blackness as an identity transform notions of citizenship within a multicultural framework. Brown et al. argue that "race is a relationship, not a set of characteristics one can ascribe to one group or another" (228), while G.E. Clarke advises that "*Blackness* is not just skin colour, but a polysemous consciousness" (*Odyssey's Home* 188; italics in original). Clarke's attention to the corporeal, "somatic" (Foster 94), and ontological qualities of blackness addresses a central problem in black Canadian writing: the relationship between the body, skin, and identity. The persistence of the question, "where're you really from," indicates the manner in which the black body is interpreted as exceeding the limits of citizenship within multicultural Canada and the extent to which even the multicultural nation is indebted to modernity's raciological definitions of national belonging. Thus each of the authors in this study attend to this relationship between black identity and the black body as they respond to Du Bois's question of "How does it feel to be a problem?" Indeed, Du Bois's original description of double-consciousness imagines the black subject trapped within "one dark body, whose dogged strength alone keeps it from being torn asunder." Similarly, in his explication of blackening, Walcott insists that the "inscriptions with which black people mark their bodies" are critical to theorizing black subjectivity in Canada.

There is a long history of critical race theory and black criticism that examines, critiques, reclaims, and resists the link between black identity and the body. Smaro Kamboureli has indicated the particular scandal of the racialized body in Canada but equally insists on its "polysemantic" nature, arguing that "'Body' refers to corporeality, but also to the body politic ... The body's desires, its traumas, its abuse are all contingent on the body politic and its various manifestations" (*Scandalous* ix). David Theo Goldberg (1990) supplements this sense of the body as discourse, arguing that "As a mode of exclusion, racist discourse assumes authority and is vested with power, literally and symbolically, in bodily terms. They are human bodies that are classified, ordered, valorized, and devalued" (306). Meanwhile, Gilroy argues that the link between the black body and racial discourse has changed such that "Nobody fills old skulls with lead shot these days" (*Against Race* 45), and Farah Jasmine Griffin (1996) insists that the contemporary "discourse of black inferiority ... stands on 'evidence' derived from cranial measurements and genital mutilation" (520). In the context of modernity itself, Sylvia Wynter forcefully elaborates the manner in which the black body was "made into the physical referent of the idea of the irrational / subrational Human Other" ("Unsettling" 266), and Cornel West (1993) confirms that "White supremacist ideology is based first and foremost on the degradation of black bodies in order to control them" (122). Griffin argues that African-American writers, from Harriet Jacobs onwards, "serve to make the wounds of ... [slavery and white supremacy] real," and that their writing of the body "is not a matter of getting back to a 'truer' self, but instead of claiming the body, scars and all – in a narrative of love and care" (521). As such, this "textual body stands as a counter to the known socially deviant black body" (Henderson 18).

These critics provide a framework for identifying the racist biological determinism which continues to inform conceptions of nation and citizenship, and is subtly and politely deployed in the question "Where are you from?" These critics show how the devalued black body is integral to modernity and they critique that devaluing by rewriting blackness and modernity.[9] Spillers addresses the struggle to find a language for the black female body, arguing that it is a signifier "so loaded with mythical prepossession that there is no easy way for the agent buried beneath … to come clean" (65). Spillers argues that the black female body constitutes an "American grammar," a "meeting ground of investments and privations in the national treasury of rhetorical wealth" (65). Thus the challenge of writing black identity regularly contends with the "investments and privations" of the body and with transforming the grammar that denigrates that body.

Yet in writing the body, many black Canadian writers do not long for a return to an unmediated corporeality, but rather attempt to transform the discourses that materialize the body. Marlene Nourbese Philip explains this difference between writing the body and writing the "grammar" of the body when she argues, "*I want to write about kinky hair and flat noses – maybe I should be writing about the language that* kinked *the hair and flattened noses, made jaws prognathus*" (*She Tries* 20; italics in original). Philip, Spillers, and Henderson all identify the difficulty of writing the black body itself and instead write the grammar, language, postures, intimacies, and performances of the body. Philip's articulation of "a profound eruption of the body into the text of *She Tries Her Tongue*" (*She Tries* 24) applies equally to each of the texts in this study where embodiment and racialized discourses of the body erupt in and interrupt practices of blackening. These writers contend with the discursive violence of representations that mediate the possibilities of embodiment, constituting the "grammar" of the black body, and look for an alternative grammar of the body.

Dionne Brand situates her own writing of the body within the history of depictions of the black female body and black female sexuality. While Brand longs for a means to write "This Body For Itself," (1994) she finds the task impossible and turns this desire for the body into an intransitive desire for language instead. Brand breaks from past feminist or womanist projects to "heal" the body or to articulate some restored black female corporeality, sexuality, or subjectivity.[10] She finds that the available grammar of the black female body is heteronormative, privileging "seamless, undifferentiated female sex" (*Bread* 30). As such, Brand builds on the work of Spillers and others in her struggle for a suitable grammar of the body, but she also draws attention to what that grammar has excluded. Brand's poetics is concerned with the absences of black diasporic life and her writing of the body renders that absence material and corporeal. In place of the recovery of the black female body, Brand insists on the manner in which corporeality is textual. She describes the black body as a "cipher of dreams, memories, horrors, and fears" (40), suggesting that she conceives of it more as a puzzle or a hieroglyph; materiality for Brand inheres in the letter rather than the body.[11]

These inscriptions of blackening are not about recovering the body itself, but about how inscriptions decipher the body as it shapes subjectivity. Thus writing the affectations and gestures of the body resists the equating of black subjectivity with the body, and disrupts a stereotypical conception of blackness. Brand and Austin Clarke, for instance, employ poetry and fiction to depict Albert Johnson's body and to illustrate how the Canadian grammar of race transforms Johnson's black body into a cipher of the "horrors, and fears" of white Canada. Johnson's death, at the hands of the Toronto police, becomes a locus for public discussions of blackness in Canada organized around the denigration of the black body. Within the Canadian public sphere, Johnson's body becomes contiguous with black deviance and criminality. Brand and Clarke transform the depiction of his body by imbuing him with a history and character that exceeds the mainstream media depiction of him as "immaculate with his disaster" (Brand, *thirsty IX*). The authors engage in a "claiming [of] the body, scars and all – in a narrative of love and care" (Griffin 521) in order to make Johnson's body matter. Brand portrays Johnson as caesura and lacuna, thereby foregrounding his physical and historical absence, while Clarke narrates Johnson's death through the collective recollections of his characters. Writing Johnson's body through figures of absence enables Brand and Clarke to resist the depiction of Johnson as a "known socially deviant black body," revealing, instead, how that deviance and that "knowing" is produced.

The texts that I have selected in this study do not attempt to recover an unmediated, original or restored black body, but rather make the gestures, longings, and postures of the black body signify something other than one-dimensional, stereotypical blackness. They engage in a blackening of Canada by making visible the abjection of black bodies from the nation and by insisting that black people belong here. Further, they are selected both because they reflect my eclectic interests and also occupy an exemplary position in the broader field of black diasporic writing in Canada. They propel the reigning motifs, themes, and formal experiments of black diasporic writing in new directions. I have selected these texts for their exemplary poetic and political practices, their interest in the possibility of rewriting the nation, and their varied inscriptions of diasporic double-consciousness. The selection has also been guided by George Elliott Clarke's call for a literate criticism of black, diasporic authors, as the texts under scrutiny merit the kind of close reading and rigorous literary analysis that Clarke calls for. Moreover, they have only rarely, if at all, been considered by extant scholarship.

Dionne Brand is a major figure in black diasporic writing in Canada and her place in this study is assured. Among contemporary black writers, Brand has received perhaps the most scholarly attention because her writing engages the questions of difference and identity that continue to intrigue Canadian critics. Brand's poetry, fiction, and criticism illustrate diasporic double-consciousness through the image of the door of no return, which informs my interpretation of her conception of diasporic temporality. The door of no return is a metaphor for the traumas of the past as well as for the possibilities of the future. Brand's attention to desire, delay, anticipation, prolongation, history, and memory within diasporic time makes her emblematic of a host of black diasporic preoccupations and places her writing on par with the works of Nourbese Philip (1989), Makeda Silvera (2003), Claire Harris (1992), and Lillian Allen (1993). Each of these writers stresses the desire to recover or return from the rupture of diaspora or the Middle Passage. Brand, however, uniquely takes up the task of speaking *from* that rupture and of desiring neither a return home to the origins of the past nor a resolution of identity in the future. The aforementioned writers tend to write the Middle Passage and the dislocation of diaspora as primarily traumatic spaces, whereas Brand intertwines the traumas and possibilities that emerge from the absences and losses of black diasporic life. Brand rewrites the betweenness of the diaspora as a productive openness that disrupts the seemingly stable temporality and border of the nation. Furthermore, unlike these other writers, Brand's texts are concerned with rewriting Canada and Canadian multiculturalism. Brand blackens Canada by locating the absences that she discerns in the diaspora within the nation, thus figuring the nation as lacking, incomplete, and in a process of "becoming diasporic." Her articulation of diasporic time in her poetry transgresses not only conventional notions of blackness and diaspora, but also engages in a blackening of the nation through her unique generic experiments and by her inscription of diasporic time and subjects within Canada.

Austin Clarke is one of the first, most widely published, and most prolific black authors in Canada. Clarke's work expresses the unspeakable and intangible dimensions of double-consciousness as well as the difference between masculine and feminine diasporic subjects through his employment of movement and mobility motifs. Clarke's blackening of Canada operates through his inscription of movement and his rewriting of the Jonah myth to locate the black diasporic subject, however alienated, within the nation, and to rewrite the nation as one route within the diaspora. Clarke rewrites the monstrous presence of the black subject in the nation as the monstrous nation that aims to devour its black citizens. "Sometimes, A Motherless Child" (1992), "I'm Running For My Life" (1996), "Canadian Experience" (1996), *The Origin of Waves* (1997), *The Polished Hoe* (2002) and *More* (2008) are singular narrations of the lives of first and second generation black migrants from the Caribbean to Canada. His work is part of a broader field of authors that includes Dany Laferrière (1985), André Alexis (1997), and Cecil Foster (1998). Clarke differs from his compatriots in his insistence on speaking from the space of the hyphen rather than desiring a resolution of that hyphenated betweenness. Unlike other writers, Clarke privileges routes over roots and movement over arrival. His inscription of movement within Canada conceives of the nation as one route within the black diaspora; one site of crossing rather than a final destination. Clarke's characters are *The Survivors of the Crossing* (1964) and throughout his body of work he details the means by which they survive, improvise, and struggle within their ongoing acts of crossing. Crossing, in Clarke's work, is polysemous as his narratives detail the geographic crossing of the diaspora, as well as the crossing of identity, language, and narrative form that emerge from diasporic life. Clarke's texts are, like Brand's, transgressive towards received notions of blackness and Canadian-ness, exceeding both categories and forcing them into a troubled dialogue with one another.

A move from fiction to history and from the semiotic to the discursive allows me to identify the public struggle over the same themes that animate black Canadian literature. The political controversies surrounding the death of Albert Johnson at the hands of two Toronto police officers in 1978 took shape in the mainstream media and in subsequent literature. His death became a major rallying point for black people in Toronto and across Canada. Brand's *thirsty* is based on Johnson's death; it functions as a catalyst in Neil Bissoondath's *The Innocence of Age* (1992), and Austin Clarke refers to Johnson throughout his corpus. Frances Henry and Carol Tator's (2002) model for analysing race in Canadian media illuminates the denigration of blackness in mainstream newspapers and the struggle over the politics of representation in black community papers. Johnson – and the black, Caribbean community more generally – are misrepresented in this discourse, and these fictive rewriting of Johnson's death transforms the smearing of blackness into a condemnation of Canadian racism. This blackening of the nation's history explicitly links the poetics and politics of these writers in an effort to intervene in the public sphere and to alter the meaning of blackness in the Canadian imaginary.

Tessa McWatt's *Out of My Skin* locates blackening and black history in Quebec through the introduction of the category of race into the politics of recognition and notions of multicultural heritage. McWatt is a member of a new generation of black diasporic writers in Canada. While her novel could be placed in dialogue with a range of other texts such as Esi Edugyan's *The Second Life of Samuel Tyne* (2004), David Chariandy's *Soucouyant* (2007), and Suzette Mayr's *Venous Hum* (2004), McWatt eschews their concern with the meaning of being black in a global and post-national Canada. Instead, McWatt's novel is a throwback to "worrying the nation" (Kertzer 1998), sharing as it does Brand's and Clarke's investment in a multicultural nation inflected by the politics of diaspora. Further, her work historicizes multicultural politics, revealing the continuities between Canadian multiculturalism and past political forms for managing difference. Her intriguing coalition with Aboriginal and Québécois claims to sovereignty distinguishes *Out of My Skin* from its transnational brethren, placing it squarely within a strategic reinvention of the historical pasts of Canadian nationality.

Each author's response to Du Bois's question "How does it feel to be a problem?" is simultaneously a response to Frantz Fanon's call to write "a new history of Man" (*Wretched* 238); it is also an illustration of blackening as the process, in Cho's sense, of becoming diasporic rather than being defined in advance of acts, inscriptions, and practices. There is a discernible development in each writer's inscription of blackening as they respond to this repeated question of "where're you really from?" The continuous staging of this question posed to black people in Canada reveals a concern with the absenting and "invisible visibility" of black people, as well as the manner in which Canada is imagined. Each author's project of blackening queries, rewrites, and intervenes in the nation from this transgressive, doubly-conscious position of the black diaspora in Canada. Brand's inscription of diasporic time within national temporality and Clarke's insertion of the themes of crossing and mobility into settled versions of nation transform Canada into a diasporic space, challenging its whiteness. Similarly, their writing of the history of Albert Johnson engages in a blackening of history that counteracts the marginalization and invisibility of historical black Canadian presences. These authors transform the interrogation of blackness in Canada into an interrogation of Canadian multiculturalism and the Canadian nation. They employ the position of the hyphen to open up new avenues of critique and citizenship that respond to the abjection of blackness from the nation and foreground the importance of race in the national imaginary. Their narratives transform black absence into a transgressive form of presence that rewrites the nation from a black perspective. Clarke and Brand trespass upon the borders of nation, whereas McWatt's version of blackening seeks both to undermine national boundaries and to carve a place within the nation. Daphne historicizes Canadian difference and, in doing so, claims Canada as a black space in ways that are not possible for the figures in Brand's and Clarke's texts. Blackening, for Daphne, is less a process of becoming diasporic and more a process of blackening the nation, suggesting that it is through the querying and transgressing of notions of Canada as whiteness that black presences can be expressed. In their responses to the question, "How does it feel to be a problem?" these writers not only reveal the strategies of improvisation, crossing, and transgression that mark black diasporic life in Canada, but also show how the "problem" is a Canadian problem with which the nation must contend.

Chapter One

Temporalities of Becoming in Dionne Brand's *thirsty*

Something must happen, something bound to come. They were waiting, after waiting for crop and pay, after waiting for cousin and auntie, after waiting for patience and grace, they were waiting for god

Dionne Brand, *A Map To The Door of No Return* 21

The vision of progress is the rational madness of history seen as sequential time, of a dominated future.

Derek Walcott, "The Muse of History" 357

Dionne Brand's writing transforms the everyday acts of "waiting for crop and pay…for cousin and auntie" into a more transcendent expression of "waiting for patience and grace." Brand's poetry makes the seemingly inconsequential and disconnected events of black diasporic life resonate with the legacy of diasporic dislocation, the unspeakable traumas of slavery, and the lost origins of the Middle Passage. Her work not only contextualizes the quotidian within the black diaspora, but also constitutes a language for these unspoken traumas, longings, and absented histories. As such, Brand's poetics indicates how any diasporic practice must contend with the inexpressible losses, historical fissures, and absent presences of the black diaspora. She reveals how "the various inscriptions with which black people…contest and resist subordination and domination" (Walcott, *Black Like Who* 125) are inflected by the irrecoverable history and lost identities of the Middle Passage and the absented-presence of the door of no return. Furthermore, Brand's representation of the everyday employs memory and narrative to intervene in the historical forms that have produced those very absences and silences. What is distinct about Brand's poetics of the quotidian is that she does not attempt to restore or fill in the fissures and lacunae of the Middle Passage, slavery, and the black diaspora. Rather, she makes those absences palpable and material, depicting them as part of the very substrate of black diasporic life. Brand's portrayal of the quotidian carefully traces the paradoxical and troubling ways in which the absences of black diasporic life are made epistemologically and temporally present. History reads those losses and absences as black silence and powerlessness, but Brand's poetry rewrites them as containing the conditions of possibility for new subjectivities. Her poetry rewrites the temporality of absence and mourning as a temporality of "waiting" for "something bound to come." This temporal shift in Brand's work constitutes an act of blackening whereby her poetics stand as a counter-narrative to modernity and history. If historical discourse has, for black diasporic people, "made the past a mystery, unknown and unspeakable" (Hartman 14) such that "Dispossession was our history" (Hartman 74), Brand rewrites absence as not strictly dispossession but also as the condition of possibility for new conceptions of black diasporic subjectivity. Waiting, patience, and grace make diasporic temporality both sustained and unpredictable, because the gift of grace is always untimely, interrupting the monotony of national temporality. As such, Brand's depiction of the quotidian rewrites that history of unspeakable losses and absences in terms that make it possible for black people to challenge their historical silencing.

Saidiya Hartman witnesses this absence and historical silencing firsthand when she visits a market in Elmina, Ghana, where hundreds of thousands of black people were sold as slaves: "I would have preferred mourners with disheartened faces and bowed heads and the pallor of sadness coloring the town. Or at least something Gothic: bloodstained ruins, human skulls scattered like cobblestones ... Instead I found myself immersed in the prosaic conduct of everyday life – the petty negotiations, squabbles, and contested transactions" (50). The "terrible beauty" (50) of this everyday scene is underwritten by the absence of any acknowledgment of the historical significance of the place and its importance to Hartman's own lack of origins. In Africa, Hartman finds no trace of her own history or mark of the trauma that has constituted her place in the black diaspora. Perhaps more terrifying, she realizes that the great trauma of slavery and the Middle Passage was everyday life for hundreds of thousands of people. In place of the grand historical narratives of oppression, resistance, rebellion, and freedom, she finds a mundane life in an unremarkable place that bears no marks of her history.

Hartman's observations of the market reveal the persistent absences of the black diaspora and the manner in which those absences permeate the quotidian. Like Hartman, Henry Louis Gates Jr. goes to Africa to understand the legacy of the Door of No Return. Brand describes her reaction to watching Henry Louis Gates Jr. interview a man in Ghana about the slave trade:

> I expect an intelligent, dispassionate discussion about the geopolitics of the time. Suddenly a plaintive and childish question from Henry Louis Gates: to paraphrase, "Why did you sell us?" The Kumasic man of course has no answer ... Gates, a usually sophisticated erudite, is completely genuine, Gates picks up after centuries as if they had spoken only days or months or even just a few years ago ... "Why did you sell us?" I switch the station ... There is no answer. The Door of No Return is ajar between them. I can see its impossibility (*Map* 31–2).

Gates's fantasy of return and recovering origins renders impossible any "intelligent, dispassionate discussion" because he feels the wounds of slavery as though they happened "only days or months or even just a few years ago." Gates and Hartman return to Africa to interrogate descendants of possible slave traders, while Brand is "embarrassed at the question and the answer." Gates hopes to heal old wounds by asking questions for which there are no answers; Brand suggests instead that the inheritance of slavery and the history of the Middle Passage cannot be cast off, but can be rewritten and "mis-remembered" in ways that make possible a different conception of black diasporic subjectivity.

Unlike Hartman, Gates, and other black diasporic writers who have detailed the traumas of living without a history and of the quotidian haunted by the lacunae and absences of the past, Brand writes about subjects caught between this haunting of the past and the possibilities of making new subjectivities in the future. Her description of black diasporic life as "a fiction" (*Map* 18) anticipates Hartman's narrating of the market scene and the manner in which Hartman tries to locate the absences and losses of her past in the quotidian. Brand argues that black diasporic life is a fiction wherein one tries to "apprehend the sign one makes yet [is] unable to escape it except in radiant moments of ordinariness made like art" (*Map* 18–19). Hartman's depiction of the everyday tries to render lost history and trauma present; however, Brand's poetics of the everyday rewrites the patience, longing, and grace that she observes in the diaspora as a hopeful expression of life that transcends the haunting traumas of the past. It is through poetry and fiction that Brand eschews this desire to interrogate and recover the past, tracing instead the complicated flux of absence and presence that constitutes black diasporic life in interstitial spaces and temporalities. Brand shifts the temporality of the black diaspora from a "backward looking conception of diaspora," forever haunted by the "endless desire to return to 'lost origins,'" (Hall, "Cultural Identity" 245) to a temporality of becoming.

Brand's inscription of this temporality repeatedly returns to the central question of "How to describe this mix of utter, hopeless pain and elation leaning against the door" (*Map* 41)? She explains the difficulty of occupying and writing the space of the door thus: "To live at the Door of No Return is to live self-consciously. To be always aware of your presence as a presence outside of yourself ... we exist doubly. An ordinary conversation is never an ordinary conversation. One cannot say the simplest thing without doubling or being doubled for the image that emerged from the doorway" (*Map* 49–50). Brand identifies the doubleness of being spoken for, predetermined, and of being haunted by a history and "torn by the ambivalence of mourning losses that are both your own and yet not quite your own" (Cho 21). In Spillers's terms, this doubleness represents a "locus of confounded identities, a meeting ground of investments and privations in the [inter]national treasury of rhetorical wealth" ("Mama's Baby" 65). Brand's poetics enable the "agent buried beneath ... to come clean" ("Mama's Baby" 65) through a language of double consciousness that does not conceive of diasporic life as singularly traumatic. Brand locates this doubleness within the quotidian partially to find a language for these unspoken yearnings and ambivalences and this tearing between the door of the past and possible transcendence in the future. Yet, Brand's poetic depiction of the quotidian also enables her to engage in a blackening of history and identity, rewriting the confounding and privation of identity as a space of expression and agency for black diasporic subjects. She explains that she is "scouring maps of all kinds, the way that some fictions do, discursively, elliptically, trying to locate their own transferred selves" (*Map* 18–19). The absences and gaps of an elliptical and fictional life are rewritten in Brand's work as the conditions of possibility for "transferred selves." These are the selves that are not located here or now, but that have been transferred across space and time such that "all names were forgotten" and their dislocation "signified the end of traceable beginnings" (*Map* 5).

The struggle to rewrite historical absence as an expression of "transferred selves" appear as early as *In Another Place, Not Here* (1996) and *Land to Light On* (1997); indeed the structural presence of absence is evident in the very title of *In Another Place, Not Here.* This novel begins with the protagonist, Elizete, saying "Grace. Is Grace, yes" (3). "Grace" functions in the novel as it does in the epigraph to this chapter, as a catch-all phrase for the inexpressible absences and longings of black diasporic life. Finding a language for that absence and a form in which to render that absence somehow present and material is one of the central themes of Brand's work. These early texts, along with Brand's later work such as *Inventory* (2006) and *Ossuaries* (2010) are decidedly transnational. Brand's *thirsty*, however, specifically locates these absences within Canada, putting them in tension with Canadian narrations of nation. The poem's sustaining metaphor of thirst inserts diasporic absence into the dream of nation. *thirsty* not only historicizes Canadian diversity but also disputes the notion of identity that Canadian multiculturalism claims to "recognize and preserve." While the longing for origins is often expressed as the absence of nation for black people, Brand rewrites the absence of origins, nation, and home as the possibilities of living as a transferred self, never wholly here nor there but always in a position of betweenness. She posits the ongoing experience of transference against the logic of origins, belonging, and arrival to show how the absences and abjections of the black diaspora push at the borders of the nation. Her inscription of the quotidian constitutes an act of blackening that rewrites the historical deprivation of black diaspora people such that the "elliptical" sense of absence is palpable and, paradoxically, becomes part of the content of black diasporic life.

Brand's writing went largely unremarked upon in both popular and academic presses until the release of *No Language Is Neutral* (1990) and its nomination for the Governor General's Award. Subsequent criticism of Brand's work focuses on the manner in which Brand gives voice to a black immigrant experience in Canada and regularly pays inadequate attention to her poetics. This continues in recent critical attempts to mine her poetry and prose (typically the latter) for textual embodiments of "Affective citizenship" (Brydon), "territorialized cosmopolitan subjectivities" (Johansen), "deterritorialization" (Dobson), "politics of ambivalence" (Forster) and "collective dynamics" (McCallum and

Olbey); in short, for alternative forms of citizenship, mobility, and political organization. The political consequentiality, these critics discern, however, tends to transcend Brand's poetics rather than emerge organically from it. Indeed, her poetics often unsettles and nuances her political claims, both tempering the anger for which she is often vilified and making it burn more intensely. The manner in which Brand's poetics reshapes the thematic tendencies that these critics identify, rather than simply exemplify or illustrate them, is often absent from their critical interpretations. Brand's project of blackening operates simultaneously at the levels of politics and poetics, and critics must consider her political claims alongside her claims about genre and form.

The limitations and problems of Brand criticism have been addressed by George Elliott Clarke, who asserts, "Bluntly, much of the criticism of [Claire] Harris, [Marlene Nourbese] Philip and Brand is irrelevant" because it elevates these authors "to triumvirate status without paying them the compliment of examining all aspects of their poetics" ("Harris, Philip" 178). Clarke argues that critics "either reduce the writers to the status of sociologists or they bleach their work of aesthetic value. The resultant criticism is tedious, inadequate, and – perhaps – insidious" (164). The pun on bleaching suggests that Clarke sees white liberal Canadian guilt operating in the critical assessment of those critics who praise the work of these authors without a thorough assessment of their poetic merits. Clarke's unapologetic critique is largely aimed at sociological readings of Brand's work that praise her politics yet have virtually nothing to say about her poetic achievements. He is also critical of scholars who turn Brand or Philip into metonyms for African-Canadian writing and ignore the long history of black writing in Canada.[1] Clarke's comments are certainly warranted, and the tedious aspects of Brand criticism is apparent both in white, liberal praise[2] of Brand's work, and in the conservative rejection of Brand's work on the grounds that her poetry is too pessimistic or political.[3]

In addition to the sociological trend, the other major strand of Brand criticism focuses on her interpretation of history and memory and the manner in which the figures in her texts are constructed through fraught acts of remembering. Erica L. Johnson describes this as "Brand's project ... of 'unforgetting'" which "addresses the extent to which the histories and individual stories of African diasporic experience have been stricken from the historical record" (1–2). Johnson and others consider the importance of memory, loss, and trauma in Brand's work and the manner in which unforgetting – indicating both the desire to remember and an irrecoverable, erased history – infuses her texts. While the first group of critics is concerned with questions of identity and alterity as they are structured by contemporary conditions of globalization, multiculturalism, and diaspora, the second group sees the subject born out of a complicated relationship with the history of slavery, modernity, and the nation. This latter group argues that Brand conceives of a poetic counter-memory to the narratives of the nation and of modernity.[4] Yet the majority of critics from both groups offer varying degrees of sociological readings of Brand's work, focusing primarily on plot with little consideration of the manner in which Brand's politics are shaped by her poetics. [5]

A critical framework that would eschew such sociological interpretations must show how Brand's politics emerges from – rather than simply reflects – her poetics. Brand's poetic meditation on the absences of black diasporic life, signified by the metaphor of the Door of No Return, inflects her political considerations as she attempts to reimagine those absences and losses as the necessary conditions for new forms of political subjectivity. Throughout her corpus, silences, erasures, and lacunae are depicted along a continuum of absence and presence. Her project of blackening illustrates how diasporic life continues to be shaped by the inarticulable elements of the black diaspora, and it is through poetry and fiction that she expresses these longings and makes absence material. At times, Brand extends the experience of loss and the presence of absence to other diasporas, as through Tuyen in *What We All Long For*. Tuyen's recurring feeling of "that anomalous void in her life" (26) stresses the inarticulable loss that her family suffered in their migration to Canada. Marie Ursule in *At The Full And Change of the Moon* (1999) describes a repeated "haunting not-enough feeling" (1) that permeates her everyday life. In *A Map to the Door of No Return* Brand argues that "The door exists as an absence" and "Every gesture our bodies make somehow gestures toward this door" (25). A criticism that takes Brand's project seriously must trace how her depiction of elliptical "transferred selves" longing for "grace" rewrites the absences and aporias of the black diaspora to bespeak new forms of diasporic subjectivity. For the figures in her work, the "haunting not-enough feeling" enables them to challenge the nation and its prescribed modes of belonging.

Even Brand's critical essays do not employ scholarly or critical prose but are written in a hybrid poetic-prosaic form. Maia Joseph describes

Brand's *Map* as an "elliptical, poetic meditation" (75), while George Elliott Clarke is critical, arguing that Brand employs "glittering, dreamy prose, also occasionally incisively intellectual, to bespeak unplumbed confusions about identity and belonging" (*Review of A Map* 557).[6] Yet it is precisely Brand's elliptical, glittering style that provides her with a means of expressing the elusive, of giving meaning to identity as absence, to the silent gestures and affectations of black diasporic subjectivity. In an earlier essay, "Water More Than Flour" (1994), Brand investigates the meaning of the titular phrase as it articulates a deep sense of absence and otherwise unspoken longing. As Brand explains, "water more than flour, to describe not only the physical but the spiritual state of want, meaning a thinness to life's possibilities, unerring hard times, an absence of joy, an absence of redemption or mercy or rescue" (124). Brand's repetition of the phrase throughout the essay accomplishes more than simply elevating the phrase to talismanic status or documenting a popular idiom. Rather, her analysis of the polyvalence of the phrase shows that given the unlikelihood of material change, often words must suffice. Language can fill in material and historical absences and provide not only an expression of the desire for change but also agency and voice in the face of material deprivation. Brand's essay turns from longing for the material plenty of flour as a respite from "the absence of redemption," to focusing on language as a kind of liquidity that can speak to spiritual and material absence and rewrite the "thinness of life's possibilities." Brand writes, "Water more than flour was their way of finding some grace, the grace of a phrase, in the hunger, in the starkness, in the bareness in which we seemed destined to abide" (124). Her repetition of the phrase reimagines the want for "flour" as part of a desire for a radical change in the conditions of everyday life. Furthermore, the words "abide" and "grace" suggest again the intersection of the ordinary and the poetic, particularly as Brand attempts to locate grace in this abiding. The essay suggests that if diasporic people are "destined to abide" then poetics and the grace of a phrase can transform the nature of absence and longing.

The "Door of No Return" is Brand's most evocative image of the absences and irrecoverable origins of the black diaspora, as well as the recurring desire to recover those origins and step back through the door to the "before" of diaspora. The Door of No Return is the actual place that Africans stepped through and entered the Middle Passage, as well as a metaphor for the loss of origins, identity, and subjectivity that resulted from slavery. Hartman has shown that to return to the site of the door does not mark a return to origins, but rather relives the traumas of that dislocation and that dissolved identity. In Africa Hartman realizes, "I represented what most chose to avoid: the catastrophe that was our past" (4). She finds that despite her struggle to return, "None of it had brought me any closer to replacing a lacuna with a name or an X-ed space with an ancestral village" (79). Hartman discovers what Brand already knows: that the Door of No Return "looms both as a horror and a romance … The horror is of course three or four hundred years of slavery, its shadow was and is colonialism and racism. The romance is of the place beyond the door, the Africa of our origins" (*Map* 22). The door is not simply a metaphor for the ghost of history but also for the irrecoverable origins of the black diaspora. It is the site where the transatlantic economy of slavery was enacted, and it marks a loss that cannot be recovered. Despite the romance of the door and the false prospect of recovery and return that it offers, Brand is at once fascinated by its haunting power and the fictions that conceive of it as a site of origins. Whether figured as horror or romance, Brand repeatedly stresses "Too much has been made of origins" (64). She writes,

> some of us want entry into the home and nation that are signified by these romances. Some of us in the Diaspora long so for nation – some continuous thread of biological or communal association, some bloodline or legacy which will cement our rights in the place we live. The problem of course is that even if those existed – and they certainly do, even if it is in the human contraband which we represent in the romance – they do not guarantee nation for Blacks in the Diaspora (*Map* 67).

Despite her disavowal of origins, Brand's poetics is doubly shaped by both the impossibility of returning to origins and the romance and promise of longing to step through the door and return to or depart from diaspora. The image of the diasporic subject "leaning against the door" (*Map* 41) suggests the absented presence of the door that Brand sees in black, diasporic life. One is haunted by the prospect of returning but that return to origins is a return to the trauma of absence and the loss of one's origins, not to the romance of the past. Brand makes this explicit when she writes, "The door exists as an absence … Every gesture our bodies make somehow gestures toward this door. What interests me primarily is probing the Door of No Return as consciousness. The door casts a haunting spell on personal and collective consciousness in the Diaspora" (25). If the door ties individual black people to a diasporic community, Brand's aesthetic project is to rewrite this process of becoming diasporic. Her work reinterprets the meaning of the door to foreground not the recovery of lost origins, stable identity, or belonging, but rather the desiring and longing for identity and nation as a hopeful gesture for change that is signified in the very longing for the door.

The door offers an image for what Stuart Hall describes as the "backward looking conception of diaspora … [that] gives rise to a certain imaginary plenitude, recreating the endless desire to return to 'lost origins,' … to go back to the beginning" (Hall, "Cultural Identity" 245). Brand's double-consciousness does not depict the diasporic subject torn asunder by the contradiction between pain and elation, but as containing both in the act of leaning against the door of no return. Her attention to posture and words is a poetic map of diasporic resilience, an acknowledgment of loss, and an embrace of hope. It is not the door that Brand finds compelling, but rather its "imaginary plenitude" and the "endless desire to return" that she identifies and abstracts as a language of longing and hope. Brand is interested in the acts of longing expressed by the subjects "leaning against the door" that "gesture towards this door," these acts of desiring and longing that on the surface articulate a desire for origins, yet also convey a desire for a more open sense of political possibility and transformation. In *thirsty*, Brand depicts the figures of the poem leaning against the door as they are personally haunted by the absences of the past, yet these absences link them to a communal longing that constitutes black diasporic experience.

Jody Mason explicates Brand's grammar of longing, arguing that, for Brand,

> the door functions as a trope for fixed forms, such as slavery and capitalism, that limit our ability to understand how past and present experience interact. Like the disabling aspect of the door of no return, the sundering of memory and history, these fixed forms cannot adequately account for the lived present. (784–5)

Mason examines "how Brand engages with this [historical] reckoning through the trope of the opening door*way*. The door*way* is the enabling aspect of the door of no return … it is the site from which Brand conceives of another kind of world that holds the emergent possibility of seeing our ghosts and, ultimately, of social transformation" (785). Mason offers a useful vocabulary for considering both the disabling and enabling qualities of the door of no return. Yet Mason's focus on tropes of haunting and historical reckoning limits the scope of her argument, particularly as she suggests that the rewriting of doors as doorways represents Brand's "new optimism about the power of reckoning with history, about the possibility of banishing ghosts" (787).[7] Brand's writing of the door/way is less a banishing of ghosts or reconciling with history than a means of expressing the unspoken longings and absences of diasporic double-consciousness. For Brand, "leaning against the door" evokes both the strain and fragility of the diasporic subject position. Nothing as complete or fulfilled as "banishing" or "reconciling" is possible for the subject in Brand's imagination. The door is still a crutch, but the posture of leaning angles the body away from the door, thus hinting of the dream of the future. In Brand's own words, the "horror" of the past begets the "romance" of anticipation and desire rather than memory and yearning. The "curiously complicated doubleness" of the door provides a metaphor that both materializes and assuages the absences and longings of the diaspora. As such, Brand's depiction of the door as bespeaking a kind of diasporic double-consciousness displaces the centrality of nation in Du Bois's formulation. Du Bois's subject is torn between nation and race, while Brand's version of double-consciousness practises a "deterritorialized strategy that is consciously aware of the ground of the nation from which it speaks" (Walcott, *Black Like Who* 15), but that locates the black diasporic subject between the horrors and absences of history and the possibilities of the future.

thirsty is a poem about memory and history. The multiple voices in the poem remember, honour, are haunted by, and attempt to forget the past. The poem's organizing metaphor of thirst comes from the dying statement of the central character, Alan, after he is shot and killed by the Toronto police. Alan's memory haunts the lives of his wife Julia, mother Chloe, and his unnamed daughter. Alan's death, while important in its own right, is also emblematic of the manner in which the traumas and absences of the past inflect black diasporic conceptions of present and future. His traumatic death is also a metonym for other disasters and forced absences of slavery, the Middle Passage, and racism. As Mason suggests, "The history of slavery and oppression forms a palimpsest over the specific, local history of the poem" (786) and these transnational histories are linked to the specific, local history of the black diaspora in Canada. Diasporic subjectivity's "romance with the past" provides an imaginative and political vocabulary for "what is / to come" (Brand, *thirsty* XX). In *thirsty*, Brand honours the real history of Albert Johnson (whom Alan's narrative is based on)[8] and his family while blackening Canadian history and poetics by not only inserting Johnson's history into the annals of Canadian history, but by making Johnson's fate that which casts a pall on the nation. This is one specific way that she challenges the "romance with the past" that she observes in both diaspora and nation. Furthermore, in her poetic meditation on longing, memory, history, and desire in the black diaspora, she makes these emotions crucial to the significance of one man's story for the fate of black diasporic subjectivity. The speaker links Chloe's and Julia's mourning of Alan and the absence of Albert Johnson to her broader observation that "Anyone, anyone can find themselves on a street corner / eclipsed, as they, by what deserted them" (XXVIII). While the two women are eclipsed by Alan's death, the speaker also explains that he "deserted them," suggesting that absence and thirst are pervasive, extending beyond the immediate loss of his death. As such, *thirsty* depicts double-consciousness temporally, positioning the black diasporic subject between a past that has "eclipsed" them and a future that never arrives. The speaker's project to write this absence transforms the backward-looking temporality of the door into an open temporality of becoming. Absence and longing become critical components of the means by which diasporic people imagine themselves anew.

thirsty is a long poem composed of thirty-three sections written in a variety of stanzaic forms. The poem begins long after Alan has been shot by the Toronto police and traces how the women in his family remain haunted by his absence. The unnamed narrator intervenes in the historical silence that has erased Alan's presence from the nation and silenced the women in the poem. The speaker is able to articulate that which remains inexpressible for the three women and render present what she detects in their gestures of longing and yearning for the recovery of an unspoken loss. As such, she recomposes Alan's history and provides a language for his absence and for the lives of the women many years after his death. In the second stanza of the first section, the speaker states,

> let me declare doorways,
> corners, pursuit, let me say
> standing here in eyelashes, in
> invisible breasts, in the shrinking lake
> in the tiny shops of untrue recollections,
> the brittle, gnawed life we live,
> I am held, and held (I)

In this opening section the speaker imagines her own place in the city in the act of historical recovery. She is explicitly located within the poem as "standing here" and being "held, and held." In the images of "invisible breasts," the "shrinking lake," and the "brittle, gnawed life we live," the speaker conceives of both the city and its subjects as decaying, vulnerable, and fragile. Indeed, the next stanza describes "wrecked boys, half-dead hours ... / inconclusive women in bruised dresses," stressing the brokenness and the fragility of the diasporic figures in the poem. These images describe the temporality of decay which turns time into process and suspension. There is also a sense of betweenness, and the absence of beginnings and endings; these figures are caught in the between time of the diaspora. Furthermore, the description of the "tiny shops of untrue recollections" shares Cho's intuition of the process of becoming "diasporic through a complex process of memory and emergence." The "untrue recollections" evoke the fictive and memorialized past of recovered absences which the speaker contests in her act of historical recovery. This is also evident in her use of transferred epithets in the "half-dead hours," suggesting that the "brittle, gnawed" quality of diasporic life has extended to time and memory. Indeed, the numerous transferred epithets in this opening section all extend a pervasive sense of brokenness and vulnerability, from individual subject to objects, spaces, and environments. This renders the process and experience described a communal one, turning affective and emotional experience into a relay. The use of transferred epithets suggests that one becomes diasporic through the cross-spatial and cross-cultural interactions of multiple geographies, affects, languages, and politics. Thus diasporic subjectivity is located neither entirely here nor there, but rather always elsewhere and in-between.

This chronic displacement finds its complement in the poem's emphasis on interstitial spaces and times (in "doorways," "thresholds," and "crossroads") and in the speaker's desire to write the history that emerges from the transferred meanings, absented presences, and unlikely connections of the diaspora. Indeed, if diasporic subjects are always out of place and in "inconclusive" places and times, then Brand expresses this interstitiality through the subject suspended between the door and the doorway. The double meaning of "I am held, and held" then becomes clear: both a moment of imprisonment and the implication of a communal embrace. The doorway represents the inbetweeneness of the diasporic subject concerned more with *there* than *here*, and with *then* than *now*. When the speaker "declare[s] doorways," she evokes the "complex process of memory and emergence" (21) whereby the history of the door no longer "looms both as a horror" of slavery, colonialism, and racism, nor as "a romance" with "the place beyond the door, the Africa of our origins" (Brand, *Map* 22). Brand's poetics of the quotidian traces the presence of absented histories in these gestures and postures of "leaning against the door" and "gesturing towards the door." Rather than disabling features of the diasporic condition, Brand turns absence and loss into the forms of excess that nation cannot imagine.

thirsty's speaker conceives of diasporic subjectivity as contending with multiple absented presences caught within a temporality that is a prolongation of the past and a delay of the future. Thirst, like the phrase "Water More Than Flour," is both literal and metaphorical, corporeal and affective, felt and unspoken. In both expressions, the intangible "grace of a phrase" communicates Alan's "brittle, gnawed life" as well as the casual horror and careless grace of his untimely and unjust death. This is evident in Alan's utterance of thirst as he dies: "he dropped the clippers to hold his breaking face, / he felt dry, 'Jesus ... thirsty ...' he called, falling" (XII). The perceived violence of the clippers contributes to his being shot; the "cut" of one responsible for the "break" in the other. The brilliance of Brand's fusion of the quotidian and the transcendent is evident in these lines: "Jesus" is an ordinary cuss word, a taking of the Lord's name in vain, but Alan's words immediately recall Jesus's exclamation in the throes of crucifixion, "I am thirsty" (John. 19.28), constructing him as a martyr figure of sorts. The shift from Jesus's "I thirst" (sometimes written as "I am thirsty") to Alan's statement of "Jesus ... thirsty ..." resituates thirst as a simultaneously dispersed and encompassing condition. Alan thus becomes a representative figure rather than a random victim of accidental violence.

Alan's parched utterance is just one of the many references to Christianity and Christian redemption in the poem. The thirty-three sections of the poem reflect the Christological calendar as well as the number of miracles Christ performed during his life. Christian imagery infuses the poem even in unexpected moments such as when the speaker describes the three women having "hoped without salvation for a trolley / they arrived at the corner impious, then, / wracked on the psalmody of the crossroad," (II). The elevated diction of "salvation," "psalm," "impious," and "cross" seems incongruous with its apparent object, the trolley, and subjects, the women. It transfigures this otherwise everyday scene while also gently mocking the pilgrimage. The conformity of life in Toronto to the Christian calendar, however, lends Alan's death prophetic weight. His utterance gestures to a world that has not yet come into being, just as his "rough Bible" (XII) contains a truth no one is willing to hear. Brand's jarring shifts in diction and her infusing of the quotidian with Biblical imagery and the Christian language of redemption confers grace upon these acts of abiding.

The speaker describes Alan as "jeremiad at the door" (XII), making his body and his speech inseparable. This links diasporic temporality with the temporalities of return and redemption found in the Christian form of the jeremiad. David Howard-Pitney offers the following definition of the rhetorical form of the jeremiad:

> The term *jeremiad*, meaning a lamentation or doleful complaint, derives from the biblical prophet, Jeremiah, who warned of Israel's fall and the destruction of the Jerusalem temple by Babylonia as punishment for the people's failure to keep the Mosaic covenant. Although Jeremiah denounced Israel's wickedness and foresaw tribulation in the near-term, he also looked forward to the nation's repentance and restoration in a future golden age (5; italics in original).

Howard-Pitney's definition expands on Wilson Moses's term "Black Jeremiad" to describe "the constant warnings issued by blacks to whites, concerning the judgment that was to come from the sin of slavery" (Moses 30–1). This African-American jeremiad adopts the tropes and symbols of American Puritan jeremiads, such as America as a "city upon a hill" and the Puritans' imagining of themselves as having "undergone an exodus from 'Egyptian bondage' in Europe to a wholly new world" (Howard-Pitney 6). Alan himself is described as a religious "man frothing a biblical lexis at Christie / Pits, the small barren incline where his mad sermons / cursed bewildered subway riders, his faith unstrained" (II). The speaker, however, is more sceptical than Alan, explaining that Alan "was thirsty, as I, ... / though we were not the same, / god would not be sufficient for me" (XIII). The disjunction between Alan's and the speaker's perspectives reveals that while their longings are the same, Alan's turn to the jeremiad and the temporality of return and redemption does not suit the speaker. Unlike Alan, her thirst cannot be slaked by god or by the promise of a restored past.

Rather, she requires another lexicon and temporality to quench her own thirst.

Alan's jeremiad, the poem's organizing metaphor of thirst, the transferred epithets of the diaspora, and the image of the door/way conceive of diasporic time as a present that is eclipsed by the losses of a prolonged past. The language of personal and political longing is deployed through tropes such as analepsis, prolepsis, and metalepsis. Diasporic time caught between the door and the doorway is inscribed in the poem through a conception of the present as an ongoing form of analepsis; that is, a notion of the present as composed out of the imaginative substance of the absences of the past. When the poem engages in prolepsis, it is imagined as a restoration, in the future, of the past. This is the condition that the speaker observes in Chloe and Julia, describing them as "limbless, handless, motionless" (XVIII) and as frozen in time "since that day which they are still standing in" (XVIII). The speaker hopes to shift this frozen temporality and move from the ongoing analepsis of the diaspora towards a time when the present and future are no longer overdetermined by the traumas of the past. Brand's literary-historical ambitions become clear once one comprehends her deployment of time. It is this feature that marks not only her disruption of linear time, but also her interruption of the Canadian long poem genre which has thus far failed to accommodate the historical presence of blackness or the tale of diaspora in the story of nation.

Poet and critic Frank Davey observes that the first, most obvious, and perhaps most important "sign we see in the long poem is its length, promising to the reader that its matter is large in depth or breadth" ("Contemporary Canadian Long Poem" 183). The critical problems of identifying the defining attributes of the Canadian long poem are numerous; indeed, its length is perhaps its only stable identifying feature. D.M.R. Bentley, in the opening essay to *Bolder Flights: Essays on the Canadian Long Poem* (1998), concludes his "Introductory Survey" of the genre with the question of whether there is "any more a justification for using the term 'the Canadian long poem,' or should every long poem written by someone with Canadian citizenship or experience be treated as a singularity" (19)? Interestingly, Bentley links the absence of innate features and the weakening of the form to what he sees as the weakening of the borders of the nation: "These are not idle questions at a time when regionalism, separatism, and globalization are working alongside multiculturalism, self-help therapies, and a host of minority and individual rights movements to reduce the Canadian nation to bite-sized chunks in the global soup of neo-conservatism" (19–20). Bentley's attributing of the alleged reduction "of the Canadian nation to bite-sized chunks" to the forces of "multiculturalism, self-help therapies" and "minority and individual rights movements" reveals, perhaps, more about Bentley than the Canadian long poem. Is the category of the nation, by Bentley's estimation, "conservative" in the good sense rather than what most contemporary critics would perceive as an "imagined community" at best and an exclusionary one at worst? Despite his puzzling argument about the nation, Bentley's observations about long poetry seem to be correct, although his bemoaning the death (dearth?) of the stable genre of the contemporary Canadian long poem was predicted by Smaro Kamboureli in *On The Edge of Genre: The Contemporary Canadian Long Poem* (1991). Brand seizes upon this generic instability to inscribe black diasporic presences within the limits of the form and to illuminate the blind spots therein. Bentley's uncertainty about the identifying features of the contemporary Canadian long poem implicitly acknowledges the formal openness and historical contradictions that enable the disruption of generic limits and the experiments with form that characterize Brand's singular reinvention.

Nearly twenty years before Bentley's comments, Robert Kroetsch argued that the contemporary Canadian long poem is organized around the thematizing of the perpetual delay of the poem's meaning and conclusion. In his postmodern, fragmentary essay "For Play and Entrance: The Contemporary Canadian Long Poem" (1982), Kroetsch contends that "In love-making, in writing the long poem – delay is both – delay is both technique and content. Narrative has an elaborate grammar of delay ... Poets, like lovers, were driven back to the moment of creation; the question, then: not how to end, but how to begin. Not the quest for ending, but the dwelling at and in the beginning itself" (117–8). Kroetsch argues that delay is both the operative temporality and generative force of signification in the long poem and of orgasm in sex. For Kroetsch, the meaning of a long poem is generated in the play between the act of signification and the perpetually-deferred arrival of meaning. Davey critiques Kroetsch, arguing that his interpretation of "the energy of the long poem as sexual energy, and delay as postponement of a terminating orgasm ... has unhappy implications for the life of the long-poem ... and contains at least a hint of exclusively male perspective" (185).

According to Davey, Kroetsch's theory of the long poem is a masculine, phallocentric formulation wherein the temporal movement of the poem is imagined as a manifestation of the sexual desire of an implicitly heterosexual, male speaker. Indeed, the very title of Kroetsch's essay announces the phallocentrism of his controlling metaphor. Davey attempts to recover Kroetsch's focus on temporality from this "exclusively male perspective," arguing instead that "we see the impulse not to delay but to prolong, to have the poem not be about time but in it" (188). Davey sees Kroetsch's "view of the Canadian long poem as a narrative of disappointment and failure," and he suggests instead that the movement of the long poem is a "movement from surprise to surprise, it is prolonged not only to delay but to continue, it anticipates more rather than postpones" (185). Davey contradicts Kroetsch's perception of lack with his emphasis on the productive and generative force of meaning in the long poem.

Davey and Kroetsch offer a vocabulary of temporality and desire with which to discuss the Canadian long poem, organized as it is around processes of delay, prolongation, and anticipation. Kamboureli synthesizes their arguments, suggesting that the Canadian long poem thematizes its own disruption of the traditional rules of genre through its inscription of temporality. Anticipating a number of the problems identified by Bentley, Kamboureli insists that this lack of generic principles is not a sign of the long poem's failure but the very grounds of its enunciation.[9] She writes,

> the contemporary long poem, while belonging to the genus of poetry, cannot be fully identified with one of its *eidoi*. By being both outside and inside the established poetic genres, the long poem participates in the category of poetry while defying its limits, the generic laws of its species. This ambivalent positioning marks the deconstructive activity of the long poem. By challenging the monism of the traditional concept of genre, the long poem invites the reader to rethink its laws (48–9; italics in original).

Bentley fears that the instability of the genre signals its demise and perhaps that of the nation itself. Kamboureli is less anxious, contending that its instability is a sign of the "deconstructive activity of the long poem," an activity which "invites the reader to rethink" the laws of genre and poetic form[10] while also enabling the poem's generation of meaning.

This ambivalent temporality gives rise to both the long poem's "deconstructive activity" (49) and formal "inscription of otherness" (101).

Kamboureli argues that "the long poem emerges from Kroetsch's essay as a desire machine (re)producing ... its 'pressure toward madness,'" (*Edge* 80). She writes, "The deferral of orgasm that Kroetsch finds inscribed in the length of poems is nothing other than the long poem's seduction by process, its unwillingness to submit to any preformalized versions of closure. Desire ... informs the quest in the long poem, but this is not the kind of desire Kroetsch discusses" (*Edge of Genre* 80). The language of becoming, of delay, and of "the long poem's seduction by process" are instances of the temporal order of the genre which represent time as openness, process, and generation rather than discrete, conclusive, or fixed. Kamboureli places Davey's and Kroetsch's temporal concepts in a continuum in order to indicate the long poem's resistance to closure and to insist on the form's drawn out, extended, and aporetic temporality. She writes,

> Delay: its meditative turns, its hesitancy to begin, its pauses, detours, and double-takes; prolongation: the rupture of what both Kroetsch and Davey call discreet occasion ... a remission of time, making a thing process ... Whereas delay and anticipation operate against a preconceived ending, prolongation functions according to momentariness, situating the long poem both within and outside a time continuum ... Delay and prolongation extend the aporetic structure of the long poem. Although prolongation comes as a riposte to delay, both of them function as engendering and not as organizing principles (85).

Kamboureli supplements Kroetsch's arguments about poetic-sexual delay (the waiting time between the moment of speech and the longed-for "discreet occasion") with Davey's logic of prolongation in order to indicate how these two temporal elements of the long poem "function as engendering and not as organizing principles."

Of course Kamboureli focuses on the contemporary Canadian long poem's postmodern deconstruction of genre, but her deconstruction can be extended to blacken the nation through challenging its representative literary form. The temporal effects of "Delay," "prolongation," "a remission of time," and "making a thing process" (85), in Brand's work, give voice to the affective experience of thirst and the chronic displacements of diaspora. These multiple poetic temporalities articulate diasporic subjectivity, connecting the poem's formal qualities (and its positioning in terms of genre) with its concerns about diasporic politics and subjectivity. Brand represents diasporic subjectivity, in Cho's sense, as one of suspension, dwelling, delay, and through the poetic act of "making a thing process" (85). Brand's temporalities of delay, prolongation, and anticipation articulate the way in which one "*becomes* diasporic," and these multiple temporalities express the combination of longing, mourning, nostalgia, and hopefulness that she sees in the black diaspora. This is neither the repetition with difference of Kamau Brathwaite's tidalectics[11] nor the endless play of the signifier expressed by Davey and Kroetsch, but a concrete, historical blackening of such play and repetition to reveal the presence of the past and the imagination of the future.

Returning to the first section of the poem, the speaker's demand, "let me declare doorways," is structured according to the temporality that Kamboureli discerns, particularly in the manner in which the fulfilment of that desire is delayed. The speaker states,

> let me say,
> standing here in eyelashes, in
> invisible breasts, in the shrinking lake
> in the tiny shops of untrue recollections
> the brittle, gnawed life we live,
> I am held, and held (I)

The temporal delay between the speaker's demand, "let me say," the numerous qualifications, and the speaker's eventual assertion, "I am held, and held" enacts the sense of delay that organizes the poem's conception of diasporic temporality. This delay occurs in the space between the speaker's expression of her intent to speak and her utterance, while prolongation and delay operate through poetic repetition. In this stanza the prolongation of a moment is evident in the repetition of the words "in" and "held," both of which signal a slowing down of temporality and of being caught in time. The repetition of the word "in" and of numerous words that contain the word "in" ("standing," "invisible," "shrinking") positions the speaker within the time that she is describing. Thus the speaker is held within and implicated in this inventory of broken things. The repetition stresses the speaker's position of being caught within this prolonged temporality, forever "held and held" and waiting. These examples suggest that *thirsty* enacts Davey's argument that long poetry is not "about time but in it" (188). Yet, the speaker is impatient with being caught "in" this time and longs for a way out, a means to break out of the prolonged suspension. Unlike Kroetsch's emphasis on the pleasures of delay and deferral, the speaker's suspension and anticipation are both intense and impatient.

The speaker's impatience and ambivalence are evident in the final line of the stanza where she declares "I am held, and held." Here being "held" suggests temporal and physical holding, predicting the speaker's later description of her project as "this embrace with broken things" (I). This simultaneous experience of being suspended and embraced is akin to Derek Walcott's "contempt for historic time ... subject to a fitful muse, memory" ("Muse of History" 354). Brand rejects the distance of history for the intimacy of memory, despite being aware of the limits of both. Like Walcott's Muse of History, Brand's speaker demonstrates the "rational madness of history seen as sequential time, of a dominated future" ("Muse of History" 357). The word "held" suggests that for diasporic subjects this "sequential time" constitutes a kind of temporal paralysis, continually eclipsed by the great disasters and losses of slavery, the Middle Passage, and colonialism. Brand explains the limitations of "historic time" to the diasporic subject when she refers to Derek Walcott's desire to "*Pray for a life without plot, a day without narrative*" (*Map* 42; italics in original). She explains that Walcott's line "described perfectly my desire for relief from the persistent trope of colonialism. To be without this story of captivity, to dis-remember it, or to have this story forget me, would be heavenly. But of course in that line too is the indifference, the supplication of prayer" (*Map* 42). The doubleness of "dis-remember" indicates the contradictory – if not impossible – impulse to escape a binding history that has defined the very diasporic community that aims to shake free of its grasp. Moreover, Walcott's words suggest that prolongation and delay constitute a forgetting, a "supplication" that history cease to remember the diasporic subject rather than an act of denial on that subject's part. Brand's poetics attempts to inscribe her desire for a "*life without plot, a day without narrative*" in the sense that poetry challenges the dominant plots and narratives of history. While history emplots her as silent, voiceless, and defined by her suffering, poetry can release her from that hold. Brand's poetics of the quotidian rewrites mourning for the absences of the past as the conditions of possibility for being dis-remembered by the haunting tropes of colonial history. In place of a narrative of history or a plot of recovery, the poetics of the quotidian makes absence material and transforms mourning and loss into the grounds for political transformation and transferred selves.

These temporal structures of delay and prolongation construct the diasporic present as a kind of empty time, in Benjamin's sense, caught between a prolonged past and a delayed future. As the poem progresses, the speaker links her own historical consciousness to the temporalities and histories of the wider diasporic community of the poem. Like Brand's longing for a life without the persistent haunting questions of origins and home, the speaker observes, in the twentieth section of the poem, the inhabitants of "this vagrant, fugitive city" and their "conditional sentences about conditional places, 'If we were home. I would …' as strong a romance with the past tense as with what is / to come … / important in the middle of the pluperfect" (XX). The repetition and multiple meanings of the word "conditional" indicate both the uncertain and contingent nature of diaspora as well as the fact that diasporic subjectivity constitutes a condition and a sentence of sorts. This condition of diasporic subjectivity is the "romance with the past tense" and the position of the subject "in the middle of the pluperfect." Diasporic longing is depicted as a kind of romance or fiction which constructs "what is / to come" based on "what they choose to remember and what they mis-forget of places / they'd known" (XX). In this sense the subject is never "here" or "now" but is caught between past and future, conceiving of the future as a return to an idealized past. The speaker expresses this betweenness in the temporalities of prolongation and delay present in the line break between "what is" and "to come." The pause between lines thematizes the temporal break between present and future tense, stressing the diasporic subject's interstitial position between a prolonged past and a delayed future. Yet the speaker complicates this attention to the past by differentiating between those who "choose to remember" and those who continually "mis-forget." This is the difference between drawing on the past as a stable resource of origins and identity, and being "eclipsed by" and unable to escape the losses, traumas, and silences of the past. Indeed, the negative activity of mis-forgetting suggests the apparently inescapable and involuntary persistence of the absences of the past and the manner in which the past continues to haunt the present and determine the future of the black diaspora. The speaker stresses the creative power of mis-forgetting, invoking the active fictionalizing of memory and beginnings that attempts to undo the absenting of origins in the black diaspora. Chloe and Julia are not able to choose what they remember, nor can they afford a romance with the past. Rather, they mis-forget Alan such that his absence is paradoxically rendered more and more present in their lives.

In Derek Walcott's terms, Chloe's and Julia's "admirable wish to honour the degraded ancestor limits their language to phonetic pain, the groan of suffering, the curse of revenge. The one of the past becomes an unbearable burden" (355). Trapped by this "unbearable burden," "in the middle of pluperfect," Brand's speaker therefore aims to provide a poetic and political language that can move from a present overdetermined by the past to one which can imagine different possibilities for the future. While the speaker is sympathetic to Chloe's and Julia's acts of mis-forgetting, as it enables them to survive their loss, she also wants to transform that romance with the past into a poetic grammar of the future. The narrator is a figure akin to Walcott's Muse of History in that she is able to name what Chloe and Julia struggle to articulate, transforming their "phonetic pain" and "groan of suffering" into a poetic language of possibility.

The speaker highlights Chloe's and Julia's temporal and physical sense of paralysis, describing them as "two women ... limbless, handless, motionless" (XVIII) who have been frozen in time "since that day which they are still standing in" (XVIII). The repetition of "less" suggests Chloe's and Julia's pervasive sense of loss and also writes them as negative presences themselves. The speaker describes "The street / now in full flight, no one notices they are arrested, / waiting for a return" (XVIII). They await the return of the unnamed daughter; for Chloe and Julia, "Time starts with her and ends when she leaves." In one sense, the two women are fixed in the past, "arrested" by their loss and the dissolution of their family. Yet despite this temporal and physical paralysis and an associated sensation of hopelessness and pessimism, there is also a sense of optimism and possibility evoked in the number of phrases expressed in the future tense. They imagine that, upon the daughter's return, "they will tell her," "they will confess their loneliness, they will / promise her," "They will dream for her," "They lust to kiss her husband," "they will love," "She will turn," "They imagine each / that they will be ready with a rare laugh ... / if she comes back" (XVIII). The complicated temporal relationship between the future tenses of Chloe's and Julia's hopes and their desire to recover the past (to have the daughter "come back") conjures the empty present they inhabit and an imagined a future that is a return to an idealized past. Alan's death is a traumatic incident which paralyses the women such that they are forever "held" "in" the time before his death, but his fate is only one instance of this lost hope and possibility. Throughout the poem, the loss associated with Alan's death becomes exemplary of a general sense of loss that the speaker observes in diaspora. Yet, the opposite is also true: the past appears in the language of the future, in the return of desire to this scenario of loss, and in the aggression that attaches itself to "lust." The insertion of the conditional "if she comes back" tempers the metaleptic oscillation between past and future by emphasizing that "they will be ready with a rare laugh." Julia's and Chloe's everyday "mis-forgetting" reveals the sense of possibility in their slightest acts of lust, longing, anticipation, and laughter. Where the signs of historical progress might be absent, Brand suggests that the nuances, gestures, and postures of the quotidian provide evidence of subtle and encouraging forms of change.

This diasporic temporality manifests itself in the metre and structure of the poem, particularly in the use of line breaks, pauses, and caesura. In the second section the speaker introduces Chloe, Julia, and the unnamed daughter as they wait, on the anniversary of Alan's death, to return to the place where he was killed:

> They had hoped without salvation for a trolley
> they arrived at the corner impious, then,
> wracked on the psalmody of the crossroad,
> they felt, the absences of a morning (II)

While the first line of this section is in perfect trochaic hexameter and the third and fourth lines are both written in pentameter, the metre of the second line is an uneven eleven syllables. The second line would be in pentameter but the metre is disrupted with the addition of "then," at the end of the line. The addition of "then" surrounded by commas, introduces a feminine, terminal caesura at the end of the line, disrupting the stanza's otherwise even metre. It is unclear whether "then" indicates the temporal past or the future. Does the speaker's use of "then" describe what happened "back then," in the past tense (as the first line of the stanza is written in the past tense), or does the speaker imply "then" in the sense of what happened next? The caesura of the temporally ambiguous "then" suggests that it also marks a temporal disruption in the lives of the three women standing at the corner. They are at once looking to the past, as this is the anniversary of Alan's death, and looking to the future as indicated by the imagery of crossroads, hope, and their anticipated movement. This caesura, both grammatical in the use of commas, and metric in the disruption of poetic metre, makes the metre of the poem bespeak its temporality.

This stanza ends with a caesura, as the final line reads, "they felt, the absences of a morning" (II). The caesura and the double meaning of "morning" invokes the absented presences of Alan and the door. The caesura in the line pauses the speaker's description of how the women "felt," thus indicating the affective experience of delay and prolongation. Their gestures, affectations, physical postures, and the very temporality of their lives depend on this sense of loss and the empty time of the present. In the same section of the poem, the sixth stanza reads,

> each her own separate weight,
> each carried it in some drenched region of flesh,
> the calculus of silence, its chaos,
> the wraith and rate of absence pierced them (II)

Alan's absence is a lived bodily experience for all three women; his absence is not lodged strictly in memory or emotion but is carried "in some drenched region of flesh," an image that expresses the intense sadness and weight of their loss. The words "weight" and "flesh" make the first and second lines metrically uneven, with seven and eleven syllables respectively. The mourning body is as much a metrical and temporal disruption as it is a surrendering of flesh to tears, and thus the prolonged past disrupts the lived temporality of the diasporic subject. This diasporic temporality is also present in the final line of the stanza where the speaker describes how "the wraith and rate of absence pierced them." The description of absence as piercing suggests both disruption and termination: Alan's life as well as their existences are cut short. This is echoed in the assonance of the strong "A" sounds in "wraith" and "rate" which disrupts the otherwise muted tone of the line and stanza, and echoes this sense of piercing and cutting that marks Alan's loss. "Wraith" alludes to the ghostliness of Alan's absent-presence, but it rhymes imperfectly with "rate," thus linking it to "calculus" in an extended mathematical metaphor that insinuates the incalculable loss they have suffered. Brand shows how poetic language's sensitivity to the inexpressible succeeds in communicating the interminable nature of the women's loss, something that the measured pace of historical progress or plot cannot comprehend or communicate.

Loss is so important to *thirsty* that Alan himself is repeatedly represented as a caesura to stress his absence in the poem, in the lives of his family members, and in the Canadian historical record. The first description of Alan occurs in the second section of the poem:

> This slender lacuna beguiles them,
> a man frothing a biblical lexis at Christie
> ...
> then nothing of him but his parched body's declension
> a curved caesura, mangled with clippers, and
> clematis cirrhosa and a budding grape vine he was still
> to plant when he could, saying when he had fallen, "... thirsty ..." (II)

Throughout these sections that focus on Alan, his absence is described in grammatical terms. Alan is first described as a "slender lacuna" frothing his "biblical lexis," an image that makes his absence rather than his presence substantial: even his lacuna is slender! The transferred epithets in this section link his "mangled" body to the history of violence against black people through the depiction of his "parched body's declension." Yet the image of the lacuna here also prefigures Alan's absence in the poem and the speaker's attempt to recreate the events of his death and of the three women's lives after his death. Alan is absent from the poem and from the lives of the three women, and his presence is only recalled, intuited, felt, and imagined. In this sense, the depiction of Alan as an absent yet beguiling presence recalls Brand's observation that "The door casts a haunting spell on personal and collective consciousness in the Diaspora" (*Map* 25). The women's response to Alan's death is "captured in individual doubt, a hesitation, / and what they could not put into words" (II). Julia, for instance, develops a "fluttering" in her hand after Alan's death, which connotes the anxieties, longings, and absences that she cannot articulate. The speaker describes "the meter / of Julia's hand more intuitive than any set of sounds" (XXIV) suggesting that poetry and the body intuit what prose cannot. The lacunae and caesuras of this passage give texture to the abstract condition of thirst and unspeakable longing that the speaker observes as the hallmarks of diasporic subjectivity. They also lend weight to the thirst while stressing the discontinuous nature of diasporic temporality. In addition to delay and prolongation, these caesuras mirror the speaker's project to break apart the temporality of the present, and to show how the present moment is inflected and delimited by the past. The caesura is thus both the representative figure of this temporality and its deconstruction and disfiguration.

The importance of caesuras to *thirsty's* poetics can be interpreted as an instance of Kamboureli's argument that "The contemporary long poem accomplishes its inscription of otherness through its temporality, specifically the present tense" (*Edge* 101). While Kamboureli is primarily interested in the generic and formal otherness of the long poem (as it differentiates itself from and engages in a "deconstruction of the lyric, epic, [and] narrative" [101]), she links this formal otherness to the otherness of the speaking "subject that enunciates it" (101). *thirsty* employs the present tense throughout the poem, beginning with the line "This city is beauty" while the speaker announces herself by saying "I am innocent as thresholds" (I). But the poetic present is in vital contradiction to the historical present which appears as the past of the "great disaster" of the black diaspora. Kamboureli's focus on the present tense illuminates the long poem's formal sense of being caught between the past and the future, particularly in its relation to past literary forms. Linking the development of the contemporary Canadian long poem with the genre's appropriation and adaptation of past forms, she writes, "Appropriation of literary kinds is characterized by both repetition and difference. The repetition of established genres recalls the already 'foreign' past within the context of a 'foreign' present. The element of difference that enters this process is accomplished through a double gaze – what we might see in Kierkegaard's terms as a looking backwards and a looking forwards" (*Edge* 25). For Kamboureli, this "double gaze" is accomplished through the employment of the present tense whereby the long poem expresses its anxiety of influence as it struggles to express itself differently. Brand's inscription of the diasporic present engages in a blackening of both poetic form and nation. Her poetics transforms the Canadian long poem, inflecting it with the persistent historical past of the Middle Passage and simultaneously expanding and pressing at the borders of the nation to include voices from its black diaspora.

Kamboureli predicts Brand's project: "Originally a textual field marked by anxiety about its foreign past, and by the emptiness and namelessness of its present, the Canadian literary landscape gradually becomes a text inscribed by new names and characterized by a more acute sense of which genres better reflect the Canadian literary sensibility" (*Edge* 26). Yet for Brand, unlike Kamboureli, the conditions of possibility for the long poem include the legacy of European forms in the shape of slavery and capitalism rather than exclusively literary traditions. In a sense, the double-consciousness of the door as "a trope for fixed forms" (Mason 784) links Brand's concern about the influence of European literary traditions with her concerns about the manner in which European political structures continue to dominate contemporary diasporic life, thus rendering the poetic and the political inextricable in her work. Rinaldo Walcott's insistence that "Any debate that seeks to seriously engage the questions of multiculturalism must take seriously that the concept is deeply bound up in a European global domination" ("Disgrace" 30) is reflected in Brand's appropriation and transformation of the form of the Canadian long poem. In this respect, Kamboureli's double-gaze can be linked to the "Janus-faced discourse of the nation" (Bhabha, *Nation and Narration* 3) which "at once gazes at a primordial, ideal past while facing a modern future" (Gopinath 186). The double-gaze of the nation is refracted through diasporic time, challenging the temporality of the nation with the diasporic temporality that pulses through *thirsty*. Kamboureli's discussion of the present tense of the long poem expresses the struggle of this national poetic genre to presently and continuously define itself against European literary norms and come into being as the voice of a nation. Meanwhile, Brand's articulation of diasporic temporality and voice dissects national literary form and time to demonstrate the differences at work in conceptions of the temporal present and of national identity. Brand's inscription of temporality is decidedly extranational and diasporic, yet challenges the temporal order of the nation in order to articulate a space of difference for diasporic agency. Kamboureli's argument that the long poem produces its inscription of otherness through the present tense can thus be usefully put into dialogue with the temporality of the nation to show how Brand's blackening of the Canadian long poem is inseparable from her challenge to narrations of nation.

Homi Bhabha has forcefully argued the manner in which the nation is imagined both spatially and temporally, and he stresses the importance of a particular temporal order to the nation's stability and homogeneity. In one of his earliest essays on the relationship between the national community and national temporality, Bhabha argues that,

> The narrative of the "meanwhile"... produces a symbolic structure of the nation as "imagined community" which, in keeping with the scale and diversity of the modern nation, works like the plot of a realist novel. The steady onward clocking of calendrical time ... gives the imagined world of the nation a sociological solidity; it links together diverse acts and actors on the national stage who are entirely unaware of each other (*Location of Culture* 308).

For Bhabha, the unitary national body is organized through this "narrative of the 'meanwhile'" which enables the "transverse, cross-time ... measured by clock and calendar" (Anderson 30) and marshals together the diverse histories, identities, and events of disparate locations via the national temporal present. It is, Bhabha argues, this "form of temporality [that] produces a symbolic structure of the nation as 'imagined community'" (*Nation and Narration* 308). Bhabha's analysis of the national temporality of the "meanwhile" recasts Kamboureli's identification of the structures of delay, process, and prolongation in the long poem as disruptive of the empty time of the nation. Indeed, Canadian multiculturalism attempts to provide "the imagined world of the nation a sociological solidity" through the production of this "national meanwhile." Yet, if the temporality of the nation "works like the plot of a realist novel," the plot and temporality of the long poem operate in an entirely different manner, cutting into the time of the "meanwhile" and slowing down, interrupting, and breaking apart "The steady onward clocking of calendrical time" which generates this perceived "sociological solidity." Indeed, if Bhabha's national meanwhile is heir to Walter Benjamin's articulation of "the historical progress of mankind ... through a homogeneous, empty time" (261), then Brand's poetics breaks apart the seemingly stable and sutured national time to create a space for black diasporic subjects in the nation.

thirsty inscribes the caesuras and ruptures of diasporic time within the nation such that the enunciation of this diasporic present breaks apart the "sociological solidity" of the national temporality and interrupts the "narrative of the meanwhile" with the voices of the black diaspora. This monological time that generates the imagined community of the nation is cut apart in the poem as the speaker and the poem's figures occupy a diasporic time that prefigures and exceeds the temporality of the nation. Thus the temporality and signifiers of the nation are present in *thirsty* only as a force that marginalizes and abjects black diasporic people from the national imaginary and temporality. One of the clearest examples of this occurs in the speaker's depiction of the newspaper and television coverage of Alan's death. In the acquittal of the police officers the speaker scoffs, "So, a cop sashaying from a courthouse, / ... history and modernity kissing here" (XXVI). The inevitability in the speaker's expression of "So" and the pause of the comma positions this clichéd image of the innocent police officer within the homogeneous empty time of the Canadian national meanwhile. Furthermore, the romance of history and modernity implicit in the kissing and strut of the police officer evokes the manner in which historical forms of racial exclusion have been reinvented and contemporized within the narrative of the nation. Whereas the diasporic figures in the poem are located in interstitial spaces such as crossroads, thresholds, and doorways, the depiction of the policeman in the newspaper supports his presence "here." In another rewriting of this national temporality the speaker describes Julia's depiction in newspapers and notes the

> extraordinary emptiness of the woman
> emerging from clusters of dots on the front page
> then the second page, then the last page
> then vanishing all together, but not vanished
> there, in the time, transparent,
> held and held, she had been held, (XXXI)

The speaker depicts "the time" of the newspaper as integral to the constitution of the imagined community, and as complicit with the national meanwhile. This is the temporal order that gives the nation its solidity, abjecting and concealing its history of racism and violence, and the "extraordinary emptiness" of this time and narrative is transferred to Julia. Throughout this section the speaker traces the manner in which Julia and Alan are rendered increasingly absent from history and the national meanwhile. Where the cop is "here," Julia is either "emerging" or "vanishing." Yet Julia's absence is not absolute, as she is still "there, in the time, transparent / held and held." There is a similarity between this temporality of the present in which Julia is held and Bhabha's conception of the meanwhile of the nation, as both temporalities admit no generative past and no possibility of future change. Black diasporic subjects in Canada are denied any history within the nation as the national meanwhile erases the history of Alan's death, the door of no return, the Middle Passage as irrelevant to the national narrative. Brand identifies this transparent national time as engendering a kind of restrictive and fixed form of politics and community; her struggle in describing diasporic lives in the pluperfect and leaning against the door is to rewrite the present such that it expresses the gaps in this "transparent" empty time, gestures towards the future, and propels her protagonists out of this experience of being "held, and held" in the empty time of the nation. Certainly the fugue of diasporic voices within the poem and Chloe's and Julia's struggle to break out of the temporality of the pluperfect disrupts this Canadian national time. By locating the temporality of the black diaspora within Canada, the speaker shows how the untimeliness of the black diaspora intervenes in and erodes this national temporality. The poem is populated with temporally "transferred selves" that imagine themselves as not here and now but rather elsewhere and in another time. Yet by locating Alan's death within Canada, Brand gives black people a sense of origin in Canada in a way that is attentive to these acts of transferal and the material and structural absences that Brand observes in the diaspora. In these respects, *thirsty* intervenes in the national temporality, transforming the caesura of black absence into a technique for cutting apart the homogeneous time of the present and inscribing a space for difference within the nation.

Bhabha theorizes this project of inscribing difference into the temporality and structure of the nation when he argues that "the performative introduces a temporality of the 'in-between' through the 'gap' or 'emptiness' of the signifier that punctuates linguistic difference" (*Nation and Narration* 299). Brand's enunciation of the Canadian long poem introduces just such a temporality of the in-between. For Bhabha, the relationship between the temporal order of the nation and the structure of the nation as "imagined community" can be disrupted by the temporality of the performative, which indicates the staging in this construction of the nation as materially and temporally "present." Bhabha argues that performative time disrupts this calendrical time, and introduces what he calls a time-lag into the symbolic order of the nation which opens a space of antagonism, revealing the nation's symbolic and political fissures. Brand's depiction of the temporality of the black diaspora intervenes in the national "present" by inscribing the persistent absences and longings of diasporic life into Canada. The empty time of the national project is recast as the in-between time of the door/way in a manner that retells the narrative of the nation and opens up possibilities for difference and change in the future. In this sense Brand challenges the abjection of black people from the nation and claims Canada as a space in the black diaspora. In a later essay that concludes *The Location of Culture* (1994), Bhabha argues that it is through the repetition and delay of the performative that one can engage in the "catachrestic postcolonial agency of 'seizing the value-coding' ... that opens up an interruptive time-lag in the 'progressive' myth of modernity, and enables the diasporic and the postcolonial to be represented" (344).[12] *thirsty*'s poetic structures of delay, prolongation, repetition, and caesura cut into the temporal present of the nation to insist that the present is haunted by unacknowledged and inarticulable histories. The broader project of *thirsty* to return to the traumatic and erased history of black people in Canada via the exemplary figure of Alan represents Brand's intervention in the progressive myth of the nation. Brand's "catachrestic" poetics operates in both senses of the term: as a productive misnaming and rewriting of the nation that opens a space for difference, and as the creation of a poetic lexicon for the otherwise unnamed and inexpressible longings, yearnings, and absences of the black diaspora.

Bhabha's discussion of temporal lag as *the* site of a critique of modernity and the nation links the prolongation and delay that Kamboureli sees in the long poem with Brand's project of blackening Canada. Indeed, Kamboureli's description of the function of delay and prolongation in the structure of the long poem is echoed in Bhabha's argument that "It is the function of the *lag* to slow down the linear, progressive time of modernity to reveal its 'gesture', its *tempi*, 'the pauses and stresses of the whole performance'" (*Location of Culture* 364; italics in original). Brand's inscription of the time of the door into the nation and her identification of the postures and gestures of diasporic life cut apart and "slow down the linear, progressive time" of modernity and nation. Bhabha's and Kamboureli's shared concerns over temporality bring to the fore the questions of diasporic agency, postcolonial critique, and cultural difference at work in Brand's long poetry. The anachronistic temporality of *thirsty*, the location of diasporic subjectivity within the pluperfect, the depiction of diasporic temporality as a kind of delay and prolongation, and the use of poetic caesuras can all be read as instances of Bhabha's time lag, particularly as they articulate an alternate temporality to that of the nation.

Brand uses caesuras as both a trope of absented-presence and as a poetic technique of delay and temporal disruption. This is one of the clearest links between her poetry and the postcolonial critique that Bhabha locates in the insertion of the time-lag into the discourse of modernity. Brand's caesuras cut apart national temporality to expose the production of the national present and "reveal its 'gesture', its *tempi*" (48). For Bhabha, the caesura marks the postcolonial moment in the time of modernity. As he explains,

> Fanon's discourse of the "human" emerges from that temporal break or caesura effected in the continuist, progressivist myth of Man. He too speaks from the signifying time-lag of cultural difference that I have been attempting to develop as a structure for the representation of subaltern

and postcolonial agency. Fanon writes from that temporal caesura, the time-lag of cultural difference (*Location of Culture* 340).

In his reading of Fanon's "The Fact of Blackness," Bhabha moves from the language of the performative to introduce the language of caesura and cutting in his analysis of the time-lag of cultural difference. The caesura cuts through calendrical time in order to disrupt the smooth national temporality. Indeed, Bhabha's description of Fanon's "jagged testimony of colonial dislocation, [and] its displacement of time and person" (*Location of Culture* 59) prefigures this disruptive caesura that he later identifies in Fanon's work. While critics have not remarked on Bhabha's turn to caesura in his reading of Fanon (from the language of the performative and the time-lag), it is particularly provocative in grappling with Brand's alteration of the Canadian long poem and the discourse of the nation. The police bullets that cut Alan apart still resonate with violence and forced absence; even more poignant, the image of Alan frozen in time with the clippers that slip from his grasp takes on new meaning in light of Bhabha's account of the postcolonial caesura in the nation. They reveal how the cutting down of Alan's body becomes a cut in the time of the nation, and thus loss provides the grounds for a different articulation of presence.

Bhabha makes the connection between the struggle to inscribe "This caesura in the narrative of modernity" and the articulation of cultural difference and diasporic agency. He argues that "The 'subalterns and ex-slaves' who now seize the spectacular event of modernity do so in a catachrestic gesture of reinscribing modernity's 'caesura' and using it to transform the locus of thought and writing in their postcolonial critique" (*Location of Culture* 353). He goes on to argue that

> The problem of the articulation of cultural difference is not the problem of free-wheeling pragmatist pluralism or the "diversity" of the many; it is the problem of the not-one, the minus in the origin and repetition of cultural signs in a doubling that will not be sublated into a similitude. What is *in* modernity *more* than modernity is this signifying "cut" or temporal break: it cuts into the plenitudinous notion of Culture splendidly reflected in the mirror of human nature; equally it halts the signification of difference. The process I have described as the sign of the present – *within modernity* – erases and interrogates those ethnocentric forms of cultural modernity that "contemporize" cultural difference (*Location of Culture* 352; italics in original).

Bhabha's articulation of cultural difference as a "problem of the not-one, the minus in the origin" indicates the way in which this temporal caesura not only opens the space for an articulation of difference, but demonstrates the presence of differences in the origin itself.[13] Brand's poetic caesuras, both as metaphors for absent-presences and as poetic embodiments of diasporic temporality, operate in a manner similar to Bhabha's description of the "articulation of cultural difference." Brand's poetics practises what Bhabha explicates, that "What is *in* modernity *more* than modernity is this signifying 'cut' or temporal break." Brand's articulation of difference and diasporic time does not merely undermine, but rather exceeds the logic of modernity and nation, enacting diasporic time's erosion of national time. Brand's use of caesura does not merely speak to absence but to a continued presence of absence, thus revealing a minus in the origin of nation. This is a more radical notion of difference than that expressed by Canadian multiculturalism and other "ethnocentric forms of cultural modernity that 'contemporize' cultural difference." This official form of multiculturalism denies the nation's history of racism, abjecting black people from the history of the nation, and rewriting the national past as a steady progression towards tolerance, diversity, and multiculturalism. In addition, these forms of nation "'contemporize' cultural difference" such that Canadian diversity becomes a sign of its modernity. The signs of visible difference may contribute to Canada's "timeliness, vitality, [and] inclusivity" (Gilroy, *Against Race* 11), but Brand's use of caesuras cuts into this national project to brandish the signs of cultural difference, showing instead how cultural difference is not merely a sign of the present but has a history within Canada. Furthermore, through Alan's depiction as lacuna, caesura, and ellipses, Brand shows how cultural difference is not contained within the meaning of multiculturalism, but instead must be understood in terms of the forced dispersals of diaspora, the dislocation of the Middle Passage, and the absented presences of the black diaspora. Thus the doubleness of the Door refracts the nation, rendering visible the caesuras of its constitution while simultaneously locating the absences of the black diaspora within the nation.

Brand's anachronistic temporality disrupts the 'meanwhile' of the nation and modernity, and interrogates the content of the present to show how it is delimited by the past. *thirsty*'s subject matter intervenes in Canadian history from a black diasporic perspective to reveal the silences and absences of Canadian history, thus disrupting the homogeneous, progressive present of Canada. Cultural difference is not contemporized by Brand, but is historicized such that the traces of the past (in the form of Alan's death and the Door) inflect the present. This alternate vision of temporality, nation, and modernity illuminates Brand's oeuvre. The speaker of *Inventory* (2006) explains that she is "not willing another empire but history's pulse / measured with another hand" (I). The speaker's stated desire to measure history's pulse with another hand links Brand's poetics with Bhabha's argument that the postcolonial articulation of difference is accomplished by inserting a new temporality into the forward-marching, calendrical time of the nation and modernity. This image of "history's pulse / measured with another hand" depicts a sick history diagnosed by the speaker who measures history according to a different conception of time. These lines resonate beautifully with – and may allude to – Derek Walcott's argument in "The Muse of History" that "The pulse of New World history is the racing pulse beat of fear, the tiring cycles of stupidity and greed" (355). While Walcott identifies the temporality of modernity with this "racing pulse beat of fear," Brand's historicizing of diasporic difference employs poetry to identify the absences of history, re-inscribe the caesura of the past and rewrite history according to another temporality. Brand's poetics measures the "pulse of New World history" that has marginalized the historical and contemporary presences of the black diaspora and marked its subjectivity as non-coeval with modernity. Walcott predicts Bhabha's observations about the temporal structure of modernity as well as the postcolonial imperative to intervene in that temporality when he explains that "The vision of progress is the rational madness of history seen as sequential time, of a dominated future" (357). Brand, Bhabha, and Derek Walcott share the view that the temporality of the nation relies on the "rational madness" of this "vision of progress." Brand's historicizing of diasporic difference employs poetry to identify the absences of history, reinscribe the caesura of the past, and rewrite history with another temporality.

Brand's poetic depiction of diasporic temporality intervenes in the temporality of the nation in ways that are unavailable to empirical or sociological analyses of diasporic subjects. Critical interpretations of Brand's work that focus strictly on plot commit the same error as strictly empirical readings of diasporic life, in that they cannot account for the play of absence and presence that Brand observes in the diaspora. The speaker of *thirsty* describes Julia as "vanishing all together, but not vanished" (XXXI), and this play between vanishing but never finally vanished provides a language for the contradictory manner in which the absences of diaspora continue to make themselves felt and present. The poetic depictions of "waiting" "willing," "longing," "desiring," and "hoping" do indeed measure history with another hand, replacing the vision of progress with a language of the inarticulable absences of the diaspora and of the longing for change. In contrast to the speaker of *Inventory* who is concerned with a far more transnational project, *thirsty*'s speaker is explicitly concerned with the historical and contemporary abjection of black people from Canada, and with rewriting black absence in ways that create a space for black people in the nation.

The speaker replaces the emptiness of the national "meanwhile" with a catachrestic grammar of longing and yearning. This shift is evident in her early declaration, "I anticipate nothing as intimate as history" (I). The intimacy of history foregrounds Brand's poetic project to write the absences of black diasporic history through the intimacy of the relationship between Chloe, Julia, and Alan. Yet, the intimacy of history also recalls Derek Walcott's desire to "*Pray for a life without plot*" (Brand, *Map* 42; italics in original) and Brand's own stated "desire for relief from the persistent trope of colonialism. To be without this story of captivity" (*Map* 42). History is not merely in the past but is intimately present and a daily, lived experience for black diasporic people as evinced by Henry Louis Gates's "plaintive and childish question … Why did you sell us?" There is also a sense of negative agency and of the lingering absences of history in Derek Walcott's desire for a "*life without plot*," in Brand's longing to be "without this story of captivity," and in the speaker's assertion that she "anticipates nothing as intimate as history." Against the narrative of historical emplotment, the "story of captivity," and the "trope of colonialism," the speaker reconceives of history as a negative present or presence; as present in the absences of the quotidian. This is evident in a later stanza where Julia recalls the day that Alan died: "lust she had lost along with the things / in her suitcases that morning," (XXXI). The speaker's passive voice in this section stresses Julia's immobility and lack of agency as well as the absence that permeates her life. Throughout this stanza Julia imagines the things that she has lost in the years since Alan's death, namely her "lust" and "the idea, the idea that she was possible" (XXXI). She recalls how once "her body was dangerous and full of liquid" and how "dance floors would bleed from the knife of her dress" (XXXI). Now, however, both Julia and Chloe are "unslaked as ghosts / They cannot summon hope" (XVIII). Towards the end of the section the speaker explains that Julia "wanted her blue skirt back, she wanted that single sense she'd lost, anticipation" (XXXI). As the absence of things lost in the past gives way to the present absence of things to come, the language of loss is transformed into the language of anticipation. In this sense the structural absence of intimate, historical loss is transformed into an anticipation of things yet to come.

thirsty ends with this felt longing and sense of anticipation. The speaker asserts, "Every smell is now a possibility, a young man / passes wreathed in cologne, that is hope; / teenagers, traceries of marijuana, that is hope too, utopia" (XXXII). The speaker, once again positioned on the street, locates hope not in the discrete identities of the people that pass her, but in the acts of exchange and transferral that she observes in the smell that they exude and that linger after they depart; "wreaths" and "traceries" communicate this web of interdependence. This sense of hopeful connectedness is also present in the speaker's musings:

> A city is all interpolation. The Filipina nurse bathes a body, the Vincentian courier delivers a message, the Sikh cab driver navigates a corner. What happens? A new road is cut, a sound escapes, a touch lasts (XX).

Interpolation, rather than interpellation, reveals how this hope is located in the anticipation of plotting new political and subject positions. It is in these new moments in this "city / that's never happened before" (VIII) that "A new road is cut." The discrete identities of "Filipina," "Vincentian," and "Sikh" give way to acts of interpolation and identities formed in exchange that constitute the kind of community that the speaker anticipates. The question "Where you from" tears the subject asunder in the act of interpellation that marks blackness as foreign and as an untimely presence within the nation. Brand rewrites this interpellation as interpolation, arguing that diasporic subjects are positioned between any stable notions of identity or belonging. In place of the desire to resolve the instability of this in-between identity, Brand valorizes it by suggesting that in these mixings, connections, and hybrid subjectivities, new possibilities of identity, community, and politics emerge. Her work demonstrates the impossibility of the question "Where are you from" for people in the black diaspora and the caesuras of both identity and nation give rise to anticipation. Like the speaker's use of transferred epithets, these concluding sections of the poem locate diasporic subjects neither "here" nor "now," but rather in the acts of exchange, interpolation, and anticipation of cutting new routes.

The speaker has detailed the manner in which the painful absences of history signified by the door, Alan's ghost, and Julia's suffering "lasts" and continue to tarnish the present moment of these lives. Yet there is a difference between the experience of being "held" in time and occupying a time that "lasts." This second condition is a hopeful temporality that is no longer overshadowed by or continually reliving the traumas of the past, but that occupies the present and anticipates the future. A time that "lasts" suggests the temporality of "interpolation" whereby the diasporic subject is not imprisoned by a longing for the past before the great disaster nor for a future that is a return to the past. Rather, occupying the present entails "living inside and outside of herself. It is to apprehend the sign one makes yet to be unable to escape it except in radiant moments of ordinariness made like art" (*Map* 18–19). For Brand, these radiant moments are the province of poetry and in contradistinction to the limits of history.

The speaker's move from the time of the door to that of the doorway is evident in the final section of the poem where she describes "From time to time … frequently, always / there is the arcing wail of a siren, as seas" (XXXIII; ellipses in original). The repetition in the phrase "From time to time" is the final repetition of the poem and evokes the prolonged temporality and the sense of being held in time that pervades the poem. Similarly, the ellipses after the repetition make delay and prolongation metrical. The phrase "From time to time" is not simply a repetition of the same empty moment in which the speaker was "held." Instead, the speaker moves from one time to another – from a time in which she was "held" to a time that "lasts" – and the phrase gestures towards change, futurity, and hope rather than a frozen or arrested temporality. The absences of the ellipses and the repetition of time open up a space of difference. At the end of the poem the speaker describes her reaction to the siren: "I wake up to it, open as doorways, / breathless as a coming hour, and undone" (XXXIII). There is a tension between the present tense in the speaker's statement, "I wake up to it" and the future tense in the speaker's description of feeling "breathless as a coming hour." The shifting of tense from the present to the future suggests the movement from one time to another and the anticipation of the "coming hour." Linking this shift in tense towards the future and the image of the doorway stresses the turn in this final section of the poem to future possibility, and to the hope of writing the doorways that the speaker wanted to declare in the poem's opening. The language of openness, doorways, and breathlessness expresses anticipation and desire, but the truly intriguing word is "undone" which suggests that the liquid future is also an undoing of the work of the past and the suspension of the present. In this sense, Brand remains true to her demand for more water than flour in her anticipation of the future.

The word "undone" reconceives of double-consciousness as not a condition to be resolved but rather a condition of possibility and interpolation. Brand's historicizing of cultural difference, her writing of absence into the narrative of nation, and her depiction of identity as "interpolation" reignite the tired debate over Canadian multiculturalism in new ways. Against the narrative of official multiculturalism that traffics in a mélange of discrete identities as signs of national "timeliness, vitality, inclusivity and global reach" (Gilroy, *Against Race* 21), Brand wants to see all identities "undone" to – in Bhabha's terms – locate the "minus in the origin" of identity and nation and to conceive of identity as open and in process. Like Du Bois who depicts the subject "torn asunder," Brand's double-consciousness gives voice to the negative identities that emerge through absence and difference. If multiculturalism is, for Brand, "relative to the state of white fear" (*Map* 79) and cannot guarantee a place in the nation, her expression of negative identities undermines these stable identities that exclude black people from the nation. Her project of blackening pushes at the borders of the nation in order to make absented, abjected, and untimely presences welcome. "Water More Than Flour," *A Map to the Door of No Return* and *thirsty* all privilege the liquidity of poetics over the solidity of empirical analyses of diasporic experience. This emphasis on liquidity also differentiates Brand's politics from Rinaldo Walcott's insistence on inscription; Brand, rather surprisingly rejoices in their undoing, in the unraveling of fixed forms. Brand's figures wait, thirst, lust, summon, and hope, evolving new forms of political community based on abiding and anticipation. Thus, Brand's writing is not merely a means to an end; her poetic meditations are acts of blackening themselves.

Chapter Two

"I'm Running for My Life": Mobility in Austin Clarke's Recent Fiction

Austin Clarke's *More* (2008) begins with the protagonist, Idora Morrison, emerging from a dream. The narrator describes Idora "Coming out of the dream, the bells are ringing, and she holds her breath" (1). This recalls the conclusion of *thirsty* in which the speaker describes awakening from a dream: "I wake up to it, open as doorways, / breathless as a coming hour, and undone" (XXXIII). The speaker in *thirsty* awakens "to it," "breathless," "open," and "undone," suggesting wonder and anticipation; Idora awakens "out of" her dream in her basement apartment to find that the circumstances of her life remain unchanged. She "holds her breath" hoping that the spiritual stasis and social paralysis that define her life have been transformed. She is disappointed and as "she is entering full consciousness, and can remember how the trees look: straight and black from the ground to the first flaring-out of limbs, dead now on the thin layer of snow that whitens the ground in these cold, teeth-shattering mornings of winter, which she hates, even after thirty years living in Canada" (1). The anticipation of the "coming hour" that infuses *thirsty* with a concluding sense of optimism and even "utopia" (XXXII) is absent in Idora's life. Instead, she awakens to recall an image of decaying, barren black trees frozen in the whiteness of the Canadian winter. If the dream at the beginning of the narrative is the migrant's dream of reinvention and a new life in a new country, that dream of reinvention is denied at the very outset of the text. In its place is the reality of black abjection from the Canadian body politic and black social immobility within Canada. Throughout *More*, and Clarke's corpus, this reality commingles with the dream of movement and reinvention to structure Clarke's deployment of double-consciousness.

As Idora awakens she goes from remembering the trees in the park to imagining her own movement through the park and across the city. This opening passage of the novel is marked by a precise and evocative oscillation between its protagonist's past and the narrative present. This striking passage, however, communicates the movement of time through physical movement across urban streets and through Idora's consciousness which mimics the agility of bodily movement. While lying in bed, Idora imagines walking

> in the short distance from her basement apartment, four streets to the south of the Park, straight as an arrow; and in her mind she crosses Queen Street, then a small street, Barton, that runs from Sherbourne to George Street; then a bigger street, Richmond, then Adelaide, and she walks through the small park and the garden patterned after nineteenth-century ones in London England, through the garbage with its smell left by dogs and homeless men; and other things that she does not like to look at, in this short walk from her neighbourhood, and she enters the huge, studded, brown, stained main door of the Cathedral that looks like the door to a castle; and sits down and settles herself in a pew whose seat is padded by a cushion and forgets her life, forgets her son, forgets "that man," forgets the Island where she was born and had left thirty years ago, as an indentured servant, a "domestic" as she was known to the Governments of her Island and of Canada; for "the loneliness, the loneliness, the loneliness," as she would complain to her friend Josephine ... the man she wanted out of her life – even though he was in America, placing him here in this basement apartment, and making him sit on one of the two red-painted chairs, talking aloud to him even though he was there only in her imagination (2–3).

The precision with which Clarke maps out Idora's movement demonstrates the traces that black bodies leave in the city through which they often move – alone, unwanted, and unnoticed.[1] Idora's movement – part pilgrimage, part personal journey – writes the spaces of the city anew from a black diasporic perspective. Idora is relegated to a marginal space in Canada, and while the spaces of the city do not reflect her presence, the city is marked with her past and present longings as she moves through it, which becomes a means of combating her marginalization. This quotation comes from the novel's opening sentence which spans the first four pages of the text and is written in stream of consciousness style, focalized by Idora. The length of this sentence and its repeated use of semicolons, dashes, commas, and ellipses indicate the leaps and movements in Idora's thinking. Like Brand's use of caesuras and repetition, the prolonged temporality at work here indicates the manner in which the present moment is overdetermined by the lingering effects and remainders of the past. Yet the length of this sentence also communicates the energetic movement of Idora's thoughts as they jump from one image, recollection, memory, and fantasy to the next.

The contrast between the activity and energy of the sentence, the energy and movement of Idora's imagination, and Idora's physical immobility within her basement apartment is equally telling. As she imagines this movement, Idora lies prostrate in her bed. The opening sentence finally ends, a few pages later, with the narrator explaining that "as she is still lying on her stomach, she cannot tell if the three red digits on her alarm clock, 7.36, refer to nighttime or daytime" (4). She imagines this vast movement across time and space while lying completely immobile, beneath the ground, in the dark. Idora's corporeal immobility is linked to her recollection of – and desire to forget – "the Island where she was born," thus linking her current immobility in Canada with the broken promises of diasporic mobility. Like the black trees in the park Idora is physically immobile, yet her imagination expresses a longing for mobility.

The simultaneous longing for movement and the feeling of immobility that animate the opening pages of *More* characterize Clarke's work. Like most of his characters, Idora is one of *The Survivors of the Crossing* (1964); she has survived the crossing from the Caribbean to Canada and now struggles to survive in Canada. The thematics of crossing pervade his work both in terms of the mixing and hybridizing of literary form, and in the ongoing movement, transference, and mobility of diasporic identities. Indeed, these two forms of crossing are inseparable in Clarke's writing and are at the heart of his expression of double-consciousness. Yet the title of his first novel also historicizes contemporary forms of movement by linking current day, transnational, and diasporic movement with the forced crossings of the Middle Passage and slavery. Clarke's texts reveal how contemporary patterns of crossing are produced by historical forms of forced movement. Against celebrations of transnational movement, global citizenship, and diasporic life, his work shows how black diasporic movement remains structured by the corporeal mobility and psychic immobility that defined the movements of the Middle Passage and the spaces of the plantation and the colony. While Idora has physically moved across continents, she has yet to arrive as a Canadian. Like Brand, Clarke's work undercuts the promises of modernity and multiculturalism by tracing the presence of the past of slavery, the Middle Passage, and colonialism in the contemporary chronotopes of black diasporic life. His characters continue to feel social immobility in Canada as they are abjected from the nation or penned in by constricting stereotypes of blackness. Yet crossing in Clarke's writings is polyvalent; the themes, politics, affects, and aesthetics of Canada and the Caribbean are wrought together through a kind of imaginative movement that exceeds the easy hybridity of official multiculturalism. His work thus eschews the fantasies of violent escape from these structures of immobility, instead detailing what it means to occupy the paradoxical and double position of being physically mobile while feeling the effects of social and psychic paralysis.

Clarke's chronotopes of black diasporic movement blacken Canada by reversing the process of inclusion. Canada finds itself within the black diaspora, rather than the black diaspora clamouring to enter the space of the nation. His characters have not crossed over but continue to engage in ongoing acts of cultural and spatial crossing with Canada. The depiction of movement transforms the nation from a site of arrival and freedom for black people, to one more route within the diaspora. Furthermore, his inscription of movement and crossing reveals the ongoing estrangement of black people from the nation as they are repeatedly imagined as en-route, originating and belonging elsewhere, an elsewhere to which they will eventually return. The mobility and crossing of diasporic life is at once the source of its vibrancy and vitality as well as a justification for black people's abjection from the nation. Clarke's work thus detours "the difficult journey from slave ship to citizenship" (Gilroy, *Black Atlantic* 31) in Canada. Walcott writes that the detour is "a method for thinking through the circuitous routes of black diasporic cultures ... Detours are the (un)acknowledged routes and roots of black expressive cultures and ... [are] both an improvisatory and an in-between space which black diasporic cultures occupy" (31). Clarke's characters' physical movement is regularly detoured by a persistent psychic and social immobility and this experience structures his expression of double consciousness.

Clarke's oeuvre aligns itself with Gilroy's premise that "The fundamental injunction" of the black diaspora is "to 'Keep On Moving'" (*Black Atlantic* 16), but rejects the conclusion that Gilroy draws from it, that the injunction to move is evidence of a "restlessness of spirit which makes ... diaspora culture vital" (16). Rather, Clarke historicizes these chronotopes and contemporary forms of diasporic movement in Canada, showing how they are not a spiritual condition but an effect of black people's psychic and social immobility. The chronotopes of the ship, the train, and the automobile reveal the continuities between the spaces of the plantation, the colony, the city, and the nation. His inscription of movement insists that black diasporic people cannot be at rest within the multicultural nation, but despite their corporeal mobility, continue to experience psychic immobility in the everyday sites of the bar, the street, the train, and the subway. Clarke's employment of those chronotopes demonstrates that the journey towards citizenship remains ongoing.

There has been a resurgence of critical interest in Austin Clarke's work since he won the Giller Prize and Commonwealth Prize for his novel *The Polished Hoe* (2002). Prior to this award, his biographer, Stella Algoo-Baksh, notes that "there has been a dearth of comprehensive examinations of Clarke's life and writing" (9). Since the publication of *The Polished Hoe*, however, previously neglected texts from his long career have been reread as early examples of a burgeoning black Canadian literary corpus. Yet, with the exception of a few critics,[2] Clarke scholarship has largely overlooked the formal and literary qualities of his writing, focusing instead on the way in which his texts "open up the possibility of cross-cultural alliances" (Casteel 132), reveal "the physical underside of urban life in Canada" (Craig 90), or "illuminate some of the blind spots of multiculturalism" (Chariandy 143). Many of George Elliott Clarke's criticisms of Brand scholarship equally apply to recent criticism of Austin Clarke's work.[3] As with Brand, Clarke's political concerns are brought into sharper focus when one recognizes how they emerge from his aesthetics; it is his rewriting of the chronotopes of the black diaspora that link his aesthetic and political concerns. He repeatedly describes the crossing of national and geographic borders as well as the traversal of cities, neighbourhoods, and the cramped inhabiting of domestic spaces. Clarke is interested in both the dream of movement that motivates the lives of his characters as well as the new and troubling forms that the dream assumes in Canada. While Brand conceives of diasporic life temporally, of the political conditions and subjectivities "to come," Clarke is primarily concerned with the spatial coordinates of identity and mobility. Clarke does not share Brand's optimism for transformation through interpolation; the routes and roots of black culture remain his focus, without utopian dreams of community, but with momentary glimpses, in the narrative present, of camaraderie and congregation.

"Sometimes, A Motherless Child" (1992), *The Origin of Waves* (1997), *The Polished Hoe* (2002), and *More* (2008) engage in a blackening of Canada by representing the putting down of roots within nation as the traversing of routes across nation and diaspora. As such, Clarke's writing of the chronotopes of the black diaspora affects a number of different registers of black diasporic life in Canada. In "Sometimes, A Motherless Child," Clarke depicts young black masculinity in Canada by contrasting the chronotope of the automobile with the immobility of the space of the jail cell. In his depiction of young and older black men, Clarke reveals how the longing for social mobility is expressed in black men's physical movement and is circumvented by the criminalization of black masculinity. *The Origin of Waves* demonstrates that older ex-colonial black men's desire for social mobility is unfulfilled by their physical movements. Clarke depicts their movement as aimless and adrift with images of an inner tube afloat at sea, a corpse that washes up on a beach, boats with no sails, and city streets covered in slippery ice. His texts broaden their scope from the consideration of the meaning of movement for the construction of masculinity to the pernicious combination of corporeal mobility and psychic immobility in black diasporic life. This shift to mobility in a general sense links his work with past theories of movement in the black diaspora as he reveals how the paralysis of the spaces of the plantation and the colony persist in these new diasporic sites. The subway, the government office, the bus, the police station, and the city street of Clarke's Canada are linked to the barracks, the plantation, the jail, and the train of Fanon's colonial environment. Clarke's work therefore contrasts the promises of reinvention and social mobility made by Canadian multiculturalism with the social paralysis that black people continue to experience in Canada.

Even before the publication of Gilroy's *The Black Atlantic* (1993) and the subsequent emergence of the Atlantic, the ship, and the figure of the exile as the definitive images of black modernity, the significance of movement, dislocation, exile, and relocation has not been lost on black writers. Of course the importance of Gilroy's work to articulate black diasporic subjectivity, particularly in his discussion of the chronotope of the ship and the space of the ocean, is immeasurable. Gilroy insists on the importance of political and geographic movements to his articulation of diasporic black subjectivity, but his work – somewhat anachronistically – does not engage with the work of Fanon despite the central importance of movement to Fanon's examination of colonial subjectivity.[4] I detour from a perhaps obvious reading of Clarke via Gilroy and instead suggest that Clarke's depiction of (im)mobility is most clearly brought into focus through Fanon's framework of movement. Gilroy's analysis of the transnational chronotope of the ship is complemented by Fanon's explication of the national and colonial chronotope of the train and the spatial configuration of race within the colony. While Gilroy focuses on figures such as Du Bois and Martin Delany,[5] a critical reading of Fanon's major works reveals the importance of movement to his theorizing of colonial power. Further, reading Fanon in conversation with Clarke's inscription of movement shows the continued presence of colonial forms of power and immobility within the nation state and how Clarke historicizes the nation's form and rewrites the nation itself as a space of movement. Fanon's colonial subject longs for the forms of corporeal movement that are commonplace for Clarke's characters. Yet the accompanying social and psychic movement that Fanon's colonial subject dreams about remains absent for Clarke's diasporic subject. Clarke's writing of the chronotopes of mobility reveals how Fanon's dream of social mobility becomes the paradoxical nightmare of diasporic paralysis. Fanon's colonial subject might dream of a violent ending to the colony that will restore his psychic and social mobility, but such an escape from immobility is impossible for Clarke's characters. Clarke's work shows how the spaces of the bar, the police station, and the government office are as immobilizing for Clarke's diasporic characters as they are for Fanon's colonial subject.

The double-consciousness of black diasporic subjectivity and the depiction of black subjects "torn asunder" is a common thread throughout Clarke's and Fanon's works. Indeed, Fanon begins *Black Skin, White Masks* (1952) with a description of double-consciousness that continues to be true of Clarke's diasporic characters: "The black man possesses two dimensions: one with his fellow Blacks, the other with the Whites ... There is no doubt that this fissiparousness is a direct consequence of the colonial undertaking" (17). Fanon's "fissiparousness" recalls Du Bois's subject "torn asunder," and this tearing pervades Clarke's depiction of diasporic double-consciousness in Canada. Unlike Gilroy who sees this doubleness as evidence of a "restlessness of spirit which makes...diaspora culture vital" (16), Fanon insists that it "is a direct consequence of the colonial undertaking" (17). In *Black Skin, White Masks* and *The Wretched of the Earth* (1961), Fanon carefully details how the colonial regime's Manichean organization of space is complemented by and enforces the immobility of the colonial subject. He argues that the colonial regime produces a physically and psychically immobilized colonial subject. Clarke, like Fanon, reveals the connection between black people's felt psychic and social immobility and physical space. Fanon insists that the colonial space is configured to enforce social and physical immobility, while Clarke transfers this colonial organization of space to the multicultural nation in which his characters are neither free nor mobile.

Fanon begins *The Wretched of the Earth* with a section on "Violence" which imagines and justifies an eruption of aggression against the enforced immobility of the colonial order. Fanon argues that "The colonial world is a compartmentalized world.... The colonized world is a world divided in two. The dividing line, the border, is represented by the barracks and the police stations" (3). For Fanon, the numerous physical and psychological divisions between colonizer and colonized not only maintain but define the colonial order. Fanon offers an extended description of the relationship between mobility and colonial power, arguing that the colonial world is "A world compartmentalized, Manichean and petrified, a world of statues: the statue of the general who led the conquest, the statue of the engineer who built the bridge. A world cocksure of itself, crushing with its stoniness the backbones of those scarred by the whip. That is the colonial world" (*Wretched* 15). This description of the colonial world as "a world of statues" excoriates the monumental history of colonialism which enshrines the achievements of the colonizer at the expense of the historical obliteration of the colonized. The petrifaction of history marked by the image of the statue is linked with the petrified (terrified) colonial subject under the colonial regime. It is this mutually enforcing petrification – immobility and terror – that constitutes the double-bind of immobility in the colonial world. Fanon outlines the psychic dimension of this immobility in his lecture "Racism and Culture," where he describes this double-bind as a social activity that "betrays a determination to objectify, to confine, to imprison, to harden. Phrases such as 'I know them,' 'that's the way they are,' show this maximum objectification successfully achieved" (44). There is a continuity between the physical and psychic structures of immobility in the colonial world, as the material immobilities of the checkpoint, the barracks, and the police station are supplemented by the ideological powers of stereotype and race. Where the dominant culture displays qualities "of dynamism, of growth, of depth," the colonized subject is socially, physically, and psychically petrified, objectified, and penned-in by the colonial regime. Like the colonial subjects who are immobilized, the colonized "culture once living and open to the future, becomes closed, fixed in the colonial status, caught in the yoke of oppression … cultural mummification leads to a mummification of individual thinking" ("Racism and Culture" 44). Whereas Gilroy's analysis of movement focuses on the transnational imagery of mobility, ships, pullman porters, trains, and the ocean, Fanon considers the explicit images of national and colonial immobility: barracks, police stations, chains, and statues as monuments to the psychic immobility of the colonial system.

Linking Gilroy's attention to the chronotopes of the black Atlantic with Fanon's discussion of colonial immobility reveals both the pleasures of mobility and the pain of enforced immobility in a nuanced account of black diasporic movement. Gilroy justifies his decision to employ the metaphor of the ship as the chronotope of the Black Atlantic:

> I have settled on the image of ships in motion across the spaces between Europe, America, Africa, and the Caribbean as a central organizing symbol for this enterprise and as my starting point. The image of the ship – a living, micro-cultural, micro-political system in motion – is especially important for historical and theoretical reasons … Ships immediately focus attention on the middle passage, on the various projects for redemptive return to an Africa homeland (*Black Atlantic* 4).

The ship is neither entirely within Africa nor the New World. Rather, the ship is located within the Middle Passage, situated in a violent, traumatic, forced, yet also "syncretic" (3) and productive in-betweenness. Gilroy's employment of the ship as a central chronotope of black modernity supports his "suggestion that cultural historians could take the Atlantic as one single, complex unit of analysis in their discussions of the modern world and use it to produce an explicitly transnational and intercultural perspective" (15). Gilroy's privileging of the Atlantic "as one single, complex unit of analysis" re-reads the violence of the Middle Passage as a possibly productive, syncretic, mobile, and liquid site that speaks to the complexities of black modernity. While Gilroy's argument is crucial, his analysis needs to be supplemented with a consideration of those forms of enforced immobility and division that restrict these syncretic acts of invention and self-making. His privileging of the ship, ocean, and mobility is complemented by Fanon's analysis of the enforced immobility of the colonial world. Indeed Gilroy's attention to transnationality and syncretism is modified by Fanon's attention to the importance of national and racial borders, immobility, and the Manicheanism of the colonial world. Whereas Gilroy sees the "fundamental injunction" of black diasporic life as a call to "Keep On Moving" (16), Fanon insists that movement is not always possible, desired, nor voluntary. Furthermore, Gilroy's analysis of movement remains largely at the level of the trope, whereas Fanon's analysis of colonial immobility describes the political, psychic, and corporeal effects of immobility on the colonial subject. Fanon's depiction of mobility and immobility operates at the level of the flesh and psyche to indicate how colonial Manicheanism isolates the colonial subject from his or her body.

Fanon's analysis of the immobility of colonial society extends not only to the social arrangement of the colony but also connects the physical and psychic immobility of the colonial subjectivity forged by that colonial order. He describes this double bind of immobility:

> The colonial subject is a man penned in; apartheid is but one method of compartmentalizing the colonial world. The first thing the colonial subject learns is to remain in his place and not overstep its limits. Hence the dreams of the colonial subject are muscular dreams, dreams of action, dreams of aggressive vitality. I dream I am jumping, swimming, running, and climbing. I dream I burst out laughing, I am leaping across a river and chased by a pack of cars that never catches up with me. During colonization the colonized subject frees himself night after night between nine in the evening and six in the morning (*Black Skin* 15).

Fanon emphasizes the missing element in Gilroy's affirmation of mobility: the colonial subject's "muscular dreams" and desire for movement are not inherent to the formation of black modernity, but rather a response to the immobility of the colonial order. As Neil Lazarus points out, "Fanon's concept of the 'native' or the 'Negro' is not to be thought of as merely *descriptive* of independently existing (African) subjects. This is a point absolutely insisted upon by Fanon: he notes time and again that the figure of the native is not autochthonous, but is rather a construct of colonialism – actually, of the settler" (169; italics in original). Lazarus's reading demonstrates that the repressive immobility of the colonial world both produces and is resisted through the colonial subject's dreams of bodily aggressiveness, physical movement, and vitality. Indeed, Fanon's description of "The immobility to which the native is condemned" (*Wretched* 51) insists that this immobility is an effect of the subject position of "native" produced by colonization. Another effect of this production of the "native" are the "muscular dreams, dreams of action, dreams of aggressive vitality" whereby the colonial subject imagines intense bodily movements that counteract the imposed immobility of the colonial order. Fanon therefore insists that this fantasy of movement is an ambivalent one, both an effect of and resistance against the enforced immobility of the colonial order, but no less felt and empowering for being so.

Clarke's depiction of black immobility in Canada reveals how Fanon's dream of violently casting off the structures of immobility is impossible for black diasporic people in Canada. Indeed, Fanon's fantasy of the mobility of the colonial subject is rewritten by Clarke in *More*. At the outset of the novel, Idora is described as "Coming out of the dream" (1), which she recalls later that morning:

> The sadness weighs upon her spirit as she tries to call to mind the dream that the ringing of the bells interrupted; and she remembers now how the dream turned terrible. There was a line of men, like soldiers on a march in a green pasture, passing her, in single file, with tall thin-bodied trees surrounding them, and that gave no shade. The horror of her dream, when she got close to the line of soldiers, all black men, and who seemed to be the age of her own son, was that they all had their right hands cut off, clean-clean, at the wrists. And she thought the end of the ringing of the bells ... was like the sudden, final slashes of a cutlass. All the men were tied to one another, by rope ... And she wondered what was the reason for cutting off their right hands. Were they all left handed? And now she remembered. The man at the head of the single file of captured soldiers was "that man," her husband, Bertram, only younger. And the man at the rear, a boy, was her son, Barrington James (22–3).

Idora's complicated dream inverts Fanon's claim that "the colonized subject frees himself night after night between nine in the evening and six in the morning," as here the dream is not one of liberation, movement, and agency but rather one of fear, anxiety, violence, and repression. While Fanon's dreaming is full of possibility, Idora's multilayered dream "turned terrible," becoming a nightmare of immobility, racism, surveillance, and powerlessness. The barren trees that Idora recalls at the start of the novel take on new connotations as she links the line of black men with the "tall thin-bodied trees surrounding them." The difference between Fanon's and Idora's dreams expresses the shift from the dreams of the colonial subject to the dreams of the post-colonial, diasporic subject, recalling David Scott's (2004) argument that contemporary postcolonial subjects "live in tragic times" (210) and that "almost everywhere, the anticolonial utopias have gradually withered into postcolonial nightmares" (2). Fanon argues that the dreams of the colonial subject are composed of "jumping, swimming, running, and climbing. I dream I burst out laughing, I am leaping across a river and chased by a pack of cars that never catches up with me." In Idora's dream, however, the mobility of the colonial subject is replaced by the immobility of black men who have their right hands cut off and are tied together, marching like prisoners. If the dream of movement is produced as an effect of occupying the subject position of the colonized, then Idora's nightmare of immobility is an expression of what it means to be black in Canada. The moving, muscular, and energetic body in Fanon's dream is replaced by the disciplined, criminalized, and brutalized black male body of Idora's nightmare. Thus Idora's nightmare reveals how the structures of physical and psychic immobility that defined Fanon's colonial world have not eroded but have persisted in new forms. Where Gilroy attends to transnational scenes of movement, Clarke demonstates the multicultural nation's indebtedness to the colony's racist arrangement of space and management of bodies. While the barriers and barracks of Fanon's colony may have been torn down, their effects are sublimated in Canada and are felt in the psychic immobility of Clarke's characters.

Idora's dream indicates the specific manner in which black men in Canada are immobilized by state violence and endemic racism. While Fanon's subject is always male, Clarke's narrating of the nightmare from Idora's perspective enables him to differentiate between the effects of psychic immobility on black men and women. Clarke's narrating of the chronotopes of the black diaspora is gendered such that Idora's immobility is felt as a "sadness" that "weighs upon her spirit," whereas the men in her life are physically and violently immobilized. Idora's retelling of her nightmare reveals her anxieties about her son and husband, and about black men more generally. Her dream and her observations of black men throughout the novel suggests the particular forms of immobility that affect black men, and also her own complicity in viewing black male bodies as criminal. While she recognizes the vulnerability of the black male body in Canadian society, and its status as a locus of power and control, she is also complicit with the dominant perspective that views black men as threats to social order. Idora's dream represents one of her many fears about her son and the stereotypes of – and violence committed against – black male youth to which she fears he is succumbing. Later in the chapter the narrator observes, "She has been thinking about her son: hoping he would stop dressing like a rapper" (24) and as she watches him in a park, she recalls her dream and "the tableau of frightened black bodies … They are bent in fear and in fatigue" (24). It is unclear whether the "frightened black bodies" are the figures in the park or in the dream, yet Idora's concerns over black masculinity and her feeling that there is an absence of men in her life (her husband leaves her and BJ is rarely present at home or in the novel) pervade the novel.[6]

Idora's fears recur when she witnesses a black man picking through her garbage and thinks "He was a black man! A black man! … The garbage-thief is a black man! It make my heart bleed … 'You come to that?' I shout at him. 'You don't know you are a black man? You come to this? You lost your dignities'" (99; ellipses in original)? Her repetition of the phrase "black man" indicates the depth of the crisis of black masculinity that she articulates. Her repeated taunt, "You don't know you are a black man" is also her lament that black men fail to live up to their name. Later in the novel, Idora describes feeling

> surrounded by her worries, quarried like an animal being hunted down; and disgusted, in her loneliness, with her son, as she would try, on many nights to locate him in the Park across the street from the apartment … And when she can pick him out from the cluster of his friends, she can see only parts of his body: sometimes his head; sometimes his legs; sometimes his torso; as if he is cut into pieces, like a side of beef, rendered headless, legless, through the dexterity of a cleaver on the carcass of a slaughtered cow. (23–4)

Idora and BJ are linked through her use of animal metaphors, yet Idora's observation also reveals her own bias and the manner in which she has naturalized a particular depiction of black men.[7] Looking for BJ, she attempts to "pick him out from a cluster of friends" as if he were part of a police lineup or an undifferentiated group of young men whose very presence is interpreted as criminal. Her worries about her son reveal the manner in which black men are socially and psychically immobilized through stereotypes of criminality, and the manner in which Idora herself is complicit in those stereotypes. Phanuel Antwi has convincingly argued that "the journey from being *a* regular black male subject to *the* black male subject under duress is a short distance" (194; italics in original). He goes on to comment on precisely the immobilizing effect of this criminalizing and stereotyping of black men: "Because we do not quite know when we will become the suspicious black (male) subject under the eye of the law or when we will escape the fishbowl phenomenon of being watched, many of our movements tend to be calculated and guarded, so guarded that each movement seems strangely immobile" (194). Idora's gaze links this criminalization and vulnerability of the black male body – read as a series of disconnected parts, or as part of a cluster of blackness – with the immobility of black male subjectivity evinced in the stereotypes of black masculinity. Her pseudo-panoptic watching of her son, along with Antwi's depiction of the "fishbowl phenomenon" indicates the immobilizing gaze that transforms BJ into "*the* black male subject under duress." Both her dream of BJ's punishment and her observations of BJ in the park reveal the pervasive depiction of young black men as criminal and problematic, as well as her own difficulty of observing and depicting black men outside that logic of surveillance and criminalization.

This tension between Clarke's depiction of black men's desire for mobility and the structures of immobilizing stereotype and criminalization is also present in the short story "Sometimes, A Motherless Child" (1993) which focuses on BJ from a number of different perspectives. In this story BJ realizes Fanon's dream of mobility as he drives through Toronto in a BMW, but his physical mobility is undercut by structures of surveillance and criminalization. The narrative is told from a number of different perspectives, including that of BJ, his mother, white people who observe him, and the police. The multiple narrators and resulting shifts in focalization display the contrast between BJ's own sense of mobility and the forms of social immobility that confine and trap him, as it does his journey from subject/agent to victim. This story, along with some of Clarke's other short stories ("I'm Running For My Life" [1996] and "Don't Shoot!" [2006]), form the outline of the plot of *More*. In the story BJ and his friend Marco win money at the race track and purchase a white BMW with the license plate "BLUE" (the name of the horse that they bet on). The movement in this narrative is largely organized around BJ's pleasure in driving his car across the city and the feeling of status and agency the BMW confers. The bulk of the narrative focuses on BJ and Marco as they drive around the city, but also includes the observations of two white women who believe BJ has stolen the car, and police officers who follow and arrest BJ and Marco. The narrator comments,

> The BMW took the first entrance on to the 401 West doing eighty. BJ settled behind the wheel, with an unfiltered Gauloise cigarette dangling at the corner of his mouth, one eye closed against the smoke, and he put the car into fourth gear, and the car still had some more power left, and it moved like a jungle animal measuring its prey, and exerting additional power because of the certainty of devouring its prey ... It was simply that BJ liked to drive fast (346).[8]

The narrative details the movement of the BMW and the pleasure that BJ takes in driving it, and one suspects that Clarke takes just as much pleasure in writing this masculine movement. There is a sense of masculine agency in this passage particularly in the way that the car signifies the kind of power that BJ desires. Yet the subject of the first sentence is not BJ but rather "The BMW" itself. Similarly, it is the car that "still had some more power left" and "moved like a jungle animal" rather than BJ. This displacement of the agency of movement from BJ onto the vehicle suggests that despite owning the vehicle, BJ and Marco will never be able to access the physical and social mobility that they believe the car offers them.

The narrator describes the pleasure BJ and Marco experience as they drive through the city: "cruising along Eglinton Avenue, passing record stores from which reggae and dancehall blared out upon them, past barbershops and restaurants and shops which sold curry goat and fish and oxtail and peas and rice, and they felt they could smell and taste the food even in this breathless afternoon" (349). Their cruising across the city, particularly as it makes the city register their presence, is a realization of Fanon's dream of mobility but with subtle restrictions. Gilroy's analysis (2010) of the chronotope of the automobile provides insight into these restrictions. In his reading of Ralph Ellison's "Cadillac Flambé" he argues that Ellison makes a "clear distinction between the traditional means of self-making – the technology of the free black self – and the forms of freedom involved in consuming objects which, though you have chosen them for yourself, effectively come to dominate you" (19). This leads Gilroy to suggest that appeals to agency via automobiles constitute nothing more than "automobile citizenship ... a kind of giant armoured bed on wheels that can shout out the driver's dwindling claims upon the world into dead public space at ever-increasing volume" (48). Yet there is no "clear distinction" between the "traditional means of self-making" and a pseudo-freedom via consumption in Clarke's works, where acts of freedom and agency are often tied to material acquisition. BJ's and Marco's driving across the city is a form of self-making that gives them temporary access to a sense of agency and power that they otherwise do not possess. Their "cruising" also constitutes a form of blackening, remapping the city from a black, diasporic perspective. The BMW enables a traversal of the city that shades Toronto with the affective experience of surprise, wonder, and pleasure: "As BJ pulled away from the curb in front of the subway station, in the East End, with Marco strapped in beside him, and laughing and turning up the volume of the saxophone solo, the BMW was so loud with the music contained within it, that Marco himself felt his head was about to explode" (346). John Coltrane's song "A Love Supreme" accompanies their drive across the city; BJ and Marco "remained quiet in the waves of this melodious tune they both liked so much ... BJ insisted ... that it was a religious chant. Marco, equally insistent, said it was a love song" (349). Both Coltrane's four-part "musical narration" and the short story are at once celebrations and elegies. Kamau Brathwaite has argued that "Jazz ... continues to be, the perfect expression for the rootless, 'cultureless', truly ex-patriate Negro ... What determines the shape and direction of a jazz performance ... is the nature of its improvisation" (336–7). The parallels between BJ's "rootless" cruising in the BMW and Coltrane's "musical narration" suggests that BJ is not participating in some form of diminished agency, but rather that his movement is a form of performance and improvisation; that his driving across the city forges new paths, mimicking the circuitous routes by which black Canadians claim Canada as their own.

While BJ and Marco are able to practise the physical movement that Fanon longed for, the structures of psychic and social immobility continue to ensnare them. The mobility which is such a source of pleasure to the men is undermined when they are followed and later arrested by the police. As BJ drives,

> he did not know that, as soon as he had pulled away from the subway at Steeles, at that precise moment, a blue sedan, with two men in it, had pulled away too, and had followed him ... The marked police cruiser was expecting him. And as he swooshed by, the traffic policeman was on the radio to another one, somewhere farther west along the 401. Conversation passed between the policemen in the cars. 'Drug dealers for sure!' (347)

The fishbowl phenomenon described by Antwi is rendered palpable here in these multiple observations that rely on stereotypes of black masculinity. When the police officer discovers that BJ and Marco are not drug dealers and did not steal the BMW, he drives them around the city trying to decide what to do with them. As the policeman drives them around the city, BJ "recognized 52 Division police station. And his heart sank. He had heard about 52 Division. Wasn't it a police officer from 52 Division who had shot a Jamaican, many years ago? … Apart from the crackling of voices from the other, invisible policemen and dispatchers, the cruiser was quiet" (352). BJ's and Marco's ride in their BMW across the city is filled with a sense of possibility in the sounds and smells of Toronto, whereas this ride in the back of the police cruiser is silent and filled with fear and the threat of violence. The narrator explains that BJ "said nothing. And Marco said nothing. Marco had been slapping his trouser legs. BJ sat with his eyes closed, his teeth pressed down tight" (353). Even the staccato sentences of this section reflect BJ's and Marco's immobility within the police cruiser. Indeed, the suspect form of mobility where they move across the city while being immobilized within the police cruiser stresses the forms of suspect movement that repeatedly affect black men in Clarke's work. This second drive contrasts with the first to highlight the curtailing of BJ's improvised movement through the city and the social immobility of black men in Canada. The first drive is written as a mélange of the sounds, smells and pleasures of black life in Toronto, while this second drive is silent but for the voices of the "other, invisible policemen." Thus Clarke repeats, with a difference, the pleasurable movement that BJ and Marco experienced in the first part of the text. It is during this drive that the invisible presence of racial profiling, surveillance, and the criminalization of youth remaps Toronto from the perspective of a criminalized black man. The story's depiction of two forms of movement give voice to the strains of elegy, lament, and love evinced by the references to Coltrane and the references to the blues.

BJ is further immobilized when he is alone in a police cell and is described as having "paced up and down, not having enough length in the square space to make his pacing more dramatic, and less of pathos … he again realized the restriction of the square space" (359). The story concludes with BJ being killed by the police, an event that is foreshadowed by Marco's feeling that his "head was about to explode" (346), and BJ's nightmare in which he screams "'Don't shoot, don't shoot!' There was terror in his pleading" (329). Fanon's dream of mobility is once again transformed into the nightmare of state violence. BJ does not have the same dreams as Fanon's colonial male subject, yet his dreams, hopes, and fears are still conditioned by the themes that Fanon illuminates. Clarke's narratives demonstrate how the desire for agency in the face of immobilizing power persists, in new forms, for young black men. In *More* and "Sometimes, A Motherless Child" Clarke reveals how, despite the physical movement of diasporic life, the psychic immobility that defined the plantation and the colony continue to persist.

If Clarke's works thus far have focused on state power's immobilizing effects on young black men, his novels that feature older black men – depicting a generational divide between figures of black masculinity – shift the emphasis to the construction of masculinity itself. The depiction of these older diasporic men is less focused on the vulnerability of the body and more concerned with a crisis of masculinity that they experience in Canada. Clarke repeatedly suggests that colonial men's desire to move is part of their desire to assert themselves as men, to stake out a new identity and territory of their own. As such, Clarke's older characters often express the failings of migration as individual failings of masculinity. As Daniel Coleman (1998) has shown, the projects of migration and of asserting one's masculinity are often intimately linked, and masculinities undergo a process of "*cross-cultural refraction*" (3; italics in original) in the act of migration. The project of becoming a man is, for many of Clarke's colonial men, dependent on leaving home and nation and making a successful life abroad. In *The Polished Hoe*, for instance, Constable Percy describes the trip he took from the island of Bimshire in a boat as akin to the

> feeling that Columbus and Sir Francis Drake and Lord Nelson … mustta had when they was sailing the high seas. A feeling that I was on top, that I was conquering something or somebody. That I was moving along. Just moving along. From one place to the next … I am sure that Sir Francis Drake and Lord Nelson, and those other sea dogs, must have had the same feeling of power of moving along. (251)

"On top" and "conquering something or somebody" indicate how the thrill of movement is, for Percy, a distinctly masculine thrill, while his allusion to Columbus and Francis Drake suggests that this male desire for movement emulates colonial male archetypes. If, as Fanon suggests, the colonial world is a "world of statues," the statue of Francis Drake in the centre of Percy's village has impressed itself upon him such that movement and power are only imaginable within that colonial imaginary. This desire to assert one's masculinity through movement inevitably fails, however, as it is undercut by racism, stereotypes, and limited opportunities in new countries. Percy's power and agency are, for instance, undercut when he feels simultaneously "collared and encircled ... surrounded by sea and sharks" (326).

This failure of mobility is also a key theme in Clarke's short story "Canadian Experience" (1986), in which an unnamed protagonist has his first job interview in five years but is unable to bring himself to attend the interview. The link between masculinity and migration is evident in the protagonist's decision to live in Canada against his father's wishes. At the end of the story the pressures of migration and life in Canada prove to be too much and the protagonist commits suicide by jumping in front of a subway car. As he dies, he thinks of the elevator in the office building where his interview was scheduled: "How comfortable and safe and brave he had felt travelling and laughing and falling so fast and so free" (39). The comfort and safety of his movement in the elevator is juxtaposed with the danger and impending violence of the subway car.[9] Both pleasure, linked to the promises of reinvention, and pain and disappointment in the social immobility that these men experience in Canada, characterize Clarke's depiction of older masculinities.

Clarke's *The Origin of Waves* (1997) is exemplary in this respect as it details a day-long conversation between two best friends, Tim and John, both of whom migrate from Barbados and are left to cope with the consequences of their decisions to do so. Both felt that migration was an essential element in asserting their masculinity, yet find that transnational movement has led to their questioning and doubting themselves as men. After a chance meeting in a Toronto blizzard, the two men go to a Yonge Street bar where they recount the stories of their lives, try to understand their decisions to migrate from Barbados, and in the process experience simultaneous crises of migration and masculinity. The contrast between their recollected transnational movement and their immobility in the bar during the snowstorm resonates with the suspect forms of movement that recur in Clarke's corpus. The dream of colonial mobility is replaced, in this text, by the repetition of two of the protagonist's childhood memories: that of his Uncle's corpse washing up on a beach and his recollection of watching an inner tube adrift at sea. Clarke's repetition of these images depicts movement as traumatic and involuntary, and the main character imagines himself as perpetually adrift. Tim's recollection of "that inner tube drowned at sea" (24) is one of the central metaphors of the novel, conceiving of movement as aimless, ongoing, threatening, and involuntary; swimming quickly becomes drowning. The inner tube metaphor also resonates with the structure of the novel which abandons chapters in favour of a single sustained narrative sequence that takes place over the course of a day. Heike Härting argues that "Both men's narratives … are frequently interrupted by the recurrence of the conch-shell and inner tube metaphors which, like the waves, recoil from and re-enter Tim's and John's narratives" (104); John and Tim are brought together because of the circularity and repetition that dominates their failed migration, and that they can ruefully turn into shared experience. They move only to find that they arrive back where they started, as the social constraints that Tim tried to leave behind are present in Canada. This circularity is mirrored in the structure of the novel itself as the narrative begins with the two men meeting in a snowstorm, spending the bulk of the narrative retelling the events of their lives in a bar, and then after leaving the bar, running into one another again in the snow. This is also captured in the title of the novel where the waves suggest repetitious movement and the impossibility of knowing one's origins. The novel's structural and thematic circularities, the absence of any chapter breaks, the continuous return of past memories and traumas, and the waves of the title all inflect the novel's concern with movement to suggest that Tim and John are condemned to return to the same questions and uncertainties.

The Origin of Waves begins in the voice of its first-person narrator, Tim, who remarks, "I am walking in the snow now … Time in this city has made this walking sail old and worn and tattered … But I am going nowhere in particular. I have no destination … the sail that gives me movement is patched with words of an old song" (13–14). He goes on to describe his attempts to navigate an icy Toronto street: "I stop walking, though I am unable to stand motionless, in this snow which shifts like an uncontrollable roller skate, for too long. My shoes are sliding" (26–7). The snow is an image for the pervasive whiteness that immobilizes black life in Toronto, and Tim later terms winter "the white darkness, the white darkness" (231). Furthermore, Tim and John's emergence from the blizzard suggests the manner in which they are denied origins or beginnings, but rather are, like Brand's transferred epithets, constantly emerging, moving, and between places. Words such as "shifting," "uncontrollable," and "sliding" reflect the contrast between emergence, transition, betweenness, and involuntary movement and stability, destination, and belonging. Yet despite the desire to move, "swim out," and "leave this place" (17), neither Tim nor John has a sense of precisely where he is going:

> "Where you was going when I bounced-into you?" John says. "Nowhere." "A man have to go *somewhere*. You can't just be walking and not going nowhere! You can't be just going from one place to the next, and not going *anywhere*! You must have some direction ..." "Every day, at the same time, in any kind of weather, I leave my house and walk down Yonge Street heading straight for the Lake, and back from the Lake up again on Yonge Street and back to my house." (69; italics in original)

Tim is compelled to move but there is no purpose, origin, or destination for his movement. Like the inner tube that haunts his memories, he is adrift and compelled to repeat his aimless movements with no origin or destination in mind.

While the plot is circular, ending as it begins, and Tim and John's movement is repetitive, the narrative also reveals how this circularity and repetition become marked by a difference. If the novel inserts a detour into Fanon's dream of mobility, it also shows how both men's acts of movement constitute a peculiar form of agency. In their second meeting in the blizzard, after having discussed their lives, dreams and memories in the bar, Tim and John are changed, having gained a sense of camaraderie in their shared condition. Near the conclusion of the novel, Tim declares, "As we stand a policeman in a cruiser the same colour of the snow passes his eye over us, and continues on his way ... 'The motherfucking *Man*, y'all!' and I feel and share the glee in his voice which shivers from the cold" (234; italics in original). The subtle link between their standing, the police observation, and the pervasive whiteness of snow and Canada indicates how their mobility is produced as an effect of social immobility. The policeman is suspicious of them standing on the street and his act of surveillance carries with it the message to move along. Yet John's dismissive and reproachful cuss becomes a means of claiming the street as his own against the blanketing whiteness. Against the state injunction to Keep On Movin', the policeman's gaze and "the white darkness" of Canada, John's language produces a form of camaraderie between the two men that makes life in Canada more bearable. If the images of white snow, blizzards, and white darkness deny John and Tim any origins and efface them from the Canadian physical and imaginative landscape, their use of language and their shared acts of narration and storytelling become the means by which they can "stand" Canada. The fragile glee of John's voice is preceded by the moment when "our laughter explodes. Out of the white mist comes shapes which pause to look, to understand, to wonder why this loud tropical laughter and equatorial joy must take place in this deadening cold" (29). Tim and John's shared laughter recalls Fanon's dream that he "burst[s] out laughing," and is an expression of their presence and a means of surviving among this "white mist" of Canada.

This repetition with difference is evident in the novel's final depiction of movement where Tim describes the two men "Like two fishing boats without sails, rudderless in the broiling white foam of the waves. We walk with our arms around each other, affection and guidance, ballast we always found in our lives; two old black men coming through a storm in a place we do not really know" (231). Although the themes of involuntary movement, the circular structure of the narrative, and the structures of "broiling" whiteness continue, there is some difference that is marked by their male camaraderie. Against the "white foam of the waves" and the "white darkness," they affectionately "walk with our arms around each other" and are "two old black men coming through a storm in a place we do not really know." While the promise of masculine reinvention through movement continues to ring hollow and the men continue to be "Like two fishing boats without sails," their camaraderie and storytelling inflect these repeated acts of movement and dislocation with a new sense of hope. Further, their acts of narration rewrite Canada by inscribing the acts of movement and the chronotopes of the diaspora within the nation. The immobility of white snow, the pervasiveness of white mist, and the paralysis of the white blizzard are rewritten as the "broiling whiteness of the waves," and this subtle rewriting of whiteness via a chronotope of the black diaspora transforms whiteness from signifying national belonging to being yet another identity that is en-route, mobile and emerging. Clarke thus blackens Canada by rewriting the nation not as a destination for some and a detour for others, but by making the transnational circuit "home." From the novel's structures of repetition emerges a re-routing and detouring of Canada as not the site of arrival or origins, but of movement and transition within broader diasporic patterns.

Clarke also revisits what is perhaps Fanon's "primal scene" (Bhabha, *Location of Culture* 109) of colonial petrifaction in which Fanon describes an encounter on a train with a white child who shouts, "Look, a Negro" (*Black Skin* 109)! Fanon writes,

> Sealed into that crushing objecthood, I turned beseechingly to others. Their attention was a liberation, running over my body suddenly abraded into nonbeing, endowing me once more with an agility that I thought lost, and by taking me out of the world, restoring me to it. But just as I reached the other side, I stumbled, and the movements, the attitudes, the glances of the other fixed me there, in the sense in which a chemical solution is fixed by a dye. (109)

In this famous colonial encounter, the white child's gaze immures Fanon in the fact of his blackness. In what is perhaps a rearticulation of Lacan's mirror stage (thus the "primal scene") of the emergence of the subject, Fanon employs the language of agility and movement to describe being consigned to objecthood. There are a series of contradictory observations in this passage: his body is at once "abraded," worn away and dissolved into non-being, yet also endowed "with an agility I thought lost." These contradictions express a "movement [that] seems strangely immobile," and are also evident in Fanon's description of the white, colonial gaze that takes Fanon out of the world but also restores him to it as an object. These contradictions express the process of having one's subjectivity "Sealed into that crushing objecthood," the process of losing one's body for oneself, and of having one's body and one's subjectivity remade as a composition of others. This passage is often read for its depiction of the body, for its psychoanalytic content, for the experience of racialization, and also for the manner in which the gaze reduces colonial subjects to objecthood. Yet implicit in this scene are the chronotopes of modernity and the black diaspora, because the staging of Fanon's intense paralysis when "the other fixed me there" occurs on a train. Both in his language of constrained agility and the setting of the train, Fanon inscribes this suspect form of movement at the core of this encounter.

Gilroy also insists on the importance of the train as a chronotope of black modernity, black masculinity, and the contradictions of movement that it evokes. He discusses the importance of the train (focusing particularly on the figure of the Pullman porter) for James Weldon Johnson and Du Bois, arguing that Du Bois "was a theorist and interpreter of African American experience for whom the compromised *public* space of the Jim Crow railroad car provided a central topos. In that absurd location, official, legal segregation touched and debased the worthy lives of black America's mobile, modernising caste. Seated there, the sublation of their freshly doubled consciousness was something they could begin to imagine" (12; italics in original). Detouring Gilroy via Fanon foregrounds the importance of the train as just such an "absurd" and contradictory site of mobility and immobility, agency, and racism. The automobile serves as a metaphor of mobility for a postcolonial generation of black men, but the train is an important image of mobility for Clarke's and Fanon's generation of colonial men and women. Gilroy reads the chronotope of the train as primarily a sign of black modernity and double-consciousness, stressing the train's importance in the routes and transformations of the black diaspora; on the contrary, Fanon writes the chronotope of the train as *the* scene of confrontation between white colonizer and black colonial subject. This confrontation suggests that both white and black identities are given meaning through these structures of mobility. Fanon's chronotope of the train reveals the contradictions of modernity's civilizing project and also shows how the psychic mobility of the white subject is an effect of the psychic immobilizing of the black subject. The child that shouts "Mama see the Negro! I'm scared" (112) and the liberal white passenger who insists "color prejudice is something I find utterly foreign" (113) both attain and secure their white identity by insisting on the immutable and immobilizing "Fact" of Fanon's blackness. As such, the setting of this scene on a train reveals the paradox for Fanon that while he is physically mobile, any form of psychic and social mobility remains out of reach. Thus the series of contradictory impulses in this passage can be read as an expression of the simultaneously enabling and disabling aspects of black, colonial subjectivity that emerge against the backdrop of the train, a symbol of the failed promises of mobility and modernity.

Fanon's depiction of the colonial gaze on a train, complete with the ambivalence of promised movement and social paralysis, is creatively reinterpreted by Clarke in *The Polished Hoe*. In this text, the main character Mary-Mathilda gives her statement confessing her murder of the plantation manager, Mr. Bellfeels. Her statement provides the frame narrative for a number of other stories she tells of her life, including a trip she takes by train across America with Bellfeels. Her pleasure in moving across the continent is undercut by her realization aboard the train that "in all this time, travelling by now hundreds and hundreds o' miles, Mr. Bellfeels is seated in a different section of the train, invisible to me, and separated from me. Mr. Bellfeels is sitting in one section, a reserved compartment of the train, a sleeper. And I in a next section they called third-class, sitting up, my back hurting me, all throughout this journey north … I was *serrigated* from Mr. Bellfeels" (188; italics in original). In this new post-plantation, but not post-Jim Crow – configuration of race, Clarke brings together Fanon's attention to the gaze and his elucidation of the Manichean organization of colonial space to undercut the pleasures and promises of mobility. Ironically, it is the great house of the plantation in *The Polished Hoe* that allows for some degree of mobility and mingling of the fixed positions of black and white, allowing Bellfeels and Mary-Mathilda to have a relationship (albeit a very violent and coercive one). The space of the train, however, is so strictly racially demarcated that the two are "invisible" to one another. Like Fanon, Mary-Mathilda gives an account of how, despite her physical movement, "the other fixed me there" (109). Yet Clarke's rewriting of Fanon's chronotope of the train also imagines that movement as a metaphor for the possibility of destabilizing racial identities as the contradictions of whiteness as a privileged racial identity are defined against a "Fact" of immutable blackness. If Fanon is the mirror onto which the white passengers gaze, then neither Fanon's blackness nor the privileged whiteness is a fact; both are mutually constitutive and imaginary.

The shift from Fanon's world to Clarke's is evident in the invisible and implicit scene of racial management and exclusion that Mary-Mathilda describes. If the encounter between Fanon and the white child precipitates the emergence of the Fact of blackness, that Manichean moment already contains and conditions the present and future that Mary-Mathilda represents. In *The Polished Hoe* the racism on the train is not staged as a confrontation with a paralysing and objectifying white gaze, but is transformed into a structure of enforced immobility that is present in the very spatial arrangement of the train. Indeed, the scene of confrontation which petrifies Fanon is impossible in this segregated train, suggesting that while the social order has shifted, the immobilities of race persist even while they have been rendered "invisible." Rather than an explicit confrontation with a white gaze, the immobility of racism makes itself felt through the segregation of the train as well as in the names of towns such as "*Lynchburg*" (194; italics in original) that the train passes through. Furthermore, where Fanon is confronted with an explicitly white gaze, Clarke rewrites the scene, removing the possible vindication of naming and resisting racism. Indeed, the structural and invisible system of racism makes the scene all the more pernicious and immobilizing. Mary-Mathilda's use of the word "invisible" recalls the depiction of the "invisible policemen" in "Sometimes, A Motherless Child" to indicate how the structures of racism and colonial immobility persist in new invisible and structural forms. The shift from confrontational racism to structural and institutional racism is one way by which Clarke transforms Fanon's chronotopes of mobility and immobility to indicate how the colonial systems of control and racial management persist in the post-colonial world in new forms.

These invisible forms of racism, psychic immobility, and apartheid take on new dimensions in Clarke's depiction of black life in Canada. In *More* Clarke returns to Fanon's primal scene on the train, yet here he writes this chronotope within Canada, showing the invisible structures of psychic immobility on the subway, bus and other forms of transit. Like Mary-Mathilda, Idora recalls a trip to America that she took with her friend Josephine. The narrator explains that "Josephine is soon sound asleep … And Idora is left alone to press her face against the cold window, to admire the Gardiner Expressway, which turns into the 401 West, and she sees the roof of a building and then more of the building, and recognizes where she is now" (127). Like Josephine and Chloe in *thirsty*, Idora cannot simply choose to forget her past. While Josephine sleeps, Idora recognizes the building as the "place she went for an appointment once about a rent-controlled government apartment. It all comes back to her" (127). She recalls being told by the supervisor that "she will have to be put on the city's List of Unfortunate Indigent Single Women" (128), and that she is a "member of a visible minority and in this office we know that you are exposed to rape and sexual abuse …. our statistics verify that profile of women like you … there's cases on file of physical abuse that you suffer, and this happens when the surrogate father, or the boyfriend, turns up, if you know what I mean" (128; ellipses in original). Idora finds the state-imposed definition of "visible minority" paralyzing, rendering her a statistic, and conspiring to label her "women like you." Josephine's easy sleep on the bus parallels the ease with which Bellfeels travels across America, and Idora's experience of being trapped within stereotypes recalls Mary-Mathilda's corporeal and psychic immobility. The immobility is formally present in the use of multiple narrative frames as the narrator describes Idora lying in her apartment recalling the bus trip she took with Josephine to America. On the bus Idora remembers her exchange with the city clerk who marks her as a "visible minority." In this passage Clarke once again reveals the continuities between the psychic immobilities of the colony, the segregated American south, and contemporary multicultural Canada. Despite the promises of change and transformation represented by Idora's migration, she remains immobilized by the fact of her blackness within Canada.

Idora describes this structural racism as an integral part of "her personal history of Canada. Her invisible visibility made her seethe with anger and rage for the police and for white people, but it also made her feel guilty, inferior, sorry to be so visible" (109). Katherine McKittrick has made the connection between Idora's "invisible visibility," structural racism in Canada, and the abjection of black people from the nation. McKittrick argues that "black Canada is lived as unvisibility" (*Demonic Grounds* 96); "black Canada is simultaneously invisible and visibly non-Canadian. This contradiction demonstrates the subtle ways in which domination shapes what has been called 'the absented presence' of black Canada and black Canadian geographies: black people *in* Canada are geographically un-Canadian" (99). McKittrick's analysis of the way in which "black Canada is simultaneously invisible and visibly non-Canadian" provides a Canadian vocabulary for the contradictions of Fanon's experience and offers a new gloss on the invisible and endemic structures of Canadian racism. Idora addresses her own unvisibility when, riding the subway, she imagines herself as "lost and without roots, without anchor; too embarrassed to admit that she is lost; too ashamed to ask for assistance. How can she confess that she is lost? A big woman like her? ... Ask for directions? And expose herself as an immigrant, a visible minority, a Jamaican, even though she is not from Jamaica" (155)? Idora's concern over being "exposed" as a visible minority indicates the structures of visibility that mark her as un-Canadian. The fear of being lost and unanchored in her origins is coupled with Idora's fear of being labelled and treated as a "visible minority." Continuing to recall her trip on the Toronto subway, Idora thinks, "I am getting a little anxious, and start to feel lost, and feel I am alone in the entire subway train; alone in Toronto on this cold morning, like how I would sometimes find myself alone in the wide sea ... My anxiety is growing" (155). Idora's reimagining of the subway train as akin to the "wide sea" links the chronotope of the train to that of the ocean and the history of the Middle Passage. The narrator describes how "She is the only black person in this coach of the subway. 'This feeling of being in the minority ... of inferiority ... not that I am inferior ... this feeling of segregation runs through my mind, each time I travel on public transportation'" (69; ellipses in original).

In addition to these explicit references to movement, in both *More* and *The Polished Hoe* Clarke is attentive to the manner in which this invisible visibility is produced through a spatial encoding of race. Clarke's expression of psychic immobility and unvisibility is evident throughout his depiction of the various spaces of home, the bar, the church, and the city. He at once depicts how black people's immobility is produced through the arrangement of these spaces and how this immobility is resisted by reimagining space through diasporic chronotopes. The depiction of "home" reveals how black people are never entirely secure or at home in Canada. Home is never a stable or secure space of belonging or retreat, but is structured by discourses of race, power, and gender. Tim and John in *The Origin of Waves* describe their respective houses but they never go there, spending the narrative in the bar or on the street. John exclaims "Home! What a sweet word! We've made this goddamn bar our home, I'd say! And what a sweet home! Home-sweet-home, home-sweet-home" (143). John's repetition suggests that the bar is not the "Home-sweet-home" that he insists it is, and reveals his worry that they continue to be seen as outsiders in the bar and in Canada. Tim confirms this suspicion later in the text when he notices, "Around us is the whispering of church and concert congregation. At times like this, after all these years, it is the quietness of this city that makes me feel different, that makes me shiver with that difference" (167). The cold quiet of the bar and the city is disrupted by their laughter, conversation, and their very presence. It is telling that John identifies the bar as "home," as this is typical of Clarke's depiction of black men in streets, bars, and restaurants, but very rarely within a domestic space; indeed it is primarily Clark's female characters who are depicted in the home. In each of the texts that BJ appears in, for instance, he is always depicted as trying to escape the domestic space. Similarly, the unnamed protagonist in "Canadian Experience" resents staying home during the week and sees it as a sign of his failing as a man. Throughout Clarke's narratives, domestic space is a decidedly female space and despite the unhomeliness of home in Canada, home remains the privileged domain of women.

In this respect, Clarke's inscription of black diasporic mobility takes on patriarchal dimensions as he paradoxically represents black people's unhomeliness within the nation alongside black women's homeliness within the home, thus further immobilizing his female characters. However, this reading is complicated by his simultaneous depiction of black female mobility; if home is a decidedly female space, movement through public space is not singularly male but practiced by both male and female characters. This aligns Clarke's work with Carol Boyce Davies's argument "that once Black women are accounted for, both 'travelling' and 'theory' can also be identified as Black women's prerogatives"

(44). She calls on critics to conceive of "Black female subjectivity ... not primarily in terms of domination, subordination or 'subalternization,' but in terms of slipperiness, elsewhereness" (36). Despite locating women within the home, Clarke's texts do conceive of travelling and mobility as black women's prerogatives and not strictly as the domain of men (as Gilroy is criticized for). As in his rewriting of Fanon, he repeatedly writes the chronotopes of the black diaspora from the perspective of his female characters. While he does write the space of the home as decidedly female, he also – perhaps paradoxically – indicates how the home is an uncomfortable, confining, and immobilizing space.

Both *More* and *The Polished Hoe* describe decidedly female domestic and circumscribed spaces. The entire narrative of *The Polished Hoe* is told in different areas of the plantation house, and each aspect of Mary-Mathilda's statement is linked to a different space of the plantation. Even when she recalls her travel, Mary-Mathilda does so from the confines of the plantation house. Percy is intimidated by the plantation, needing Mary-Mathilda to serve as his guide, even though her position is that of accused criminal and servant, and she is in the throes of confessing to the murder of Bellfeels. In a curious way, she is more at home here than either Percy or Bellfeels. She was born in the north field of the plantation among the sugar cane, and after being raised by her mother on the outskirts of the plantation, eventually moves into the plantation home after she is raped by Bellfeels. Mary-Mathilda makes the link between slavery, race, and the plantation when she explains, "this Plantation touch all of we. All our lives was branded by this Plantation" (18). The plantation is both a menacing and repressive space, but also a place Mary-Mathilda knows intimately. Her statement thus provides a history not just of slavery but of what the specific panoptic space of the plantation signifies: "The Main House have three floors, to look over the entire estate of the Plantation, like a tower in a castle. To spy on everybody ... the lay of the land of things; the division of work and of household" (4). Towards the end of the novel Mary-Mathilda describes a collective experience of imprisonment that binds black people together, "no matter which Plantation we are to call home-prison, as Ma always referred to her life on *this* Plantation" (367; italics in original). The language of home-prison evokes the disabling, immobilizing, and unhomely aspects of any home for those characters.[10] Indeed, Mary-Mathilda reveals to Percy that the plantation was once an actual prison when they move from the main floor to her bedroom and then into the dungeons beneath the kitchen. Moving through the dungeons she tells the story of three men who demanded higher wages and were locked up and severely beaten and whipped.[11] The spatial configuration of the dungeons beneath the kitchen mirrors the buried history of the plantation, as well as the spatial encoding of race and power in the great house. While the dungeons are underground, their presence cannot be isolated from the above-ground space of the plantation. Mary-Mathilda explains that the night the men were whipped, "the plantation was having a birthday party ... they could hear the cowskin, the bull-pistle whip ... tearing-into flesh, *plax! plax! plax!* In a rhythm as if the man wielding the balata was looking at the hand of a metronome, or a clock, measuring-off time in seconds" (340; italics in original). The history of slavery and colonialism has not passed but is recorded in the bodies of the men in the dungeon and in the spatial arrangement of the plantation house itself. Mary-Mathilda's recollection of the rhythm and time of the balata and whip is akin to Brand's "history's pulse / measured with another hand," yet here it is the markings of space and memory that remember history from a black diasporic perspective. Her recollection of the whipping and her graphic depiction of the "tearing-into flesh" indicate how the history of violence against the black body is not buried in the dungeons but is alive and well in her recollections. Mary-Mathilda's narrating of this incident of violence, captivity, and immobility therefore becomes a means of revealing the history of the space of the plantation, the unhomeliness of home, and the manner in which space produces the violence against and immobility of the body.

Despite the apparent differences between plantation and urban apartment, Clarke reveals how both spaces are imprisoning. Unlike the plantation house which is at the centre of the village, and Mary's bedroom which looks out over the entire village, Idora's apartment has a partial and obscured view of the street. The narrator of *The Polished Hoe* describes Percy's amazement when he looks through Mary's window which has a panoptic view of the village below: "He walks this Village at the level of the centipede and the worm, on bare ground, on roads in the darkest of nights, patrolling. Now, from this window, he has a new elevated knowledge of his Village" (304). There is a sense of agency and power in being able to survey the land from this position of elevated knowledge. The visual power associated with Mary's window and the overseer's gaze contrasts with the subterranean window wells of Idora's basement apartment. Idora lives beneath even "the level of the centipede and the worm," and the narrator observes,

> Her apartment has two windows on the south side, facing the Park. They look like portholes to her … looking through them to see the people passing, they make her feel she is on a schooner, watching the waves, and the fish beside the boat swimming faster, passing her in their silent, surer confidence. So, when she looks through the two rectangular windows, it is as if she is in a submarine; and it is the people, men and women and children, in prams and strollers, who pass her, in front of her subterranean window-hatches. They are moving, and she is standing still. She is not tall enough to see the entire bodies of the people passing, at all hours of the day and night, in all months of the year, in all temperatures. She never sees their full stature. She has to stand on her bed to see three-quarters of a person's body. (44)

Living underground, Idora's inability to see the entirety of her street, her neighbours and her city, renders her spatial position in the city analogous to her experience of immobility and unvisibility. She imagines herself as completely cut off from the above-ground world of movement and life. Indeed, her subterranean perspective is connected to her physical and figurative immobility, as it is the passers-by that "are moving, and she is standing still."

David Theo Goldberg has analysed these spatial configurations of racism, arguing that "Racism becomes institutionally normalized in and through spatial configuration, just as social space is made to seem natural, a given, by being conceived and defined in racial terms" (185). Idora's "subterranean" position in a basement apartment, cut off from the city that passes by, is a spatial encoding of her marginalization and social immobility in Canada. Goldberg describes this link between racial and spatial configurations as a kind of "*periphractic* space … It does not require the absolute displacement of persons to or outside city limits, to the literal margins of urban space. It merely entails their circumscription in terms of location and their limitation in terms of access – to power" (188; italics in original). Idora has not been pushed outside the city but rather relegated to just such a periphractic space whereby her presence goes unnoticed and her invisible visibility is compounded. Her position in the city is analogous to the dungeons in the plantation house of *The Polished Hoe*, yet Idora's spatial marginalization is an effect of class and implicit racial-spatial arrangements rather than explicit colonialism or slavery. As Fanon explains, "apartheid is but one method of compartmentalizing the colonial world" (*Wretched* 15); Idora is not subject to apartheid but is relegated to a periphractic space through economic and invisible racial structures with the effect that she is rendered unvisible in Canada. This passage, with the fish and ocean imagery, recalls Toni Morrison's argument in *Playing in the Dark* (1992) that "It is as if I had been looking at a fishbowl ... and suddenly I saw the bowl, the structure that transparently (and invisibly) permits the ordered life it contains to exist in the larger world" (17). Morrison's gaze shifts from seeing the fish moving to seeing the fishbowl that constrains and regulates their movement. Like Morrison, Idora's partial perspective makes her aware of the fishbowl she is in and the way in which race in Canada functions "transparently (and invisibly)." In this sense, Idora's diasporic and marginalized perspective offers a unique, critical view of her society.

Clarke's depiction of the periphractic space and endemic immobility of black life in Canada reveals the continuities between the spaces of the plantation, colony, and the nation. His work traces the encoding of subtle forms of racism and racial exclusion in the very spaces his characters occupy. His characters may cross national borders and continents, but they remain trapped within an immobilizing Fact of Blackness. Fanon's argument that the colonial subject's psychic immobility is "a direct result of colonialist subjugation" is transposed in Clarke's work to reveal how Idora's, Tim's, BJ's, and his other Canadian characters' psychic immobility is a direct result of the social order in Canada. Clarke's depiction of each characters' "personal history of Canada" makes apparent the mechanisms of unvisibility and immobility that attempt to exclude black people from the nation. In McKittrick's terms, Clarke's texts "hold place and placelessness in tension, through imagination and materiality, and therefore re-spatialize Canada on what might be considered unfamiliar terms" (*Demonic Grounds* 106).

Reading Clarke via Fanon reveals how Clarke's texts correct some of Fanon's blind spots. Khachig Tölölyan has critiqued the manner in which theories of diasporic life lack a certain "richness," particularly the manner in which diasporic identity becomes too often "an occasion for celebration of multiplicity and mobility" (28), without consideration of the manner in which that mobility is a "fundamental injunction" rather than an actual choice. Clarke's texts add to the richness of theories of the black diaspora and undercut this celebration of unexamined mobility by indicating the persistence of the immobility of race in Canada, and insisting on the importance of narrative to complicating the theories of black diasporic double-consciousness in Canada. Fanon is often critiqued for his overly-simple invoking of 'the people' or 'the masses' as a stable assembly of uniform subjects. Neil Lazarus has suggested that Fanon's work involves a "certain unwarranted 'speaking for' – that is, ventriloquizing, speaking 'in the place of' or 'instead of'" (179). Whereas Fanon's work is often described as lacking "a critical and dialectical analysis of the process of the formation of consciousness," (Clegg 239) or as engaged in a "ventriloquizing" of the black colonial subject, Clarke's dynamic style gives his characters both depth and vitality. Their anguish is visceral, their anger explosive, and their laughter loud. Clarke's depiction of double-consciousness differs from that of Gilroy who imagines the black subject negotiating and engaging in a syncretic blending of national and diasporic perspectives. Clarke's narratives also disavow Fanon's fantasy of violent rupture and complete liberation of the black subject from forms of social and psychic immobility. Rather, his work shows how the fantasy of violent rupture is untenable and how the psychic immobility of the colony and the plantation persist despite the promises of independence, multiculturalism, and citizenship. The unfamiliarity that McKittrick discerns is at once the cause and the grounds for Clarke's character's sense of exclusion, outrage, and critique. Furthermore, the doubleness of Clarke's crossing inheres in his simultaneous attention to the repetition of past historical forms of racism and the inventive and creative means by which his characters struggle to transform those forms through memory, language, and story. Memory functions doubly in his work: both enabling his characters to reveal the contemporary persistence of the past, and to insert difference and change into that memory. Mary-Mathilda's recollections do not merely trace her own social immobility, but through the act of narration, bespeak a form of mobility and agency of her own. Clarke's narratives thus employ the chronotopes of the diaspora to depict double-consciousness in Canada and thus transform the conditions in which nation and citizen are imagined.

It is in Clarke's most recent novel, *More*, that he most discernibly employs the chronotopes of the black diaspora in order to blacken Canada. Certainly Idora's basement apartment is a marginalized and periphractic space, yet her depiction of that space through the chronotopes of the black diaspora transforms it into something less immobilizing and confining. Comparing her windows to "portholes" and the apartment to "a schooner," Idora reimagines her space as mobile, thus gesturing towards Clarke's project of writing Canada as a less immobilizing space for his characters. Later in the novel the narrator describes Idora lying "in the belly of a fish. And her basement is the fish, and she is engulfed and enveloped in its darkness and its hollowness" (241). The narrator's use of sea, sailing, and fish imagery recall Idora's migration from the Caribbean to Canada and her own use of nautical chronotopes to comprehend and retell the events of her life in Canada. In addition, the narrator's description of Idora lying "in the belly of a fish" alludes to the Biblical narrative of Jonah and the whale. The Jonah narrative parallels Idora's in their shared themes of suspect mobility, exile, and social critique, and the chronotope of Jonah in the belly of the whale is *the* central metaphor of corporeal mobility and psychic immobility in the latter portion of *More*. Idora recalls that "the one story in the Bible which touched her admiration best ... if not worst ... was the story of Jonah in the Belly of the Whale" (191). The Jonah narrative both frightens and appeals to her as it offers such an apt depiction of her own mixture of adventurousness and seemingly self-inflicted paralysis. In addition to the connections between Idora's migration from the Caribbean and Jonah's exile from the ship, the narrative of Jonah in the belly of the whale connotes the mixed sense of movement that pervades Clarke's corpus. Jonah's imprisoned movement in the whale is the most evocative chronotope for Idora's life in Toronto, expressing both her compulsion to move and the structures of psychic and social immobility that bind her. Indeed, Tim in *The Origin of Waves* describes the night he spent with the only woman he loved as being "like Jonah in the belly of the whale. The seas parted, like the seas that rise-up and tumbled-over the bow of *Galilee* that tossed my uncle overboard. Those seas of that night's story were filled with sharks that kill, the seas that washed-him-in, big, bloated, and bulgeous" (82). Tim invokes the Jonah narrative to substantiate the feelings of danger, anxiety, pleasure, and excitement that he felt that night. Yet for Idora, the story of Jonah not only refers to her anxiety towards her own immigration and transnational movement, but also her relationship to Canada. The feelings of immobility and unvisibility produced by the Canadian state, in the marking and management of "visible minorities," and the persistence of racism, construct Canada as a kind of whale in which Idora is trapped. Just as Jonah preaches to the city of Nineveh and calls on its residents to repent, Idora preaches to her own community and her city of Toronto, thus transforming these places through her language. Like Jonah, Idora feels that her exile and social marginalization have given her insight into the workings of Canadian society. Similarly, Idora sees – in Jonah's desire to defy God's command and escape Nineveh – a parallel narrative to her own flight to Canada and to the general condition of black diasporic life.

The Jonah narrative leads Idora to escape the immobility of her basement apartment. After spending three days in her basement apartment remembering and retelling the narrative of her immigration to and life in Canada, she leaves her apartment on the third day, a Sunday, to preach the story of Jonah to her congregation. She tells the congregation that,

> out of the fish's belly, Jonah was crying out to God, "I am the reason for my own affliction ... amen!" ... "Jeeees-sus" Idora screams. "I'm running for my life!" "We're all running for our lives, Sister!" Ole Jonah cried out "... amen! ... out of the fish's belly ... amen!" ... and said ... "amen! ... The Lord hath given unto me, another chance! I am going to pray! And maybe" ... amen! ... "maybe, the Lord will hear my prayer ..." The church is shaking. Everybody is standing and clapping ... Idora begins to lead the congregation in the altar call, in song. She begins with the song she has been singing in her basement apartment ... "I'm Running for My Life." (272–3; ellipses in original)

This section of the text is remarkably different from the rest of the novel as the multiple voices, disrupted speeches, and interjections mark this passage as dynamic. The energy of this passage is in stark contrast to Idora's previously stated desire to "lie low, and to remain 'dead'" (191), a desire that is evinced in her immobility and in the languorous temporality of the narrative up to this point. The heteroglossia of the narrative, Idora's preaching, and the numerous voices and shouts of the congregation infuse this passage with an energy that has been otherwise absent. The narrative focus expands to include the diverse and unnamed voices in the congregation. The bulk of the novel alternates between direct and indirect focalization, whereas here the narrator records only Idora's voice along with the voices of the other parishioners, offering no access to Idora's thoughts. This shift in form is signified by the use of ellipses which indicate moments of disruption and of the narrative voice outpaced by the voices in the church, thus providing a palpable sense of vibrancy and energy. Michael Bucknor has argued that Clarke's use of "ellipses ... expose the gaps within the text not as failed representations but as translations. Thus, a lack of success in attaining full equivalence, total containment, and faithful rendition of experience in language is laid bare in empty spaces" (152). Bucknor argues against critics that read Clarke's work as realist, sociological accounts of black Canadian life, and instead demonstrates the manner in which Clarke thematizes the struggle to represent, as well as the presence of the absent or unsaid, in the form of his prose. The immobility evident in the earlier sections of the novel breaks apart here to express a formal openness that parallels Idora's newfound mobility. The omniscient narrator in the earlier sections of the novel offer complete access to Idora's thoughts, while the ellipses in this section mark the oral, corporeal, and imaginative energy and vibrancy that the narrator cannot wholly convey.

Clarke's use of the Jonah narrative locates the collective struggle to keep "Running for My Life" within the Canadian narration of nation. Northrop Frye has famously observed that "Canada has, for all practical purposes, no Atlantic seaboard. The traveller from Europe edges into it like a tiny Jonah entering an inconceivably large whale, slipping past the Straits of Belle Isle into the Gulf of St. Lawrence ... To enter the United States is the matter of crossing an ocean; to enter Canada is a matter of being silently swallowed by an alien continent" (217). This image of the all-consuming Canadian leviathan is repeated throughout Canadian criticism such that Jonathan Kertzer generalizes Frye's articulation as a statement that "Canadians often feel [that] ... They must all become Jonahs ... who give themselves to the Canadian leviathan" (5). Kertzer further transforms the Jonah narrative to contend with the concerns of immigrant writers in Canada, arguing that "To the ethnic, feminist, Native writers, the bourgeois nation is a monster, an ideological aberration to be corrected, rather than a natural habitation" (133). Clarke's use of the Jonah narrative functions in yet another manner, linking Jonah's involuntary and constricted movement with the ambivalence towards movement expressed by the diasporic subjects in his texts. In this sense, Clarke's use of the Jonah narrative creatively rewrites this tradition of Canadian Jonahs such that he makes the narrative relevant to the lives of Idora and the other diasporic figures in his narratives.

Clarke's repeated use of the Jonah narrative in his writing marks a point of connection between the imaginative vocabularies of Canada and the black diaspora, thus locating black diasporic themes and motifs within Canada rather than as decidedly external. If this is a repetition of standard Canadian themes, it is a repetition with difference or repetition detoured. The paralyzing anxiety expressed by Frye's European traveller is rewritten as the doubly-inflected form of movement of the diaspora. Where Frye, Kertzer, and others use the Jonah narrative to describe how one becomes Canadian, Clarke uses Jonah to blacken

Canada and render it diasporic by transforming the stability of place into one more route in the diaspora. The longing for rooting is transformed into the practices of routing in Clarke's work in such a way that black abjection is transformed into a rewriting and blackening of the nation itself. Like Brand's blackening of the Canadian long poem, Clarke's rewriting of the Jonah narrative not only provides an appropriate form for articulating black diasporic experience in Canada, but also shows how the concerns of his black diasporic characters are decidedly Canadian ones. Like Brand, Clarke exploits the openness of Canadian motifs and forms to reimagine the Jonah narrative as giving voice to black diasporic experience within Canada. Clarke crosses the forms of Canadian writing with those of the black diaspora to resist any strict demarcation between black and Canada; instead, he offers crossing as an appropriate form for thinking of black presences in Canada. Blackness, in Clarke's work, is not external to Canada, is not here only temporarily, and does not reflect negatively against the "white darkness" of Canada. Rather, his use of Jonah, his inscription of psychic immobility in Canada, and his identification of the continuities of the spaces of the plantation, the colony, and the multicultural nation, write black diasporic concerns as central to the Canadian imaginary. If *More*'s opening image of the paralysed, frozen, and barren black trees expresses the impossibility of rooting in the nation, then the vibrancy of Idora's sermon and her rewriting of the Jonah narrative gestures towards the possibilities implicit in routing the nation. In this sense, the Jonah narrative, more than any of Clarke's other chronotopes, detours the narration of Canada. Clarke's detours disavow the logic of origins or belonging and rewrite Canadian space via the chronotopes of the black diaspora.

The novel concludes with Idora running *for* her life, and taking the congregation to which she preaches with her. Both Alan, in Brand's *thirsty*, and Idora are mad prophets, and it is unclear – despite the rousing tone and communal intent of Idora's jeremiad, and because she is the only one who both speaks and sees in the novel – whether the salvation in question is hers alone. Alan's "ravings" get him killed, even if they bear the truth of suffering. Clarke and Brand share the desire to make their lowly characters exemplary figures and to grant both meaning and value to seemingly banal, imprisoning lives. Brand and Clarke are the voices of their communities, not in the sense that they speak *for* those whose lives remain unremarked, but in the power with which they *imagine* the rich, inner lives of their characters in acts of extraordinary empathy. They perform the necessary and difficult task of writing characters exemplary of the condition of migration without imagining them as mouthpieces for the authors' anxieties and political concerns. This empathy is a consequence of their supple command of words and their respect for silences. Their literary repertoire exploits voice, accent, idiom, diction, register, and genre to communicate their characters' distinct perspectives on common predicaments. After reading their work, it is no longer possible simply to observe with distant sympathy the lives they describe; instead, one lives their joy and agony, but with an unsentimental understanding of the consequences of The Middle Passage and of the ethos of migration. Like Chloe and Julia, Idora abides her time, yet her recollections of migration employ memory and desire to transform and blacken the nation.

Chapter Three

Writing Life-Worlds: Canadian History and the Representation of Albert Johnson

Dionne Brand and Austin Clarke re-route and blacken the nation as they simultaneously write for their community, transforming individual struggles into a collective ethos and articulation of the everyday experience of migration and crossing. They give meaning to notions of blackening and becoming diasporic in their depiction of "the varying experience of the pains and pleasures, the terrors and contentments, or the highs and humdrum of everyday lived culture" (Brah 192). Yet in describing the affective experience of being black in Canada and being at once "within and without" the nation, Brand and Clarke both write for their community and write *against* broader structures of racism and exclusion that otherwise denigrate and marginalize black people in Canada. Thus their fiction, poetry, and critical essays locate black diasporic subjects within the multicultural nation while also attacking the policies that bespeak inclusion while in practice exclude black people. Brand criticizes the manner in which public discourse affirms a banal notion of multiculturalism while internalizing racial inequality within that discourse. She writes,

> Now the revisionists went to work, the great legitimizing machinery of liberal democracy set about inserting itself as always in favour of racial equality ... The newspapers said immigrants were taking away white people's jobs, the newspapers said black youth were running amok, the newspapers said before black people came here there was no racism, the newspaper said before black youth there was no crime, the newspapers said we live in a multicultural society. (Bread 103)

Brand's critique of the "great legitimizing machinery of liberal democracy" indicates the importance of narrative to disrupting this dominant representation of historical and contemporary Canadian multiculturalism. In addition, Brand's criticism, here and elsewhere, indicates that it is just as inadequate to attend to her politics at the expense of her poetics, as to focus solely on her aesthetics; the two do not complement but generate one another. Brand's and Clarke's projects of blackening are both literary and public struggles to inscribe blackness in Canada and to work against the smearing, misrepresentation, and erasure of black presences in Canada. As such, these narratives of blackening must be situated within their political contexts and must be read as part of the blackening of the Canadian public sphere. Integral to this is the manner in which their work responds to and is inflected by public debates over the relationships between race, citizenship, and nation. As Kamboureli notes, "A multicultural critical idiom is of necessity comparative, for it attempts to interrogate the diverse forces that comprise the representation of diasporic subjectivities" (*Scandalous* 37), and thus one must keep in view the distinctions and similarities between Brand's and Clarke's conceptions of blackening as both poetics and public intervention. Bed Prasad Giri insists that for diasporic discourse to retain its vitality as an "alternative site of sociality and belonging" (216) it "should be understood in the content of its *worldliness*" (223; italics in original), a concept that Giri borrows from Said to evoke "a means to steer away from the tendency to turn literary criticism into a rarefied, 'scientific,' and priestly pursuit" (Giri 223). The worldliness of Brand's and Clarke's projects of blackening is brought to light by reading the case of Albert Johnson and the resultant devaluing of blackness in the Canadian public sphere. This attends to, in Stuart Hall's terms, the "*semiotic* and *discursive*" aspects of blackening that transform the Canadian public sphere. Hall writes that "the *semiotic* approach is concerned with the *how* of representation, with how language produces meaning – what has been called its 'poetics'; whereas the *discursive* approach is more concerned with the *effects and consequences* of representation – its 'politics'" (Hall, *Representations* 6; italics in original). The semiotic and discursive, and the poetic and political aspects of blackening regularly overlap, particularly as public discourse and conceptions of Canadian citizenship are mediated by an invisible whiteness.

The politics and poetics of blackening and of white Canadian civility (Coleman 2006) come into view through the depiction of Albert Johnson and the events leading to his death in 1979. Johnson's death serves as a worrying reminder of how pre-multicultural Canada coped with increasingly difficult questions of cultural difference and race, and of the manner in which Canadian public discourse continues to neglect black Canadian histories. Johnson's death – prior to the passing of the Official Multiculturalism Act, the controversies of the "Into the Heart of Africa" exhibit, and the "Writing Thru Race" conference – represents the discourse of race in Canada before the heady days of multiculturalism and indicates Canada's failure to account for its own historical racism. Indeed, Brand insists on the importance of historicizing multicultural Canada in her description of how the historical "revisionists went to work" to erase this history of racism in Canada. Newspaper accounts of Johnson's death reveal the manner in which neither "liberal democracy" nor white people in Canada were always "in favour of racial equality" or even multiculturalism. A critical reading of the mainstream newspaper coverage of Johnson's death reveals how the public discourse of race in Canada is based on a structural opposition between a conception of whiteness as civility and blackness as deviance. This smearing of blackness is challenged by Austin Clarke's, Dionne Brand's, and Neil Bissoondath's narratives of Albert Johnson as they intervene in this public and historical discourse, thereby contributing to a blackening of Canadian history. Moreover, the case of Albert Johnson challenges George Elliott Clarke's suturing of African-Canadian, revealing that black Canadians are often not depicted through the logic of the hyphen, but are excluded from the Canadian national imaginary outright.

Benedict Anderson (1983) has famously argued the importance of print media in imagining a national community, and the case of Albert Johnson shows the racial exclusions at work in such imaginings. Similarly, if Stuart Hall is correct in his observation that "the media's main sphere of operations is the production and transformation of ideologies" ("Whites" 81) and the creation of a "grammar of race" ("Whites" 83), then analysis of the media coverage of Johnson's death identifies the manner in which the public sphere in Canada is shaped by particular racial ideologies. While it would be incorrect to draw a stark and definitive division between the space of literary production and interpretation and that of the public sphere, newspaper representation can be said to constitute an *explicitly* and *intentional* public discourse whereas literary representation is perhaps only latently so.[1]

Henry and Tator in *Discourses of Domination* (2002) employ Critical Discourse Analysis to analyse this grammar of race in the Canadian public sphere and mainstream media. They uncover the mechanics of public discourses concerning race and cultural difference.[2] They plainly demonstrate how concepts of "Tolerance, equality and freedom of expression – central concepts in liberal discourse – have immensely flexible meanings" (38), and how this democratic language can produce racially exclusive practices. Furthermore, they show how the Canadian discourse of race marks whiteness as invisible, rational, and normal, and blackness as deviant, criminal, and problematic to produce a unique form of racial exclusion within liberalism and multiculturalism. They define this as "democratic racism,"

> an ideology in which two conflicting sets of values are made congruent with each other. Democratic principles such as equality, fairness, and justice conflict with, but also but [*sic*] coexist with, racist attitudes and behaviours – including negative feelings about minority groups and differential treatment of them ... It is an elusive concept because the rhetoric of dominant discourses is hidden within the mythical norms that define Canada as a white, humanistic, tolerant, and accommodating society. However ... beneath the reassuring notions of liberal arguments and justificatory lines of reasoning remain deeply problematic ideas about minority populations. (228)

Liberalism and racism are the two "conflicting sets of values" that are "made congruent with each other." Democratic racism describes how liberalism's language of equality and individuality enables particular forms of racism to persist because they cannot be identified or understood through liberalism's critical vocabulary. The concept of democratic racism undermines the arguments of the "racial realists" (Brown et al. 7) who insist that the alleged colour-blindness of contemporary liberalism and multiculturalism will inevitably eradicate racism by treating all individuals as equals. Brown et al. argue that this is a form of democratic racism, and counter that "the color-blind ideal actually impedes efforts necessary to eliminate racial inequality. Formal color-blindness fails to recognize or address the deeply rooted institutional practices and long-term disaccumulation that sustains racial inequality" (58). Furthermore, democratic racism obscures "white supremacy" particularly as it camouflages "the existence of a system that not only privileges whites but is run by whites for white benefit" (Mills 31). This is why democratic racism remains so hard to define, because the political language that defines "Canada as a white, humanistic, tolerant, and accommodating society" obscures persistent racial inequalities and discrimination in Canada and does not provide an adequate language for comprehending racism within a liberal democratic state. Albert Johnson's death, though, reveals the particular manner in which the "mythical norms that define Canada as white" rely on a devaluing of blackness and an exclusion of black people from the national imaginary.

Henry and Tator's theory of democratic racism can be usefully linked to the work of critical race theorists such as Michael Brown, Sherene Razack, Richard Dyer, David Theo Goldberg, and others. This is particularly true of their analysis of whiteness in Canadian media and the manner in which democratic racism relies on the notion of whiteness as invisible, disinterested, and racially unmarked. In place of this conception of whiteness as neutral, recent analyses have shown "the obvious and overlooked fact that whites are racially interested and motivated" (Hartigan 1). Richard Dyer explains that "There is no more powerful position than that of being 'just' human" (2), and Steve Garner argues that while white must be understood to be a racial category, it is a category of identity that is crucially "*unlike any other*, because it is the dominant, normalised location" (6; italics in original). Henry and Tator's analysis reveals the unique position of whiteness as invisible, dominant, and normalised within Canadian media, and they also show how liberalism's language of equality cannot account for the particular forms of privilege and power that are accessible to white Canadians. For instance, Brown et al. analyse the effects of accumulated advantage for white people in the United States, arguing that over the past 360 years, "whites have gained or *accumulated* opportunities, whereas African Americans and other racial groups have lost opportunities – they suffer from *disaccumulation* of the accoutrements of economic opportunity" (22; italics in original). Thus, "Understood this way, affirmative action has been in effect for 360 years, not 39. For the first 330 years, the deck was officially and legally stacked on behalf of whites and males" (25). The unique and privileged identity of whiteness and the accumulated advantage that white citizens enjoy under liberal democracy are rendered invisible by democratic racism.

Linda Alcoff, commenting on the work of David Theo Goldberg, has argued that liberalism is unable to adequately contend with questions of difference through its language of rights and equality. She writes, "the universal sameness that was so important for the liberal self required a careful containment and taxonomy of difference. Where rights require sameness, difference must be either trivialized or contained in the Other across a firm and visible border" (5). Sherene Razack sees an inherent colour-blindness at the core of liberal concepts of rights, contracts, and the individual as the subject of liberalism. She argues that

"Rights thinking is based on the liberal notion that we are all individuals who contract with one another to live in a society where each of us would have the maximum in personal freedom. Starting from this premise, there then are no marginalized communities ... and no historical relations of power" (17). She goes on to argue that "in any discussion of rights, it will be exceedingly difficult to introduce the notion of oppression of women by men (and whites by non-whites [*sic*]) because this oppression is the hidden cornerstone on which rests individual autonomy" (30).[3] These criticisms of liberalism provide a political and sociological framework that gives weight to Henry and Tator's theory of "democratic racism." This framework, alongside Henry and Tator's methodology, illuminate the representations of race in the mainstream media coverage of Albert Johnson's death, and the subsequent manslaughter trial of the two policemen who were charged with his death.

While it is difficult, if not impossible, to claim to know the facts concerning the life and death of Albert Johnson, there are some basic details which are generally agreed upon. On Sunday, 26 August 1979, Johnson was in the laneway behind his home at 52 Manchester Ave in Toronto. Around 1 p.m. the police received a complaint from a neighbour who reported that Johnson was being loud and disruptive. Johnson was known to police as they had had numerous encounters with him in the previous six months. Johnson claimed that he was a victim of police harassment on a regular basis, whereas the police claimed he was mentally ill and was routinely involved with them. Three police officers agreed to meet at the Johnson residence as none of them wanted to confront Johnson alone. The first two officers who arrived on the scene, Walter Cargnelli and William Inglis, decided to confront Johnson while the third officer, Gary Dicks, was en route. It is at this point that the events leading to Johnson's death come into dispute. The following is a list of the major claims made by the police and by Johnson's family that are under dispute, in approximate chronological order:

- Johnson was cursing, shouting and being aggressive before the police arrived. One neighbour testified that he heard Johnson shouting "Kill all police" in an alley behind his home before the police arrived. Other neighbours claimed that they heard no swearing, shouting, or aggressive behaviour coming from the back alley. One neighbour told reporters that he was sitting and talking quietly with Johnson minutes before the police arrived, while another reported seeing him at church ten minutes before the shooting (Mironowicz and Lavigne P1).

- Johnson cursed and shouted at the police officers when they arrived on the scene, and their presence seemed to put him in a rage. Officer Cargnelli testified that "I said, 'how's it going today?' He said, 'Why don't you – - off, you bumbo clat.' I asked him what he was cooking on the fire in the garage, and he said 'Why don't you – - off, you bumbo clat? – - off. If I had the chance, I'd kill you all.'" Some neighbours testified that they witnessed no such exchange while another neighbour testified that he heard Johnson say "'get off my so-and-so property.' Johnson then closed his garage and went inside his house … the officers then threw their hats on the hood of the car and ran towards the house. Finding the door locked, they broke it down" (Clarke, "Johnson killing murderous" 1).
- Police allege that Johnson ran into his home and spat on police from a second-floor window. Forensic evidence revealed no saliva on any of the officers' uniforms or on the screen of the window out of which Johnson is alleged to have spat.
- The police kicked in the locked back door of Johnson's home and entered to arrest him because they feared for the safety of his family. Officer Cargnelli claimed that Johnson's family was very frightened of his behaviour and that his children were screaming and crying. They allege that they entered the home to protect the children from their father. Neighbours testified that the scene inside the house seemed calm.
- Johnson resisted arrest after the police officers entered his home. Johnson's wife, Monica, claimed that she attempted to protect Johnson from the police. Mrs. Johnson claims that the police attempted to arrest Johnson inside his home for disturbing the peace. When she asked Albert Johnson to go with the police, she recalls him saying, "No Monica, I'm not going this time. When I'm wrong I'll go but this time I didn't do anything" (Clarke, "Johnson killing murderous" 1). The police claim that Johnson resisted arrest, struggled with the police in the kitchen, and then ran upstairs.
- The police followed Johnson to the bottom of the staircase at which point he reappeared, at the top of the staircase, holding what they believed was an axe. The "axe" was a lawn edger which, after being forensically analysed, revealed no fingerprints (forensic testing was not performed until nearly one month after the shooting and the evidence had not been properly handled). Witnesses claim that they heard a policeman say "he's got an axe" moments before the police shot him. The police claim they told Johnson to "drop it" while Mrs. Johnson and other witnesses never heard such a request.

- Johnson's daughter claimed that she saw the police force Johnson into a kneeling position at the bottom of the stairs before shooting him. She claims that he was surrendering to police when he was shot. Johnson's daughter's claim matches with ballistics tests which confirm that the policeman's bullet entered Johnson's "abdomen at a 45 degree angle and travelled in a downward direction, meaning he had been lower than the gun" (Blatchford, "Blacks cry 'shame'" A10). Johnson's daughter's testimony was discounted both by the Ontario Provincial Police (OPP) investigators (they felt she had been coached despite evidence indicating otherwise), and by the judge in the trial who instructed jurors to treat her testimony "almost with suspicion" ("What Judge Dunlop told the jury").
- The police changed their story, initially claiming that they shot Johnson on the staircase. On the day of the incident Cargnelli claimed he fired a warning shot at Johnson on the staircase and then fired the second, fatal, shot at him when he was on the second step of the staircase. One month after the incident, during an OPP interview, Cargnelli "changed his version to say Johnson jumped down the stairs and landed in a crouched position before he was shot" ("Cop changed statement, Johnson trial told"). This second version accords with the ballistic findings while the first version does not.

After the shooting occurred, police closed off access to the house to Johnson's family, and an ambulance rushed Johnson to Toronto Western Hospital where he died, at 7:30 p.m.

In addition to these disputes there are a number of disagreements concerning Johnson's character; particularly his mental health, the reasons behind his unemployment, and whether he was harassed by the police in the months leading up to his death. Johnson lost his job in May of 1979, and after being laid off suffered an increasing number of mental breakdowns.[4] While police maintain that they were called numerous times to arrest Johnson during these incidents, Johnson and his family allege that the police harassed him and that his mental illness provided a convenient justification for that harassment and the killing. Johnson was, in fact, arrested a number of times in the summer before his death but the charges were routinely dismissed by judges who saw no evidence of a substantial crime being committed. Johnson was also involved in a physical altercation with police in May 1979 and was injured so severely that he was hospitalized. Jim Arger, a high school teacher, shared a room with Johnson in the hospital and described Johnson as being "in terrible shape" as a result of a beating he claimed he received from police. Arger said Johnson told him then "they (the police) are going to kill me" (Hluchy A3). Johnson reiterated his fear that the police wanted to kill him to the Ontario Human Rights Commission four times in the summer before he was killed. Ten days before Johnson's death, Gail Guttentag of the OHRC wrote,

> Mr Johnson appeared increasingly desperate due to the increased harassment that he felt he had been subjected to. He had not been working, had lost his job following the incidents in May and had fallen behind in his mortgage. His biggest fear, he admitted, was that police would shoot him down. He repeated that he thought the police are trying to kill him, and have been making a concerted effort to continually and increasingly harass him. He feared that this would culminate in his own death. (Blatchford, "What the jury didn't hear in the Albert Johnson case" A10)

The question of Johnson's mental health would be one of the main concerns of the trial, with the police alleging that Johnson was mentally unstable and family members alleging that what appeared to be mental instability was a response to losing his job and police harassment. The media coverage of Johnson's death and the subsequent trial of the two police officers focus on his mental health, linking it to his status as an immigrant and his blackness, all of which denigrate his character and position him as the problematic other to conceptions of white Canadian normality. The coverage of the trial shifts from focusing on the white police officers to Johnson's deviance, which becomes a broader comment on black deviance from a white, Canadian civil order. Within this public discourse Johnson becomes an exemplary figure of black deviance, and the denigration of his character becomes part of a broader smearing of blackness in the Canadian public sphere. Johnson's mental instability, his blackness, and his status as an immigrant all provide the materials that enable the media's discourse of white civility and black deviance.

The main headline on the front page of the *Toronto Star* on Monday, 27 August 1979 reads, "Police Gun Down Father of Four Waving Lawn "Tool." The article, by Don Dutton, sensationalizes the details of Johnson's death. Dutton writes, "Blood was running from a cut on Albert Johnson's face and he was swinging what looked like an axe as he came down the narrow stairs in his old Manchester Ave. home – into a police bullet" (A1). The second paragraph describes how

> The policemen, standing at the bottom of the stairs with their guns drawn had told Johnson to "drop it." A warning shot was fired into the wall half-way up the stairs but the tall, black man kept swinging the "axe," police said, and a second shot from Constable William Ingles' gun slammed into his chest. The weapon was later found to be a lawn edger – about the size of a small spade with a crescent shaped blade about six inches long. (A1)

While these two opening paragraphs aim at an objective and factual tone, they also establish the interpretive frame within which Johnson's death is reported. The headline that describes Johnson as a "father of four" who has been "gun[ned] down" by the police sympathizes with Johnson and also sensationalizes the events of the killing. Yet despite this sympathetic headline, the article's point of view is closely aligned with the police account of events. Later court testimony reveals no evidence that Johnson is "swinging" the axe or that the police "had told Johnson to 'drop it'." The image of Johnson as he descends the staircase with blood "running" down his face and swinging his lawn-edger is one of an aggressive, mentally-disturbed man, an image that is reasserted in the following paragraph: "Johnson ... had shouted a few minutes before the shooting, 'I can't take this no more'" (A1). Johnson's mentally disturbed state is reaffirmed a few sentences later by Inspector Robert Stirling who claims that police received a complaint of a man "acting disorderly – creating a disturbance." From the outset of their coverage, the *Star*'s perspective is closely aligned with that of the police, although it is not marked as such. Instead, this opening description of Johnson's death, which is contested in a number of substantial ways by his supporters, is unmarked, unassigned to any speaker and given the authority of objective fact. From the front page of the paper, the article continues on A3 where a photo of the shocked and frightened Johnson family (Monica and four children) is juxtaposed with an image of uniformed police standing guard outside their home.

It is on page A3 that the article moves from the police narrative to include the perspective of Monica, her children, and Mary McBean, Johnson's sister. It is after the police account of Johnson's death, which is presented as fact, that Dutton writes, "Johnson's sister ... blamed his problems on frequent visits by the police and wondered if racial prejudice were behind the complaints" (A3). Henry and Tator's analysis of media coverage of black Canadians and the police repeatedly finds that "The 'black' point of view in the article is referred to only later, in a 'comments' section of the article ... minority group speakers ... are seen as partisan, whereas white authorities, such as the police or the government, are simply seen as ethnically 'neutral'" (188). Whereas the police account of the killing is presented as fact, McBean is described as weakly having only "wondered" about the racism of the initial complaint against Johnson (the potential racism of the police, in shooting Johnson, is never raised), and as attempting to "blame" someone for his death. Similarly, Johnson's nine-year-old daughter Colsie claimed that "the policemen made him kneel on the floor and that he was shot moments after he turned to a policeman to say he wasn't going to do anything" (A3). This account of Johnson's death, which directly contradicts the police account, is not mentioned until the fourth column of A3, long after the narrative is framed by the official police version of events. Despite these two contradictory accounts, the paper treats Colsie's account as a matter of opinion overshadowed by the facts. The discursive framework employed by the *Toronto Star*, the *Toronto Sun*, and the *Globe and Mail* reveals each paper's alignment of their own viewpoint with that of the police. The *Toronto Sun* completely accepts the police account at face value, with *Sun* columnist Morton Shulman insisting (having only heard the police account) that if he were in the policeman's position, he would have shot Johnson in the exact same manner (Shulman). The *Globe and Mail* at least canvassed homes in the area in an unsuccessful attempt to find the complainant who called the police. Like the *Star*, they privilege the police account over that of Johnson's daughter. Police Inspector Stirling describes Colsie's version of the killing as "completely inconsistent with what we've got here. She's 7 years old, not a credible person" (Mironowicz and Lavigne P1), and these newspapers do little to challenge this discrediting and silencing of Colsie Johnson. Indeed, the fact that her account would later be proven to be credible by ballistics tests whereas the police account would be later revised to match the ballistic evidence was given little attention in subsequent coverage. This alignment between the police account of the events of Johnson's death, and the mainstream press's reporting of the details of his death continues throughout the coverage.

The *Toronto Star* coverage and the police trial continued from August 1979 to December 1980. The paper offers detailed reporting on Johnson's life, his background as a Jamaican immigrant, the circumstances of his death, and the trial of the two police officers. While Johnson's history is completely open to public scrutiny, the race, cultural backgrounds, religious beliefs, and political leanings of the three police officers are never discussed in the press. Indeed, the police officers are somewhat invisible figures throughout the coverage of the trial. The coverage is decidedly focused on Albert Johnson and this is part of the same discursive framework that privileges the testimony of white authority figures over that of black people. Whereas 'the black perspective' is seen as inherently biased by special interest concerns about racism and injustice, the white perspective is seen to be completely unencumbered by such concerns. The coverage in the mainstream press aligns itself with the police version of events particularly in the link between whiteness and normalcy and their privileging of white perspectives. Johnson's blackness signifies irrationality, deviance, and criminality while the police officers' whiteness is never raised in the trial, and is seen as invisible, objective, and civil.

The *Toronto Star* repeatedly raises the question of Johnson's possible mental illness and links it with his blackness and immigrant status[5] with the effect of marking Johnson as deviant. For instance, the headline on 29 August 1979 reads "Albert Johnson 'needed help': *Neighbours say police shooting victim sometimes 'frightening'*" (Dutton and Mietkiewicz A2; italics in original). The reporters interview Johnson's neighbour, Robert Lackaye, who insists that since Johnson lost his job in May 1979, his "mental problems ... seemed to be getting worse." Lackaye goes on to describe Johnson as sometimes "'frightening' because [Johnson] often carried a big stick in his hand and was shouting and cursing" and describes how, on the Friday before he died, "He was up on the garage roof, wearing a hat and well, a cape like Superman's and waving a big stick." Not only does Johnson's alleged deviance demonstrate the implicit coding of white normality and black deviance in the media coverage of his death, but Johnson's deviance is employed to render his death acceptable. The coverage of the trial transfers the deviance from the white police officers – who have killed a civilian – to the black victim in order to render Johnson's death reasonable and justified under the circumstances. Henry and Tator note that "In a racially divided society, the assumptions and beliefs that underpin the dominant discourses of much of the media ... serve an important function: they explain, rationalize and resolve insupportable contradictions and tensions in society" (227). The contradictions of democratic racism that persist in liberal Canada and are made apparent by the shooting of Albert Johnson are, in this case, explained and rationalized by marking Johnson as deviant. This has the effect of transferring the criminality of his death from the police onto Johnson, and turns his death into an unavoidable tragedy.

In addition to Johnson's mental health, his blackness is also one of the foremost ways in which he is constructed as deviant. The *Toronto Star* focuses not only on the link between Albert Johnson's deviance and his black identity, but extends that coverage to the black people who support him and his family, making blackness one of the dominant signifiers of deviance and criminality throughout the mainstream media coverage. Like Johnson's character, the collective black community in Canada comes under scrutiny, and black Canadians are depicted as an irrational, problematic group. For instance, the headline on the Thursday after Johnson's death reads "Angry Jamaicans shout at slaying probe team" (Hluchy). The headline of the article links "Angry" with "Jamaican" to depict black Canadians as irrational and problematic. It is unclear how the author knew that all of the supporters at Johnson's home were Jamaican, but it doesn't actually appear to matter as "Jamaican" becomes a catch-all signifier for angry, black, West-Indian, Caribbean, immigrant. These supporters are not identified as Canadians, citizens, friends, or mourners, but rather are marked as extra-national Jamaicans and thus not Canadian. Identifying all of Johnson supporters as Jamaicans (because they are black) and marking them as angry and deviant contributes to the depiction of "Jamaicans as people from a crime-ridden and poverty-stricken country who are good at sports and entertainment but who consistently present Canadian society with a myriad of social problems" (Henry and Tator 168). The deployment of the word Jamaican creates an image of uncontrollable, irrational, and aggressive black immigrants. The reporter writes that the group of supporters "became enraged when Johnson's widow Lemonica, 29, told them her daughter Colsie, 7, was 'getting mixed up' during 1½ hours of OPP questioning" and that some of the group "shouted to detectives that the OPP was trying to intimidate and confuse the child in order to discredit her story." The supporters are described as having "shouted" and become "enraged" in their protestations over the O.P.P. interview, indicating the palpable threat that they pose to the officers. The *Globe and Mail* engages in the same practice, repeatedly describing Johnson as "the volatile Jamaican" (*Globe*, "Had 'Nowhere to Go'" P5). The merits of Johnson's supporters' complaints are neither addressed nor assessed in the article; rather, their tone, mood, and affect is the reporter's central concern.

This representation of blackness as signifying irrationality continues in the *Toronto Star*'s coverage of police testimony about the day of the killing. Cargnelli describes his initial encounter with Johnson, alleging that Johnson was "screaming 'You – -ing bumboclat (a Jamaican curse)' His eyes were bulging, his cheeks were puffed, and with that, he spat on us" (Blatchford, "I Would Have Shot" A2). Cargnelli then describes Johnson running, "chuckling and swearing" (A2) and Blatchford transcribes what Cargnelli and Inglis reportedly saw next: "as he and Inglis passed the window, Cargnelli told police they saw Johnson and heard 'kids screaming and crying, an hysterical woman,' and decided they'd better act (A2)." Blatchford goes on to include Officer Gary Dicks's claim that "the scene inside the house was frantic," that "Johnson himself was 'Ranting and raving, aggressive, very aggressive,'" and that "Johnson dangled one of his daughters from a railing overlooking the stairs." (A2). The article, which aligns with the perspective of the police officers, depicts Johnson as irrational and mentally disturbed, and this irrationality is extended to the rest of the family in the depiction of the "kids screaming and crying, [and] an hysterical woman." The only rational agents on the scene are the white police officers who "decided they'd better act." Blatchford offers minimal journalistic framing of the officer's account and instead presents it as verifiable fact such that her article reads like a transcript of their testimony. Unlike Johnson's relatives and supporters who are marked by their blackness, their physicality, their gestures and their alleged emotional outbursts, the police officers' accounts are retold, transparently, such that they become linked with the authority of Blatchford's reporting. Indeed, the headings in her article read like a guide to the police account, reinforcing Johnson's instability and maligning his character: "Lawn edger," "Very violent," "Dangled daughter," "Mentally ill" (A2). The only instance where the police are marked physically or in terms of emotion occurs in an article the following day where Blatchford describes, "Visibly nervous and frequently stumbling over his words, Cargnelli insisted 'women were screaming, children crying, and Albert Johnson ranting and raving'" (Blatchford, "Police feared 'berserk' man would hurt family" A2). This portrayal of Cargnelli evokes sympathy for the officer. This is in direct contrast with the depiction of Johnson given in the headline of the same article: "Police feared 'berserk' man would hurt family, trial told." Johnson is a "man gone berserk," whom police feared would hurt his own family, whereas Cargnelli is "visibly nervous."[6] Further, the article is framed by focusing on what the "Police feared," which has the effect of constructing the police officers as the victims and Johnson as the deviant aggressor.

This focus on the alleged aggressive and emotional behaviour of black people persists throughout Blatchford's coverage of the trial. After the trial when the policemen are found not guilty by the all-white jury, the headline reads "blacks cry 'shame' as jury finds policemen not guilty." The emotionality of the black supporters is once again foregrounded and presented as an irrational response to the jury's finding. Blatchford describes the defeated Mrs. Johnson's departure from the courtroom: "With her four young children clutching to her coat and her 27–year-old sister, Bevolyn Williams shrieking at her side, 30-year-old Lemona [*sic*] Johnson was ushered to the escalator by the hostile group. Carefully watching were at least 15 uniformed Metro policemen" (A1). Her description of the mob of amorphous, dangerous blackness recalls Idora's view of her son vivisected; the black Canadians are described as crying, "shrieking," and "hostile," while the police and reporter are "Carefully watching." In the same article Blatchford writes that some of the jury "appeared upset by the emotional outburst from Johnson relatives, though there were similar scenes throughout the trial. Almost daily witnesses were heckled by a handful of spectators in the second-floor courtroom, and at least a half-dozen times, Mrs. Johnson, her sister or Dudley Laws … ran muttering and yelling from the room." The black spectators and supporters are depicted as being unable to observe the court proceedings rationally and prone to "emotional outburst." This is also present in The *Globe and Mail's* coverage which focuses on the black spectators: "During his charge to the jury, Judge Dunlap studiously ignored a subdued chorus of clucks, whispers, moans and groans from the audience that rose slightly in volume whenever the judge mentioned the possibility of an acquittal" (Carriere and Fluxgold P1). The description of the white judge who "studiously ignored" the black "chorus of clucks, whispers, moans and groans" is exemplary of the recurring link between white rationality and objectivity, and black emotionality and bias.

Blatchford's linking of blackness, irrationality, and deviance continues after the trial in her summary article entitled "What the jury didn't hear in Albert Johnson case":

> the half-dozen blacks who regularly attended the trial … were vocal in their disapproval of the way the trial proceeded. During testimony from Johnson's 30-year-old widow, Lemona [*sic*], other relatives moaned and cried out, "Oh, my brother! My brother"! When police officers gave

> evidence about Johnson's bizarre behaviour, Mrs. Johnson was among those who grumbled and hissed.
>
> Outside the court, the scenes were often even more theatrical.
>
> "Why didn't Albert kill one of them [the police]" Mrs Johnson shouted, weeping. "Than [*sic*] I would know justice is being done …"
>
> "This is a circus," one [policeman] whispered. It was one of the scenes the jurors never saw. There were others. And there was information about Johnson that was never presented to them. (A10)

Blatchford juxtaposes the supporters' behaviour with the policeman's observation that "This is a circus," further aligning the newspaper's perspective with that of the law. That she is physically close enough to the policeman to hear him whisper reveals her own bias. The details and language of this scene portray Mrs. Johnson and her supporters as a mob of black stereotypes who are "theatrical" who "grumbled and hissed" and "moaned and cried out." The white police officers "gave evidence" while the black observers turn the trial into a "circus." What possible reason could there be for the jury to witness the scene described by Blatchford other than to indicate the irrationality of Johnson's black supporters? Blatchford's depiction accords with Henry and Tator's observation that the "criminal activities of racialized minorities, although perpetrated by isolated individuals, are often interpreted as 'group crime'" (154). Steve Garner confirms this in his observation that "the dominant white gaze on black peoples conflates them into an undifferentiated mass" (19), and indeed Blatchford repeatedly links Johnson's individual deviance to a collective black deviance and criminality. She writes at the beginning of her article that the jury "weren't asked to return a verdict on Albert Johnson … sometimes known as 'The black Dragon,' but if they had been, they might have found him guilty of unhappiness and desperation and ruled his death almost unavoidable" (A10). While the jurors "weren't asked to return a verdict on Albert Johnson," the media coverage was concerned solely with passing judgment on Johnson's character.

In the reporting on this case, there is a discursive sliding between black, irrational, immigrant, problematic, deviant, and criminal such that the police violence against Albert Johnson is read as a tragic, yet unavoidable, response to black irrationality. Consider, for instance, Sol Littman's article, "Assessing the effects of the Johnson case" where he writes that "The small villages and urban slums of Jamaica give rise to large numbers of religious eccentrics. Nurtured on the Bible, driven by poverty, they look to Armageddon and maintain an uneasy relationship with the authorities of this world" (B4). The logic of the stereotype informs the colonial-sociological gaze of Littman's article, enabling his argument that it is Johnson's cultural origins in "the small villages and urban slums of Jamaica" that are responsible for turning him into a "religious eccentric" who maintained "an uneasy relationship with the authorities of this world." The clashes he had with police leading up to his murder are seen as problems inherent in Johnson's Jamaican (which, when necessary, is synonymous with blackness) culture and identity. The question of whether there are cultural or racist problems in "the small villages and urban" centres of Canada is never considered, as white Canada is depicted as rational and normal. Dudley Laws, a regular supporter of Johnson and a leading figure in the black Toronto community, sums up the manner in which Johnson's race, immigrant status, and mental stability became the focus of the case: "*Albert Johnson* only was on trial in court. The police were never on trial. It is a disgrace" (Carriere and Fluxgold P1; italics in original).

The discourse employed by the *Toronto Star*, the *Globe and Mail* and the *Toronto Sun* in their depiction of Johnson relies on a particular construction of race which conceives of whiteness as rational, invisible, and objective and blackness as irrational, emotional, deviant, and foreign. Henry and Tator describe this as "*The Discourse of Otherness*" (231; italics in original), in which the discourse of the newspaper positions the deviant subject as "other" to the reader, separating the (racially-coded white) readers, reporters, and officials and the "other". The media depiction of Johnson employs a discourse of otherness whereby his mental illness, his status as an unemployed immigrant, his size, and his behaviour are all marshaled under the sign of his blackness to mark him as foreign, criminal, and deviant from a white Canadian norm. The mainstream media's concept of whiteness is described by Coleman in his analysis of *White Civility* where he argues,

> what has come to be known as English Canada is and has been … a project of literary, among other forms of cultural, endeavor … the central organizing problematic of this endeavour has been the formulation and elaboration of a specific form of whiteness based on a British model of civility. By means of this conflation of whiteness with civility, whiteness has been naturalized as the norm for English Canadian cultural identity (5).

Coleman analyses the manner in which whiteness in Canada is defined according to a certain form of British civility, thereby elevating white Canadians over both First Nations people and non-white immigrants. Within multiculturalism, civility is a means of differentiating "real" Canadians from the rest. Coleman argues that "civility itself is a positive value that is structurally ambivalent. This is to say that at the same time that civility involves the creation of justice and equality, it simultaneously creates borders to the sphere in which justice and equality are maintained" (9). Coleman's stressing of the ambivalence of the concept of civility necessarily supplements democratic racism in Canada; Coleman's ambivalent civility gets to the heart of how civility at once enables a discourse of liberal "justice and equality" and "creates borders" that regulate whom that justice and equality will include. The depictions of black people as deviant, emotional, and irrational in the media's coverage of "the Johnson trial"[7] reveals how the structures of white civility police access to the Canadian public sphere by marking certain subjects as uncivil (not white) and thus un-Canadian. The media coverage employs a grammar of white civility that excludes black people from the public sphere and the national body proper.

In one sense the killing of Albert Johnson reveals the contradictions in white civility as it is the white police officer, perhaps *the* figure for the border between Canadian, civil whiteness and un-Canadian, irrational, uncivil otherness, who is charged with the unlawful killing of a black man. This figure of the white law-enforcement official who has crossed over into criminal activity, perilously blurring the lines of civility, brings to the surface the contradictions, the simultaneous appeal to universality and acts of exclusion, of white civility. Yet, in another, more chilling sense, perhaps the police killing of Johnson and the discourse surrounding his death is consistent with the logic of white civility, revealing how this discourse renders Johnson's killing possible. Sherene Razack has made the link between the production of whiteness as a privileged and exclusive identity and the devaluing of non-white subjects, arguing that "the evictions of racialized peoples [from legal protection, citizenship and categories of civility] make possible the production of white identities – as kin groups, families, nations" (*Casting Out* 7). To borrow Achille Mbembe's term, perhaps there is an element of "necropolitics" within the discourse of white civility such that the uncivil quality of non-white Canadians can be used to justify the state killing of a non-white subject. The discourse of white civility evicts Johnson outside the borders of civility which, in turn, renders his killing, in Blatchford's terms, "almost unavoidable." The project of white civility relies on the exclusion of non-civil, non-white others, and that in the case of Albert Johnson: he is "marked as outside humanity" (Razack, *Casting Out* 6) and as the *"living dead"* (Mbembe 40; italics in original) such that his killing becomes tolerable.[8]

While the voice of white civility is often invisible during the trial and only implied in the marginalization of black perspectives and devaluing of black opinions, there are occasional moments when it announces itself quite explicitly. For instance, after the not guilty verdict is announced by the jurors, the black supporters of Johnson "Walked from the courtroom, shouting and crying" (Blatchford, "Blacks Cry 'shame'" A1). Judge Dunlap is described as having "told the jurors that he … regretted the demonstration they observed in response to their verdict … I had wanted to say I was most pleased by the way the blacks and the whites and all the people who have come here have behaved" (Carriere and Fluxgold P1). The judge's differentiation between the behaviour of black and white people and his paternalistic disappointment in the behaviour of black people further indicates his concern with the codes of civility. Similarly, the *Globe* reports that after the jury had delivered their verdict, "Judge Dunlap told the jurors their verdict 'restores my faith in Canadian human beings, to see how you've behaved'" (Carriere and Fluxgold P1). The judge's strange observation that his "faith in Canadian human beings" has been restored by both the jury's verdict and their behaviour suggests how white civility is at the crux of this trial. This is just one of Dunlap's many statements throughout the trial where he indicates that he wants the jury to rule in favour of the police officers. Sol Littman writes that Dunlap "left little doubt that he trusted the policemen's account of the incident and discounted the Johnson family's evidence. On matters of law, the judge instructed the jury, he was supreme. His interpretation of the law left little room for the jurors to find the officers guilty" (Littman B1). The *Globe* confirms this, reporting that "Dunlap told the jury that if Constable Inglis felt himself in danger when Mr. Johnson appeared with the lawn edger, he was entitled to use force … 'It's hard to have detached reflection in the face of an uplifted knife,' Judge Dunlap told the jury" (Carriere and Fluxgold P1). While Dunlap's bias is evident throughout the coverage of the trial, his statement concerning the fate of "Canadian human beings" gestures towards the very structure of white civility which posits that there are "Canadian human beings" and other "human beings" organized according to barely-visible codes of civility. The statement indicates the racism that frames the discourse of the trial both within the courtroom and in the media's coverage. That the judge decides to link, in praise, the jury's acquittal with the way "they've behaved" reveals that it is their behaviour, their reaffirmation of the codes of white civility, that confirms them as "Canadian human beings." The implicit contrast between their behaviour and the decidedly un-Canadian, non-white behaviour of the Johnson supporters is clear.

The discourse of white civility is also present in readers' responses to coverage of the trial. Many readers are outraged at the manner in which the media covers the Johnson killing, and their anger suggests the crisis of white civility that organizes the discourse of the trial. Letters to the major Toronto newspapers are uniformly outraged when police are challenged, and are silent or approving when police are supported and Johnson is portrayed as deviant or criminal. From the outset of the coverage, readers play a major part in reaffirming the discourse of white civility and repeatedly link blackness with crime and deviance. In Hall's and Douglas Kellner's terms, the readers virtually uniformly reproduce "Dominant readings" (Hall, "Encoding" 233) of the discourse of white civility, only disagreeing with the newspaper's account when it conflicts with that discourse of white civility. In the "Letters to the Editor" section in the *Toronto Star* on 3 September 1979, the week after Johnson's death, readers express anger towards not only the black community for their claims that the police are racist, but also towards the *Toronto Star* for their sympathetic depiction of Johnson. V. Henry writes, "I sincerely hope that I am not the only *Star* reader who was dismayed and outraged at the headline 'Police Gun Down Father of Four' ... would not attach any blame to them for shooting a man in the circumstances described. Nor do I understand what being a 'father of four' has to do with it." The next letter, from Kenneth Thomson Jr., calls on reporters and readers alike to "put yourself in the police officer's situation" and suggests that anyone in the position of Inglis and Cargnelli would have shot in self defence. Both Henry and Thomson are happy to accept the police account of events, and indeed the majority of letters call on reporters and readers to "put yourself in the police officer's situation." Other readers are angered by the suggestion that race was a factor in the shooting at all. Pearl Miller writes, "I'm getting sick and tired of the continual cries of 'racism' against our police force. In the latest regrettable shooting of Albert Johnson, given the same set of circumstances and under the same situation would the outcome have been any different if Johnson were white? I think not!"[9] Robert Smith echoes Miller's comments when he writes, "The Jamaican community can best serve justice in this case by treating the shooting as a matter of defence of life, instead of the catch-all excuse of 'racism'. It has become by now the cheapest word in the English language and long stale." Both Miller and Smith insist that not only should race be ignored as a factor in assessing Johnson's shooting, but both also presume police innocence in the matter. Albert McKay invokes race in a (barely) coded manner: "I can walk down any street in Toronto and not be attacked by a policeman. I cannot be sure of this regarding some other elements of our society. Instead of calling for a judicial inquiry ... I think we should call for stricter immigration laws." Here race is invoked to group black Torontonians together and mark them as criminal, deviant, and potential threats to white civility and order.

While Henry and Tator never address the media coverage of Johnson's death, their analysis of the infamous 1990 "Just Desserts" killing in Toronto offers a useful counterpoint to the media depiction of Johnson. In the Just Desserts killing, three black men robbed a café in midtown Toronto and killed a white patron. From the outset of the media coverage, the media employs a discourse of white civility and black criminality. In this instance, where the criminals are black and the victims are white, the language of unavoidable tragedy used to describe Johnson's death is replaced with a language of outrage and anger towards black and Caribbean communities. Christie Blatchford, the *Toronto Star*'s lead reporter in both cases, titles her lead article on the Just Desserts case "*Good and Evil*" and suggests that an "epic contest ... was being waged in Toronto between 'the forces of good and evil'" (Henry and Tator 174). In a hyperbolic moment that is excessive even for Blatchford, she writes that the Just Desserts killing is "not the end of the world, and there will always be much to like about Toronto. But changed it is and a city's safety and self-confidence, like a woman's virginity, is lost only once and is never retrieved" (Henry and Tator 174). Part of Blatchford's outrage results from the location of the killing: an upscale café on the border of Toronto's elite Yorkville neighbourhood. That this crime occurs a mere 2.5 km from the site of Johnson's death demonstrates, again, the periphractic spatial management of race in Canada. The contrast between the discourse adopted by mainstream press in this case and in the case of Johnson's killing is revealing. In the Just Desserts case the white victim is portrayed as sympathetic, and the black criminals as violent thugs who have destroyed Toronto's innocence. Johnson, however, is portrayed not as a victim but as a troubled, deviant subject such that the white killers become the sympathetic figures who have been given the impossible task of having to manage this black man. In the Just Desserts case, the death of the victim is reprehensible and morally outrageous whereas Albert Johnson's death is "tragic" yet "unavoidable."[10]

The discourse of white civility and black criminality is completely disrupted within the alternative press coverage of Albert Johnson's death, particularly in the Toronto black community newspaper *Contrast*. *Contrast* was the major black newspaper in Toronto from the mid 1960s until the early 1990s. Its reporting on Johnson situates his death within a discourse of Canadian racism, police violence, anti-immigrant sentiment, and white supremacy. Throughout the coverage of Johnson's death, *Contrast* reporters, letter-writers, and editors link Johnson's killing to the killing of Buddy Evans the year before and cite both as examples of a pattern of racism and violence committed against black people in Canada. While the writers in *Contrast* have a variety of views, and openly disagree with one another in the paper's letters and editorials, what is repeated throughout is an awareness of the structures of power and racist violence that white civility enacts upon black Canadians. Errol Townshend asks "is 'racism' or 'racial tension' really the central issue in this [Albert Johnson] situation? It is not. The central issue here is abuse of power by a cherished and potent agency of the state in its dealing with a powerless minority. That's the issue Canadians must face, but won't" (9). In the following issue of *Contrast*, John Harewood writes, "In our liberal democratic tradition we are brought up to believe that the state exists to serve the better interests of all its people. The truth is that the state serves the interests of those who have authority in it. And since the protection and security of the citizen often depend on those who are in authority, the citizen may hardly ever expect to receive them without their consent" (9). What is striking in each of these articles is how the writers link the language of race to a language of power. In contrast to the semiotics of white civility that justifies Johnson's death, Harewood, Townshend, and others read his death through the lens of power relations. The intersection of race and culture with power identified by these writers presents a decidedly different understanding of Johnson's killing than the one offered in the mainstream press which attributes Johnson's death to his own individual failings and to the un-Canadian behaviour of black immigrants and black Canadians. These writers employ the language of "our liberal democratic tradition" to critique that same tradition's ongoing racism.

Mainstream accounts of Johnson's death construct a narrative of a tragic misunderstanding between cultures, whereas *Contrast* indicates that power in Canada is distributed and affects subjects according to race. Johnson's death, therefore, is an effect of this racist power imbalance.

Austin Clarke writes an editorial for *Contrast* concerning the Johnson killing in which he openly expresses his anger over this abuse of power. Clarke originally wrote the article for publication in the *Toronto Star*'s "Insight" section but it was rejected as "the article did not present the editor's opinion" (Clarke, "Johnson Killing" 12). Entitled "Why I Call Johnson killing Murderous," Clarke begins his letter with the argument that "People with power do not have to give reasons for their conduct. They usually do not. And when their conduct is injurious to the powerless, such as the immigrant in this society, their explanation of their conduct is usually not logical. Their explanation is often unacceptable to the powerless. It tends to be, also, tendentious and patronizing" (12). While Clarke describes the immigrant as "powerless," his insistence that the white "explanation" is "often unacceptable" suggests that there is a form of power in holding the police and white people to account. Clarke's editorial, along with the other articles in *Contrast*, are a way of writing against the felt powerlessness of the mainstream media's discourse of white civility and black deviance, and of insisting that black people not only be treated as part of Canada but as full and equal citizens. The editorials and letters in *Contrast* express a form of power that enables black people to critique the smearing and devaluing of blackness in the public sphere, and engage in a blackening of that public sphere. This capacity of writing to call power to account is evident in Clarke's article when he writes that black Canadians "may have to stop asking the power, the people in authority, to put an end to racialism. We must instead, illustrate with the blood of Albert Johnson, the result of racialistic conduct. And then all we can do is to leave the society, including the powerful and the politically powerful, to face the naked evidence of their indecency" (12). Clarke's call to "illustrate with the blood of Albert Johnson, the result of racialistic conduct" suggests the capacity of writing and narrative to disrupt the discursive formation of white civility that devalues black Canadians. Clarke locates Johnson within the broader contexts of transnational and Canadian black struggle and links his death to historical and contemporary racism in Canada. He initiates this act of illustration at the end of his article where his tone shifts from plainly political and analytic tone, to a more emotive and poetic language. He writes:

> Anytime. Anytime I have to expect. that a policeman. who dislikes my love of flowers. who feels that I am man. can kick in my door: overturn my Sunday pot of rice and peas: beat me while I am on bended knee. and then kill me. He can kill me in the presence of my children and my wife. He can do all those things to me. because he has the power. and the authority. Because he has determined. on his own. that I am his enemy. And also because he feels that his conduct. his indecency may not be chastisably reprehensible by his colleagues and his superiors. (12)

The shift in tone and the staccato sentences in this final section of the article indicate Clarke's anger at the police shooting, as well as the way this injustice renders a generic political discourse inadequate to expressing this anger. While the article begins with a careful and philosophical statement about the relationship between power and race, it concludes in far more personal tone in which his anger towards the police violence is palpable. Certainly Clarke's description of the police officer's "indecency" reads like a parodic rewriting of the discourse of white civility. This parodic rewriting constitutes an act of blackening of the Canadian public sphere that employs narrative to work against this smearing of blackness and sense of powerlessness.

Clarke's representations of Albert Johnson begin with his editorial in *Contrast* and continue such that Johnson seems to haunt his corpus. The most regular references to Albert Johnson appear in *More*, which Clarke wrote and revised over a thirty-year period. While early versions did not include references to Johnson, later versions of the text – revised to focus primarily on a Caribbean domestic worker – include repeated references to Johnson's death. In first drafts of the novel from the early 1980s, reports of Johnson's death are heard on the radio, while later versions of the novel begin with the main character dreaming of the imprint of the policeman's boot that remains on Albert Johnson's back doorway. After Clarke was unable to get early versions of *More* published, he transformed the early drafts into short stories which he released in the collection *In This City* (1992), where there are numerous references to Johnson. In "Sometimes, A Motherless Child," which focuses on an older domestic worker and her son in Toronto, there are explicit references to his death, such as when the unnamed domestic worker goes to a hair salon and listens to conversations about Johnson. There are also references to him in "I'm Running For My Life," in which the episode of police violence that concludes the narrative mirrors Johnson's death. References to Albert Johnson pervade both the early and final verions of *More* as Idora is haunted by what happened to "poor Mr. Albert Johnson" (100). Sitting at the intersection of Yonge and Dundas, Idora sees a police officer patrolling and she imagines taking the policeman's gun out of his holster and shooting him. As she fantasizes about this she thinks, "My mind is remembering the fate of poor Mr. Albert Johnson, whose picture of crucifixion I have on a wall in my apartment" (101). Idora imagines taking the policeman's gun and shooting him "Three times. To make sure that if the first bullet did not hit him, the second one would! And the third one would kill-him-off! Dead! Yes! One for Mr. Albert Johnson. One for the other Jamaican, the Prince of Africa. And one for the future – for my son, as worthless as he is" (100–1). The repetition of threes in Idora's fantasy and her elevation of Johnson's death to a "crucifixion" links her desire for revenge with the novel's theme of religious and spiritual redemption. Idora insists on remembering these black men killed by the police and she retells their death through this religious imagery as part of her heretical blackening of Canada.

Idora continually returns to the figure of Albert Johnson, spurred on by her small collection of newspaper clippings, memories, and by the links she makes between contemporary and historical violence committed against black people. Idora offers the following first-person account of her discovery of Albert Johnson's life and death:

> one afternoon, it was a Thursday, years ago, I was still working as a domestic … [on] the four floors in that mansion, including the basement floor, where I first came upon the name Mr. Albert Johnson, a Jamaican. Lord have His Mercy! I saw the photograph of the killing. On the front page. And I had to read the full story. I read the story in a newspaper, the *Star*, I think. The newspaper told how the police went into that man's home, on a Sunday, and shoot him dead! My God. My heart burned when I saw the picture in the newspaper … I still can't get that picture out o' my mind. I cut-out the clipping with a pair of scissors. It was from the newspaper in a drawer I found it in, and I have it in my bureau, up to today. I looked at it every night; for nights, at the beginning; and then, after a while, when the worse wore off, I would look at it just to remember the past, every November when I have to search for my Labello Lypsyl, to prevent my lips from chapping and cracking, I would look at Mr. Johnson in the bureau drawer … just to remember. Even though I was told years later that he was killed in the month of August, I nevertheless associated his murder with the month of November, which was one of the most miserable months of my life in this country, because of the dreadful weather. And why, you tell me, why still can't I get his face out o' my

> mind? And I will tell you why. Every time, every year, every beginning of winter, every November, my mind goes back to that face. It was a August when the policeman blew his head to smithereens! Simple as that, the reason, I mean. Mr. Johnson's head was covered in blood, in a drawer in the servants quarters my employers had assigned for me to sleep in. (55–6)

This complicated passage is very important in terms of Clarke's conception of black history in Canada, as well as the way in which he depicts Albert Johnson as both a figure for and the content of that history. Certainly Idora's first-person narrative indicates the importance of oral storytelling to preserving black history in Canada. Idora affirms Brand's observation that "oral history opened up that vast and yet untapped well of events, knowledge, and experience that black women live and have lived in this country" ("factory" 171). Idora's role in the mansion indicates the position of first- and second-generation black Caribbean women in Canada who often arrived as domestic servants in the 60s and 70s. Both Idora and the newspaper that records the details of Johnson's life are relegated to the periphractic space of the basement and forgotten within a decidedly white Canadian history. The link between Idora's status as a domestic and Johnson's history is made again when Idora describes discovering an image of "Mr. Johnson's head … covered in blood, in a drawer in the servants quarters my employers had assigned for me to sleep in" (56). Linking Johnson's death with Idora's position in the servant's quarters, Clarke positions Johnson's history as part of a broader history of marginalization of and violence against black people in Canada. Yet, while both Idora and Johnson appear to be powerless, Idora's recovery of Johnson's history and her linking of his history with her position in the Rosedale mansion reveals how power can be appropriated. The black presence in Canada is one that is barely tolerated, disavowed as it is by white Canadians and relegated to the basement of national history. Yet Idora traverses that home, and although she and Johnson have been marginalized, their presence and her narration of their presences constitutes a form of blackening that transforms these spaces.

The article on Johnson's death takes on a talismanic quality for Idora, providing her with a vocabulary for remembering and narrating her migration to Canada. She explains, "I looked at it every night; for nights, at the beginning; and then, after a while, when the worse wore off, I would look at it just to remember the past, every November … just to remember." Finally, she explains, "Even though I was told years later that he was killed in the month of August, I nevertheless associated his murder with the month of November, which was one of the most miserable months of my life in this country, because of the dreadful weather … Every time, every year, every beginning of winter, every November, my mind goes back to that face." Idora's memory of Johnson is linked to her own memory of immigration and of her domestic work. Furthermore, her shifting of the month in which Albert Johnson was killed from August to November (the month in which the police officers were acquitted) and linking Johnson's death to the oncoming "dreadful weather" is Idora's creative reimagining of his death. If the dreadful weather of November can be read as not only a sign of the inhospitable Canadian environment but also of the cold reception of black people by white people in Canada,[11] then Idora's reimagining of Johnson's death as occurring in November suggests his killing is a pronounced example of white discrimination that she has encountered in Canada. More than mere archival work then, Idora also transforms this act of terrifying violence into a sign of the struggle and resilience of black people in Canada.

Idora's accidental discovery and subsequent preservation of the Albert Johnson article thematizes the erasure of black Canadian history and Clarke's project of blackening Canadian history. George Elliott Clarke describes this subaltern and repressed quality of black Canadian history, arguing that "The perpetual, white denial of Canada's own history of slavery, segregation, and anti-black discrimination accents black invisibility" (*Odysseys* 35). G.E. Clarke discusses Canada's denial of its own history of racism, slavery, and discrimination, but he also indicates the manner in which black Canadian subjects are rendered invisible or seen as outsiders in Canada through the repression and disavowal of black Canadian history. In this sense, Idora's archival work of finding the newspaper and preserving the article for nearly thirty years in her drawer, indicates the manner in which both she and Austin Clarke preserve an otherwise forgotten black Canadian presence and give voice to Johnson's enforced silence, thus making absence speak. In Idora's preservation of the article and Clarke's fictive recreation of the struggle to preserve Johnson's memory, both are blackening Canadian history through their acts of recovery and narration.

McKittrick complicates this notion of black Canadian history as rediscovery in her insistence on the importance of "surprise" as the "outcome of wonder" (91) in the discovery of black Canadian history. She writes,

> The element of surprise, then, holds black Canada in tension with the nation's ceaseless outlawing of blackness: blackness is surprising because it should not be here, was not here before, was always here, is only momentarily here, was always over there ... black people in Canada are also presumed surprises because they are 'not here' and 'here' simultaneously: they are, like blackness, unexpected, shocking, concealed in a landscape of systemic blacklessness. (*Demonic Grounds* 93)

This is the surprise of white Canada "discovering" black people in Canada before the advent of multiculturalism, or that there are black Canadians outside of Toronto, Montreal, and Vancouver. Yet this surprise is also the surprise black people provoke when they disrupt stereotypical and monolithic blackness. This wonder is present in Idora's discovery of the Albert Johnson article as she exclaims, "Lord have His Mercy! I saw the photograph of the killing. On the front page. And I had to read the full story ... The newspaper told how the police went into that man's home, on a Sunday, and shoot him dead! My God. My heart burned when I saw the picture in the newspaper." Idora's exclamation is not just the surprise of discovering the details of Johnson's death, but also the surprising way in which she renders his death productive and makes it significant to her own experience of migration and marginalization. Idora's surprising rewriting of Albert Johnson's death transforms the erasure of blackness in Canada into a blackening of Canada. Her reaction expresses the absented presence of Johnson's history, and her rewriting of his death reveals how that absented presence can be reimagined as black expression rather than immobilizing powerlessness. As such, Idora's reimagining indicates the strategies of adaptation that have enabled her to survive in Canada despite the deep discrimination and violence that she experiences.

Surprise and wonder as forms of blackening are present throughout *More* and throughout Clarke's deployment of the story of Albert Johnson. Later in the novel, Idora goes to a hair salon on Eglinton Avenue where the discussion turns to Albert Johnson:

> the conversation turned and settled on their remembering the Jamaican man shot dead by the police. "And child! All that blood! What a thing, eh?" "And did you see the pictures in the *Star*?" "In all the papers, too!" "Yes, they show you how that police went in with guns blazing ..." "Toronto is the new Wild Wess!" "And the two thrildren hiding behind she! Scared as hell! ... Two girls, I think I read in the *Star* ..." "And his

> wife, poor soul, down behind the table, hiding. From the bullets … her two hands covering her head and her two ears!" "One picture show how the street was empty. And it was a morning. It must have been seven or eight. And the garden in the back was so nice, with such lovely red –" "Roses!" "Yes! The paper said they were roses!" … "My God, his roses, I hear, were so pretty! Just like back home in Jamaica … And all of a sudden two police appear, called by Mr. Johnson's malicious neighbours! And you're charged for breaking the peace! They complain your music is too loud …" "Sometimes I does wonder 'Why worry'?" "Yeah! Why break my ass?" "Were they two police, or t'ree?" … Idora didn't think so many others knew, and cared, and remembered poor Mr. Johnson, even though none of them seemed to know him personally. For the first time, she learned that his wife, Mrs. Johnson, had to hide behind the dinner table! Or was it the chairs? … "Here in Toronto, they say your home is your castle …" "What kind o'bullshit is that?" "… no home is no castle, if it own by a Negro …" (253–5; ellipses in original)

The narrative gives voice to the concerns and memories of black people in ways that the mainstream media discourse never does. The closing statement of the passage, "no home is a castle, if it own by a Negro," marks a contrast between the mansion that Idora worked in and the basement apartment she lives in (as well as Johnson's home), and gestures towards this general sense of unhomeliness for black people in Canada. Yet what this passage reveals most clearly are the ways in which black diasporic communities engage in a blackening of the nation's history through their interpretations and retellings of the experience of marginalization and racism. Narrating the events of Johnson's death becomes a source of community empowerment that counters Canadian racism. The interpretation of newspaper articles and the sharing (and misreporting) of the details of Johnson's death is a crucial means by which black Canadians affirm their presence in the nation. In the act of narration, of telling the story of Albert Johnson's death, Idora and other people in the salon claim a space for themselves in the nation, creatively reinterpreting and blackening this narrative of violent racism and drawing strength from it. Clarke's articulation of wonder and surprise in his rendering of Johnson's historical presence is one method by which he resignifies Johnson's history, extricating it from a discourse of white civility that erases black presences in Canada. In place of this construction of Johnson as black tragedy and part of a general history of black powerlessness, Clarke elevates Johnson's history in order to illuminate the absences and struggle that constitute black diasporic life in Canada. Johnson's history is narrated and improvisationally used by black diasporic people in Canada to challenge the erasure of black histories in the nation, blackening its contours with their surprising and creative imputations of violent racism, and drawing strength from this strategic smearing of national unity.

In place of this construction of Johnson as one more figure in a general history of black powerlessness, the improvisational use of historical fact allows Clarke's characters to challenge the erasure of black histories and force a place for themselves within the nation. Clarke's historical narratives express the forms of resistance that black Canadians use to combat that erasure, and also record the actual existences of black history and black presence in Canada. His narratives include not only the details of Johnson's death but also the manner in which those details are preserved, remembered, and transformed by other black Canadians into a blackening of the nation.

Neil Bissoondath also writes the narrative of Albert Johnson – albeit in a concealed way – into his novel *The Innocence of Age* (1994). Bissoondath's largely forgotten (and forgettable) novel is a coming-of-age narrative for middle-aged men, focusing on a number of men in Toronto who attempt to find their place in the city. Although there are some considered moments in the narrative, Bissoondath's characters are too often flat, singular mouthpieces for clichéd political perspectives. Indeed, the plot reads much like a fictive case study in support of Bissoondath's argument in *Selling Illusions: The Cult of Multiculturalism* (1994). The symbolic overloading of his novel is present at the outset: the text begins with a group of men of diverse cultural and ethnic backgrounds in a downtown bar, The Starting Gate, where one of them reads Plato's *The Republic*. United in their masculinity and their common desire to succeed in Canada, these men are uniformly uninterested in the multicultural experiment of which they are a part. Throughout the novel the recurring themes of unity among men, desire between the sexes, and a hope for a better life transcend any discussion of politics or racism. Indeed, the very name of the bar "The Starting Gate" has all the implications of liberal equality, meritocratic thought, and "colour-blindness" that Bissoondath advocates in *Selling Illusions*. The implication is that, placed together at the starting gate, this group of men have equal opportunity to succeed and it is up to them to ensure that they do.

Clarke's narratives link the lives of his characters to broader contexts, but Bissoondath's novel is suspicious of linking individual concerns to the politics and history of race and multiculturalism in Canada. When Bissoondath does represent politics, history, or racism, they are depicted as irrelevant to the lives of his characters. The protagonist, Pasco, watches "the seven o'clock news on television. There was nothing new. Native unrest, immigration policy, the Soviet economy, African starvation, Ottawa corruption, lake-water pollution: each topic got its thirty or forty seconds, not enough to inform but quite sufficient to ensure that the world was, as ever, lurching from one crisis to another" (43). The narrative voice treats politics as an irrelevant, media-driven sideshow of disaster, crises, and celebrity that has little to do with the lives of the characters. While Pasco's perspective is not necessarily Bissoondath's, this scepticism towards politics pervades the narrative. This cynicism towards politics exemplifies Davey's (1993) arguments about the features of the contemporary "post-national" Canadian novel which, as a group, disavow the relevance of the Canadian state and instead "suggest a world and a nation in which social structures no longer link regions or communities, political process is doubted, and individual alienation has become normal" (266). This is largely the Toronto described in Bissoondath's writing, one that exists at the expense of any meaningful history of Canadian racism.

Bissoondath's rendering of Albert Johnson follows the novel's pattern of scepticism of linking the political with the personal. Montgomery, one of Pasco's drinking buddies at The Starting Gate, is the figure in the novel whose life and death mirrors Johnson's. Montgomery is a black Grenadan immigrant who finds that his masculinity and patriarchal status are in crisis after his daughter begins disobeying his instructions. This undermining of his masculinity leads to him arguing with his wife, developing a drinking problem, and having trouble at work. Montgomery's anger eventually renders him uncontrollable and violent and he is shot, in his home, by two police officers on a Sunday afternoon. Pasco's friend and fellow Starting Gate congregate, Pushpull, relates the events of Montgomery's death to Pasco: "'They say he came at them with a knife in the corridor outside his apartment. So they pumped two bullets into him. Self-defence' 'What the fuck were they doing there?' ... 'They say he threatened a neighbour. You believe that?'" (279). Bissoondath appropriates the details of Albert Johnson's death for his novel but obscures them such that it becomes difficult to identify their historical origins. Yet the similarities between Montgomery and Johnson make it clear that Montgomery's death is partially based on Johnson's (some of the details seem to be borrowed from the history of Lester Donaldson who was also killed by Toronto police). Bissoondath's re-narration of Johnson's death completely decontextualizes the narrative from any broader discourse of racism in Canada or from a history of police violence, and instead constructs the shooting as a tragic yet isolated event resulting from a confrontation between two confused and frightened people (Kurt the police officer and Montgomery). Bissoondath foreshadows the shooting by repeatedly describing the police officer who shoots Montgomery as an ultimately good but misguided individual. Kurt and his older partner, Sean, are regulars at Pasco's diner and Sean confesses to Pasco that "Kurt's a nice kid. Good name for him, by the way. Young and kind of high-strung, y'know? Granpa was in the force, dad was in the force, older brother's in the RCMP up north. And now here's junior lookin' real nice in his uniform and packin' a pistol. Likes to keep his hand on the butt whenever there's a situation" (73). This effort to humanize both the police and Montgomery, comes at the expense of identifying the structures of racism that make Montgomery's death possible. Kurt is depicted as a "nice kid" who is "Young and kind of high-strung," and Pasco observes that he has "watery and unsure eyes, eyes that undercut, even for a young boy, the confidence with which he spoke" (121). Later in the novel, Sean describes a "nightmare of being confronted by a gunman bursting from one of the apartments. 'With all those doors … there's no place to go, nothing to do except crouch and fire' (158–9). Bissoondath repeatedly foreshadows the eventual confrontation between Montgomery, Sean, and Kurt, and Pasco's positioning between the two parties renders him an ideal liberal observer who is able to see all sides of the event while attributing blame to neither. Bissooondath's rendering of the events of Albert Johnson's murder, with his humanizing of both Kurt and Montgomery and his portrayal of their confrontation as an inevitable tragedy resulting from fear and misunderstanding, severs the link between the killing and the history of police violence against black people and Canadian racism more generally. In effect, Bissoondath's novel decontextualizes Johnson's death such that it becomes tragic and terrible, perhaps the underside to the Canadian multicultural program, but is never seen as part of a larger pattern of racism and violence against black people in Canada.

Both Pasco and the narrator are dismissive of any attempt to attribute Montgomery's death to racism. The novel's broader suspicion of media discourse and anti-racist politics is evident in its depiction of the public response to Montgomery's death:

> Cut to a group of solemn young people, many blacks with a few whites sprinkled among them, holding up signs: END RACISM NOW! CHARGE HIM WITH MURDER! KURB KOP KILLINGS! Cut to a man familiar from the news, the lawyer Pushpull had mentioned, a grave and elegant man: 'Today is a day of sadness and anger for us ...' Cut to another man, yet another face grown familiar in recent days, identified as a black activist, less polished than the lawyer but a dapper dresser still: 'We will not take this lying down. I put this racist society on notice ...' Cut to a police spokesman announcing that the constable involved – cut to a photograph of Kurt – had been suspended with pay pending the outcome of an internal investigation. (284–5)

This barrage of clichéd images of protest, dismayed public leaders, rhetorical black activists and solemn police spokesmen indicates a total disaffection with any attempt to link the shooting to a broader political discourse. The clichés offered by both the police and the protestors are seen as empty, self-serving responses to a crisis that is far more complicated than their rhetoric suggests. Even the language of "Cut to" reveals the narrative's cynicism with both the content and the form of this media coverage, suggesting that it aims to scandalize and focus on the crisis, but has little to offer in terms of real understanding. Pasco reaffirms the narrative's perspective when he looks at "a copy of the *Sun*, the front page taken up with a colour portrait of Kurt on the left, a black-and-white one of Montgomery on the right. Pasco glanced at it briefly, rolled it up and put it ... in the garbage can" (283). For Pasco and for the narrative more generally, Montgomery's death is not a political issue and is not connected to broader questions of race, power, or violence in Canada, but is a tragic result of a confrontation between two equally well-intentioned, yet confused men.

This decontextualizing of Johnson's killing is also present in the statements given by Montgomery's son after his father's death. The exchange at the end of the novel between Pasco and Montgomery's son articulates the narrative's view of the correct response to Montgomery's death:

> "she's found herself people to listen to now." "What d'you mean?" "They keep shoving cameras and microphones in front of her." Pasco didn't have to ask who "they" were. The controversy continued with demonstrations and press conferences, accusations flying back and forth. "Even Mammy's getting caught up in it. She's planning on joining a demonstration at Queen's Park tomorrow." "And you?" "I've told 'em to fuck off, I don't plan to be anybody's victim. My sister, she likes that, eh? She likes being told she's a victim" ... Montgomery had had the kind of determination he was hearing in his son's voice, the steady strength it took to insist on leading his life as he saw fit. He said, "I think you're going to be all right." (306)

The sister described in this passage is the same woman that disobeys Montgomery which leads to his breakdown and his eventual shooting. After disobeying her father she runs away from home and becomes a prostitute. Setting aside the tortured dialogue and absurd gender implications of the plot, the narrative depicts the sister's (and even the "Mammy's") participation in protest and demonstration as "getting caught up in" (and enjoying) victimhood. Bissoondath's retelling of Albert Johnson's story decontextualizes the events of the shooting, disconnecting them from any broader understanding of police violence or racism in Canada. In place of an attempt to understand the links between the shooting and systemic discrimination and racism, Bissoondath's novel portrays Montgomery's death as an isolated incident, and the narrative praises the capacity of individuals to cope with trauma. Pasco sees that both Montgomery and his son have a "kind of determination ... the steady strength it took to insist on leading his life as he saw fit" (306), and this abstract, male, individualistic determination is valued over the response given by Montgomery's daughter. It is telling that at the end of the text, the novel is focalized on white Pasco assessing Montgomery's death and Montgomery's son's response. This narrative implicitly endorses the liberal values of the determined individual triumphing over their social circumstances, and it does so by erasing the history of systemic discrimination and violence against black people in Canada. In a sense, Bissoondath's rendition of Johnson's death reinforces the codes of white civility, but simply attempts to read this civility in a race-neutral manner. *The Innocence of Age* constructs the shooting as a tragedy but admits no links between this shooting and any broader systemic discrimination, and suggests that to claim that there are is to play politics and celebrate one's own victimhood.

Dionne Brand takes up the history of Albert Johnson's death in a far more nuanced and challenging way, as her texts thematize the historical erasure of Johnson's death and convert that erasure into a surprising articulation of black history in Canada. The speaker's claim in *thirsty*, that "History doesn't enter here," can be read as an ironic statement about the manner in which Canadian history excludes the histories of black people. Similarly, her statement that "life ... / on this small street is inconsequential" suggests that Johnson's life had no consequences for the police and remains historically irrelevant and a matter of no consequence to the national narrative that ignores him. Brand's task throughout the poem seems to be to render Johnson's life consequential to history and to identify the erasure of black history in Canada. Not only are the events of Alan's death very similar to those of Johnson's, but the speaker also explains that "The house is still there, on Hallam Street, / still half-sleeping, ramshackled like wintering / bear" (XXI).[12] The speaker's task, and perhaps the task of Brand's poetry more generally, is to awaken the sleeping rage of the "wintering / bear" that is black history and consciousness in Canada. Brand has also explicitly discussed her own personal experience in the Albert Johnson case in a number of texts. In her essay "Bathurst," she links the space of Bathurst and Bloor streets ("Bathurst Subway. I say it like home. It's an uneasy saying" [*Bread* 67]) to her memories of black collective struggle and her involvement in advocating justice for Albert Johnson:

> In 1978 we were working the four corners of the intersection just after the killing of Albert Johnson by the cops. Only months before they had killed Buddy Evans down on Spadina Avenue. And those who could have saved his life had said that he was just a nigger and left him to die. Now Albert Johnson was shot on the staircase in his house on Manchester. A Jewish sister and I were flyering the corners, she on the south-west, I on the north-east. It was for the rally to protest the killing of Albert Johnson. The rally would start on Manchester, go to Henson-Garvey Park (in 1978 some of us called Christie Pits the Henson-Garvey Park), then up Oakwood to the police station on Eglinton near Marlee ... The day of the rally not a cop showed up in uniform and the police station was locked and ghostly. We wanted to break down the doors but Dudley [Laws] said no. When Albert Johnson's sister sang "By the rivers of Babylon," water came to our eyes. We've been weeping ever since. One killing after another, one police acquittal after another. (74–5)

Brand remembers the details of the rally vividly, although she incorrectly states that it was held in 1978 when it was actually held in 1979. What is both compelling and puzzling about Brand's description of her involvement with the Albert Johnson Defence Committee is the vivid details that she recalls and the documentary-like attention she gives them. She names the numerous activist groups operating around Bathurst and Bloor in the 1970s, and describes many of the major events and figures in the black community in Toronto, all in the interests of documenting the fullness and complexity of black life in Toronto. Yet this insistence on recording black lives and history contrasts with the decidedly undetailed and abstract manner in which she represents Johnson's death in *thirsty*. In the poem she renames Albert Johnson as Alan and changes his address from Manchester Avenue to Hallam Street. Also, the description she gives of the Albert Johnson rally is recalled by the speaker in *thirsty* but with none of the same detail that appears in the prose piece: "Chloe sang *By the Rivers of Babylon*, then broke like cake into a falsetto of grief / raised in the air to summon an inattentive God" (XXI). While Brand and her speaker are clearly describing the same events (although in the poem it is Alan's mother who sings, not his sister), it is up to the reader to make the necessary links. While Brand's essays reveal a desire to record, archive, and preserve the histories of black people in Toronto, her poetry abstracts these histories and does not explicitly link her critique and political intervention to these particular cases of racism, violence, and discrimination.[13] Perhaps Brand's obscuring of the details of Johnson's life and death thematizes the erasure and absenting of black presences in Canadian history. This is not necessarily contradictory to her stated project of "recovering history, history important only to me and women like me" (*Bread* 10), but rather complements that recovery by attending to the paradoxical presence of absence in black history in Canada. This paradox that structures Brand's historical writing is evident in her depiction of Alan as a "slender lacuna" and "a curved caesura." Furthermore, Brand's rewriting of Johnson's life and death renders his history relevant to black diasporic women as it focuses on his wife, daughter, and mother and attempts to give them agency and a voice outside the shadow of his death. These images of absence are rendered present in *thirsty* not simply to critique a metaphysics of presence or to gesture towards the irrecoverability of history, but to foreground the ongoing absenting of black histories in Canada.

Clarke and Brand recover the history of Albert Johnson in order give voice to black diasporic communities in Canada. Brand's obscuring of the details of Johnson's death enables her to productively reconstruct his history and situate it within a broader narrative of black life and struggle in Canada. Like Austin Clarke's attention to the acts of improvisation and narration that transform powerlessness into a form of agency, Brand's obscuring of the details of Johnson's history links his death to the broader struggle of black diasporic people. She writes, "black people ... living in Canada ... have the task of the necessary retrieval of our stolen history. We do not wish to run from our history but to recover it; our history is to us redemptive and restorative; in as much as it binds us in a common pain it binds us in common quest for a balm for that pain" (80). Both Clarke and Brand depict Johnson's death as a kind of transfiguration that rewrites the otherwise tragic events as redemptive for black people in Canada. Their rewriting details the doubleness of the "common pain" as well as the "common quest for a balm for that pain" in a way that locates black histories in Canada and that suggests a broader thematic of black diasporic history. This is evident not only in the religious themes of Clarke's and Brand's rewriting but also in their depiction of the collective dimension of diasporic history. Brand's repeated use of the terms "we" and "common" bespeak her desire to abstract individual instances of historical suffering and make them speak to a collective history of "common pain" and struggle. In this respect, Brand obscures the details of Albert Johnson's death in order to articulate a collective language that can express shared black historical suffering and possibility. When she describes the collective mourning she notes, "We have been weeping ever since," and it is this articulation of "we," of the collective black diasporic experience, that Brand hopes to "illustrate with the blood of Albert Johnson."

In a seemingly paradoxical way, Brand's lack of historical details in her decidedly historical poem contextualizes Johnson's killing within the history of the black diaspora in a manner that is unavailable to the mainstream media discourse. As the speaker of *thirsty* mockingly describes,

> So, a cop sashaying from a courthouse,
> his moustache wide and bristling,
> his wool coat draped across his body ...
> all muscle and grace, his virility in hand

> his striking the match like a gunslinger, ...
> history and modernity kissing here (XXVI)

The speaker links the image of the policeman with the repository of images of cowboys and gunslingers to deconstruct the realism of mainstream media discourse, revealing it to be a white romance between "history and modernity." The repetition of "his" in "history" marks the speaker's suspicion of historical discourse and its privileging of white, male perspectives. This image of the white police officer celebrating and smiling after his acquittal is actually taken from another police murder of a black Canadian which Brand describes in an earlier essay: "the image on national television of the white officer acquitted in the Lester Donaldson killing, a victory cigar in his mouth, triumph over and disdain for black people on his face, smiling for the cameras" (*Bread* 156). Here the details of the Lester Donaldson killing are obscured and linked to Albert Johnson's killing. By obscuring the details of Johnson's death, Brand's *thirsty* articulates a more general history of violence against black people in Canada, and the killing becomes one focalizing instance of that violence. Brand's narrating of the events of Johnson's death enables her to make white civility visible and show how it is supported by mainstream media discourse. Her depiction of the cop with "triumph and disdain for black people on his face" reveals the structures of racism that lie behind the death. Brand retells the events of Johnson's death in a manner that contextualizes it within other instances of racism in Canada, making visible the process by which black history is both erased and preserved. Her abstraction constitutes a blackening of the entire nation, as she elevates the death such that it is not merely a local, isolated event, but rather, relevant to black diasporic people across Canada, helping to give voice and identity to that community.

Brand's poetic rendering of history also allows her to depict the details of Albert Johnson's death that would be otherwise deemed irrelevant by traditional historical discourse and in the mainstream media. The speaker explains, "It would matter to know him as a child, / after all, he's dead when this begins / and no one so far has said a word about him / that wasn't somehow immaculate with his disaster" (IX). Brand sets herself the task of writing about Johnson and the women in his life without deeming them "immaculate with his disaster"; they are real people with full lives. Cutting through the mainstream discursive construction of Johnson as one-dimensional, mentally ill, and deviant, Brand depicts him as a complicated subject with hopes, dreams, and desires. Her portrayal of Johnson as a real person rather than just a cliché of violence, suffering, and tragic black masculinity supports McKittrick's argument that there is an element of surprise and wonder that marks black lives in Canada, particularly the surprise that black people can "exist in a landscape of blacklessness and have 'astonishingly' rich lives, which contradict the essential black subject" (93). Also, the poem's focus on the lives of Julia, Chloe, and the unnamed daughter accords with Brand's (and others') criticism of historical accounts that either exclude women altogether or locate them strictly within the home or the family. Brand writes that black women "are rarely seen as historical actors in their own right. In effect, the work that these women performed and the energies they expended in the survival of those early communities are minimized" (*We're Rooted* 6–7). Her focus on these women elevates them from the familial context and clichés of mourning wife or fatherless daughter, and instead provides them with real lives, desires, hopes, and suffering. Brand's poem works against the silencing of black women in the media depiction of the Johnson trial. Police Inspector Stirling's description of Colsie Johnson's testimony as "completely inconsistent with what we've got here. She's ... not a credible person," and Judge Dunlap's instructions to the jury to "disregard evidence from Johnson's 9 year old daughter Colsie" (Blatchford, "Blacks Cry 'shame'" A3), reveals the silencing of black women within the media. Brand rewrites this history to give voice to these women. As such, *thirsty* recontextualizes Johnson's death by simultaneously recovering the details of both his life and death and rewriting his killing in such a manner that renders that history productive and enabling for black Canadian women.

Brand's and Clarke's semiotics of blackening respond to and are structured by both authors' discursive concerns, particularly the manner in which their projects transform the public sphere and resist the discourse of white civility. Their poetics are inextricable from their political and discursive concerns, particularly as they reconstruct and reinterpret Johnson's life and death in order to resist the erasure of black presences from Canadian history, and to provide a full and surprising account of that life. Brand fills in the details of Johnson's life and of the women in the poem to demand that black Canadian history is not interpreted as an endless repetition of tragedy. Chloe, Julia, and the daughter each develop their own senses of hope, desire, and longing and a sense of the possibility of moving beyond the shadow of Alan's death. Clarke reconstructs Johnson's existence in a manner that depicts him as more than just the "essential [and tragic] black subject." Rather than detail the silences and exclusions of black people in and from the public sphere, as Henry and Tator painstakingly do, Brand's and Clarke's narratives break that silence through their illustration of surprise and wonder. Brand's and Clarke's acts of narration and reinterpretation work alongside acts of historical recovery in order to articulate black histories in Canada in a manner that disrupts discourses of white civility, black invisibility, and black deviance. George Elliott Clarke, discussing the importance of recovering and preserving figures in black Canadian history, insists that black authors "have to recover their bodies. They belong to us" (Wyile 149). Clarke's stated desire to "recover their bodies" is simultaneously an act of recovery, preservation, and the constitution of a community in the name of that history. His call to "recover their bodies" is supplemented with Austin Clarke's insistence on the need to "illustrate with the blood of Albert Johnson" to express the recovery of black history in Canada alongside the necessary reinterpretation of that history to work against the discourse of white civility. The necropolitics of white civility are challenged by Clarke's and Brand's recovery and narrating of Johnson's life and death. If Mbembe sees, in "Necropolitics," the "creation of *death-worlds*" (40; italics in original), Brand's and Clarke's rewriting of Johnson's death signifies *life-worlds* whereby the violent necropolitics of the state are productively rewritten in a manner that at once exposes Canadian racism and that offers a narrative of resistance against that racism. Brand's and Clarke's texts intervene in the publics constituted by the mainstream media discourse and white Canadian history, and narrate counter histories which challenge white civility. By rewriting the history of Johnson's death, Clarke and Brand at once gesture towards the historical facts of his life, but also re-narrate his life such that his death productively re-situates black people within Canadian history.

Chapter Four

Race, Heritage, and Recognition in Tessa McWatt's *Out of My Skin*

The analysis of democratic racism in the media coverage of Albert Johnson demonstrates how a discourse of otherness and white civility informed notions of Canadian citizenship prior to the recognition of multiculturalism in *the Canadian Charter of Rights and Freedoms* in 1982 and the passage of the *Canadian Multiculturalism Act* in 1988. Yet Henry and Tator have also shown the continued presence of democratic racism in Canada long after the passage of the Act, and the manner in which the discourse of otherness informs contemporary notions of race in Canada. This discourse seems to be challenged by the Government of Canada's stated claim in the *Canadian Multiculturalism Act* that "all Canadians, whether by birth or by choice, enjoy equal status, [and] are entitled to the same rights, powers and privileges" (Preamble 1988 n. pag.). Further, the Act states that the Government of Canada "recognizes the diversity of Canadians as regards race, national or ethnic origin, colour and religion as a fundamental characteristic of Canadian society and is committed to a policy of multiculturalism designed to preserve and enhance the multicultural heritage of Canadians while working to achieve the equality of all Canadians in the economic, social, cultural and political life of Canada" (Preamble 1988 n. pag.). The *Canadian Multiculturalism Act* introduces a "*Discourse of Tolerance*" (Henry and Tator 234; italics in original) that aims to supplant the discourse of otherness but that, in some instances, works in tandem with the abjection of black people from the nation. As with democratic racism, the discourse of tolerance renders the discourse of otherness compatible with multiculturalism by stressing that "Canadian society is a model of tolerance and accommodation. The emphasis on these values suggests that though one must accept the idiosyncrasies of the *others*, the dominant culture is superior" (234; italics in original). Despite multiculturalism's recognition of diversity, the claim that Canadians possess a "multicultural heritage" implicitly gestures towards "The ubiquitous *we*...the white dominant culture" (Henry and Tator 231; italics in original) who claim that heritage as their own. Further, the acts of recognition, preservation, and enhancement enshrined in the Act seem to be performed by just such an invisible and "ubiquitous *we*." The Act attempts to name this Canadian "we," but this effort is undermined by its enunciative position which reinforces the hegemony it alleges to challenge.

Dionne Brand's and Austin Clarke's work insists that Albert Johnson's history is part of this "multicultural heritage of Canadians." They question the meaning of that multicultural heritage by narrating the marginalized histories of black people in Canada and revealing how, despite what "The newspapers said," (*Bread* 103) this discourse of otherness has a long history in Canada. In *Out of My Skin*, Tessa McWatt continues their project of writing back to and blackening this multicultural heritage to reveal how it continues to affect contemporary notions of citizenship and race. Like Brand's and Clarke's projects to write life worlds and "illustrate with the blood of Albert Johnson," McWatt's novel conjures diasporic memory in order to combat the erasure of black people from Canada. She thus blackens Canadian heritage by asking who decides what constitutes Canadian heritage and how the language of heritage functions to exclude black people from the nation. At the heart of McWatt's critique of multiculturalism is the question of what constitutes Canada's national heritage. McWatt expands Brand's and Clarke's exclusive focus on black Canadians to consider the effects of heritage, racism, and nationalism on a much broader group of people including Francophone Canadians, First Nations people, black Canadians, and white, Anglophone Canadians. McWatt's novel extends the project of blackening in new ways by suggesting coalitions between aboriginal, raced, and sexed subjects in multicultural Canada. Her return to the meaning of heritage challenges Canadian multiculturalism, citizenship, and nationalism on their own terms.

The language of heritage in the *Canadian Multiculturalism Act* and the *Canadian Charter of Rights and Freedoms* indicates the cooperative relationship between the discourses of otherness and tolerance within Canadian multiculturalism. Similarly, the language of recognition in the Act separates those who share in Canadian heritage (and what that heritage includes) from those who do not. Constitutional scholar Peter Hogg argues that Section 27 of the *Charter*, which states that "This

Charter shall be interpreted in a manner consistent with the preservation and enhancement of the multicultural heritage of Canadians" is little more than "an interpretive provision, not offering any guarantee" and "may prove to be more of a rhetorical flourish than an operative provision" (71–2). While this section has rarely been used as a basis for legal arguments, the recurring emphasis on heritage within the *Charter* and the *Multiculturalism Act* gesture towards the hegemonic voice that pervades the discourse of both documents. This emphasis on heritage suggests an unbroken chain of Canadian values and a homogeneous conception of community that contrast with the stated diversity of Canadian multiculturalism. The *Charter*'s enshrinement of the "multicultural heritage of Canadians" performs a historical rewriting that simultaneously disavows Canada's colonial and racist history while rendering national diversity a "sign of the present" (Bhabha 352). Heritage also suggests generational continuity, biological uniformity, and notions of citizenship as birthright; all concepts that multiculturalism claims to critique. Among the definitions of heritage in the *OED* is the "fact of inheriting; inheritance, hereditary succession," "That which comes from the circumstances of birth," "the condition or state transmitted from ancestors," and "Heirs collectively; lineage" ("heritage"). Both the *Charter* and the *Act* paradoxically assert that Canadian identity is one of diversity and multiculturalism, but do so using the language of heritage which suggests birthright, "hereditary succession," and biological descent. *Out of My Skin* seizes upon this tension and doubleness in the *Act* to insist that the heritage of the black diaspora, as well as Canada's racist history, are both part of the contemporary "multicultural heritage of Canadians."

From its beginnings, the notion of heritage has troubled Canadian multiculturalism. Perhaps Canada's first official multiculturalism publication, *Book IV* of the 1969 Royal Commission on Bilingualism and Biculturalism, set out to understand "the Canadian Confederation on the basis of an equal partnership between the two founding races" (Dunton *Book IV* 3). This document assesses the merits of preserving the cultural and linguistic heritage of the "two founding races" along with the cultural heritage of "other ethnic groups" in Canada. The national forgetting implicit in this conception of Canadian heritage is evident in this early document as the Commission, crucially, does not consider the historical and contemporary presence of Aboriginal peoples. The Commission insists that "it is obvious" that "Indians and Eskimos [*sic*]... do not form part of the 'founding races'" (Dunton *Book IV* xxvi) nor are they included among "other ethnic groups" (xxvi). The contradictory assertion that Aboriginal people are simultaneously the "first inhabitants of this country" (xxvi) yet not one of its "founding races" belies the Commission's inability to cope with Canada's own colonial history.

Yet Aboriginal people are not completely absent from the Report: the first use of "heritage" in *Book I* of the report asserts that "everything possible must be done to help the native populations preserve their cultural heritage, which is an essential part of the patrimony of all Canadians" (Dunton *Book I* xxvii). While the "cultural heritage" of Aboriginals is an "essential part of the patrimony of all Canadians," Aboriginal people themselves are relegated to the margins of both historical and contemporary Canada. They are neither a "founding race" nor are they a part of the growing number of "other ethnic groups," but rather are marginalized within the Commission's reassessment of Canadian heritage. Indeed, Eve Haque's analysis of the Commission and its subsequent reports shows how

> Submissions by "Indians and Eskimos" and "other ethnic groups" during the preliminary hearing reveal the counter-stories, deviations, and disjunctures to both the commission's terms of reference and its singular notion of a crisis in the history of the country. It is in these counter-stories and disjunctures that the fault lines of an emerging racialized hierarchy between founding races, Indigenous groups, and other ethnic groups can be detected. (53)

In addition to this tension surrounding this notion of "founding races," the Commission's attention to "cultural heritage" in place of history erases the violent history of colonialism, broken treaties, and the forced assimilation and genocidal practices of the Canadian state. Thus the pre-multicultural language of "cultural heritage" enacts a rhetorical sleight of hand that enables Canada to repress its own history, and to marginalize Aboriginal people's claims on the nation while appearing to honour and memorialize that history. "Diversity" further obscures white supremacy in Canada by transforming theft and violence into "heritage."

It is telling that in the same moment that Canada was developing its proto-multicultural policy in the form of the Royal Commission, it also attempted to rewrite its relations with Aboriginal people with the infamous *Statement of the Government of Canada on Indian Policy* (1969), otherwise known as *The White Paper*. *The White Paper* was written under then Minister of Indian Affairs, Jean Chrétien, with the intent of redefining the relationship between Aboriginal people and Canada. Among other recommendations, the paper suggests abolishing the *Indian Act*, enabling individual Aboriginal people to alienate their land, and encouraging the gradual assimilation of Aboriginal people into Canadian society. The *White Paper* describes a "simple reality that the separate legal status of Indians and the policies which have flowed from it have kept the Indian people apart from and behind other Canadians" (n. pag.). Thus it proposes to attack Aboriginal people's "burden of separation" by ending "the legal distinction between Indians and other Canadians." In order to effect this change of status, the Paper insists that the history of relations between Canada and Aboriginal people must be transformed and that Aboriginals must recognize that "The significance of the treaties in meeting the economic, educational, health, and welfare needs of the Indian people has always been limited and will continue to decline." In place of treaty rights and separate status, Aboriginal people are promised access to material resources and full membership in Canadian society, but also "recognition by everyone of the unique contribution of Indian culture to Canadian society." The section entitled "The Indian Cultural Heritage" insists that "Rich in folklore, in art forms and in concepts of community life, the Indian cultural heritage can grow and expand further to enrich the general society." Thus in the *White Paper* as in the Commission's report, history is transformed into heritage, and the historical grievances of the past are ignored while Canada celebrates Aboriginal folklore, culture, and language.

The Aboriginal response to the *White Paper* was swift and derisive. Harold Cardinal and the Indian Chiefs of Alberta issued a response paper entitled "Citizens Plus," colloquially known as the "Red Paper."[1] "Citizens Plus" begins by asserting, "To those of us who are Treaty Indians there is nothing more important than our Treaties, our lands and the well being of our future generation" (189). In place of notions of cultural heritage, the authors insist that "Justice requires that the special *history*, rights and circumstances of Indian People be recognized" (192 italics mine). The authors demand that Canada recognize its own history and historical obligations and that it not attempt to erase Aboriginal histories from national consciousness. Yet for the authors of "Citizens Plus," the importance of Canada's historical and contemporary obligations does not detract from the possibility of a different form of Canadian multiculturalism. They explain that "There is room in Canada for diversity. Our leaders say that Canada should retain her 'pluralism,' and encourage the culture of all her people. The culture of the Indian peoples are old and colourful strands in that Canadian fabric of diversity" (194). The authors do not deny Canadian diversity but rather insist on a deeper notion of multiculturalism that goes beyond banal proclamations of "pluralism" and cultural heritage, and instead attends to the nation's history as it shapes the representation and politics of diversity in contemporary Canada.

Together, these three documents provide a lens that reveals how the development of Canada's multicultural policy not only transformed the relationship between Canada and its immigrant and non-white population, but also marked an attempt to renegotiate the relationship between Canada and Aboriginal people. Specifically, the discourse of Canadian heritage at once celebrates a vague notion of Canada's "multicultural heritage," while simultaneously substituting for Canada's history of racism and colonialism. This erasure of Canada's history of racism and its historical obligations via the rhetoric of "heritage" adds another dimension to the absented presences of Canadian history that Brand, Clarke, and McWatt contend with. Furthermore, it suggests the value of coalitions between Aboriginal and black people in Canada in the struggle to render that absented history present in contemporary Canada. Tessa McWatt's *Out of My Skin* explores the possibilities of such coalitions as they insist upon the importance of Aboriginal and black diasporic history to notions of Canadian heritage. The Charter insists on the historical reality of Canadian diversity and brandishes that diversity as a sign of Canada's shared history. Yet this is an empty notion of diversity and one which attempts to bury Canada's history of racism and colonization. McWatt's novel shows, therefore, that while the diversity of national origins is obvious, it is the narration of that history, the exposure of the fissures and cracks in the national narrative, and the alchemical process by which it is transformed into national myth that matters in defining the nation today.

The protagonist of *Out of My Skin* is Daphne Baird, an adopted mixed-race woman in search of her biological family. Daphne was adopted by a white Scottish-Canadian couple as a child, and the novel begins with her attempting to learn about her own familial and cultural heritage. The question of what constitutes Canadian heritage and history and the possibility of alliances between diasporic and aboriginal people is present in the friendship between Daphne and Surefoot, an Aboriginal woman involved in the Oka resistance. Surefoot's name suggests the sure presence and belonging that eludes Daphne, while also parodying the claim of the *White Paper* that "The weight of history affects us all, but it presses most heavily on the Indian people." Furthermore, the narrative links Daphne's questions about her own heritage to the truth of her identity as signified by her body and skin. Daphne continually attempts to decipher her body in the hope that it signifies her true origins. Whereas the government of Canada "recognizes the diversity of Canadians as regards race, national or ethnic origin, colour and religion," Daphne herself cannot recognize her own racial, national, or ethnic origin as these positive elements of identity are unknown to her. The process of recognition fails when confronted with Daphne's skin, which she reads as an undecipherable hieroglyph of muddled origins.

Although Daphne searches for identity in her body, her search for origins is mediated by memory and language. Cho's argument that "one *becomes* diasporic through a complex process of memory and emergence" (21; italics in original) takes on a new meaning in *Out of My Skin* because Daphne herself has no memory or personal history of black diasporic life. While in Montreal, Daphne meets her biological aunt, Sheila Eyre. Sheila gives Daphne her grandfather Gerald's diary that he kept while in a mental institution for multiple nervous breakdowns and his belief that he was white.[2] Daphne pores over the diary to learn about her own biological heritage and the reason behind her adoption. As Daphne reads she notes the similarities between her own unknown origins, Gerald's ambiguous identity, and the manner in which both identities are damaged by an imputed blackness. Further, Gerald's diary details the gradual erosion of his memories and destruction of his selfhood as he undergoes electroshock treatment. This sense of lost origins and absent memories is compounded when Daphne discovers that knowledge of her biological family cannot offer the easy, comfortable identity that she desires. Her hope for a sure and stable identity rooted in family and biology is shattered when she learns that she is the product of an incestuous relationship between her grandfather and his daughter. This distressing revelation locates violation at the origins of identity because the incestuous relationship is itself the product of colonialism's violation of his dignity as a black man, coercing him to desire the gift of civilization.

Perhaps the central image of belonging and identity that Daphne contends with throughout the novel is that of the family, particularly in the sense that the family, as an organizing concept of identity, promises a single and secure heritage. While Daphne's immediate concern is with her own familial origins, the narrative links these individual concerns to national identity and belonging through its setting in Quebec, and its depiction of multicultural Canada and the Mohawk struggle at Oka. The narrative critiques the metaphor of nation-as-family, showing how it relies on an exclusive notion of heritage and justifies particular modes of exclusion from the nation. The metaphor of the family subtly evokes racial difference to link biological homogeneity with national heritage, constructing categories of citizenship around racial and phenotypic lines. For instance, the novel depicts the Francophone residents of Chateauguay protesting the Oka occupation: "In front of Quincaillerie Boucher a group of men wrenched open a fire hydrant, letting the water shoot across the road. Shop windows were shattered by teenagers who accompanied the rioters. A family affair" (146). The narrator links the stable identity and belonging of family to the exclusionary and violent actions of the rioters whose concept of familial and national homogeneity allegedly justifies their claim over the land.

Out of My Skin shows how the conception of the nation as family is a fantasy of unity constituted through acts of exclusion, and this is evident in the Canadian government's pre-multicultural document *Notes on the Canadian Family Tree* (1960). *Notes on the Canadian Family Tree* collates information on cultural, racial, and ethnic groups in Canada with the apparent aim of assimilating them into the fabric of the nation. The anonymously written Foreword highlights the tension between neutralizing and marking difference, because it claims to do no more than "provide factual information on many of the ethnic groups that comprise the Canadian population" (i). The text specifically excludes, however, "Anglo-Saxon and French groups" because "much material [on these groups] is available in other forms" (i). The effect of this exclusion is that their presence becomes normalized and they are ethnically unmarked and racially invisible. Further, their exclusion supports the discourse of otherness such that this group of "Canadians proper" constitutes the observing, gazing *we*, the ideal reader of the text who observes the ethnically, racially, and culturally marked remainder of the Canadian population. This strategy that marks white, British Canadians as invisible and ethnically neutral is a recent instance in a long history of managing Canadian diversity. Richard Day's (2000) analysis of *notes* and similar texts shows how Canadian concepts of managing diversity have retained the same basic features that can be traced back to Herodotus's first forays into cultural anthropology. He writes that techniques of marking, recording, and managing difference in Canada comply with "both the method of Herodotan ethnography and its obsession with the seven categories of cultural fact: place of residence and climate, language, dress, food, dwellings, religion, and political organization" (Day 128). These Herodotan categories structure *notes* and mark these groups as internal-others, at once part of the "Canadian family tree" but also as distinct from the unmarked, culturally neutral, white Anglo-Saxon and French Canadian readership. These groups are identified as particularly and excessively ethnic, through repeated acts of "comparison with a standard assumed to be shared with the reader, but not with the object of the text" (Day 129). Anglo and French white Canadians are seen as occupying the central trunk of the family tree, and each ethnic group's celebrated "Contributions to Canadian Society" are primarily examples of how that group has successfully assimilated itself to Anglo and French Canadian norms. Similarly, while the metaphor of the family tree replaces the hierarchy of previous ethnic and racial studies (so much so that ethnic groups are listed alphabetically), the study is not completely able to eradicate the language of race from its analysis. The chapter entitled "Negroes" attempts to account for all black Canadians despite their varied ethnic, cultural, and national origins. Black Canadians prove to be an exception to the rule that otherwise replaces race with ethnicity and culture; their blackness becomes the dominant (if not only) marker of their identity, trumping any national, religious, or cultural identifications.

The image of the family tree naturalizes nation and heritage, concealing the historical genesis of both. As Anne McClintock argues, "Historical progress is naturalized as an evolving family, while women as historical actors are disavowed and relegated to the realm of nature. History is thus figured as *familial*, while the family as an institution is seen as beyond history" (*Imperial Leather* 39; italics in original). McClintock goes on to argue that "The family trope is important for nationalism in at least two ways. First, it offers a 'natural' figure for sanctioning national *hierarchy* within a putative organic *unity* of interests. Second, it offers a 'natural' trope for figuring national time … The family offered an indispensable metaphoric figure by which national difference could be shaped into a single historic genesis narrative"

(*Dangerous Liaisons* 91; italics in original). The metaphor of the family thus naturalizes a national "genesis narrative," privileging certain national constituencies as central to the nation and marking other groups and histories as peripheral.[3] *Notes on the Canadian Family Tree*, for instance, makes no mention of Aboriginal people in Canada. Thus, in both *Notes* and *Book IV* of the Royal Commission on Bilingualism and Biculturalism, Aboriginal people are erased from this familial narrative of the nation. Kymlicka (drawing on the work of Shulamith Firestone and Susan Moller Okin) has also described how the family is constructed as a microcosm of the political order in liberal discourse. He argues that while mainstream liberal thinkers "have officially proclaimed that their theories are based on the natural equality of individuals, they have in fact taken the male-headed family as the essential unit of political analysis; women's interests are defined by, and submerged in, the family, which is taken to be their 'natural' position" (*Liberalism* 92). Both Kymlicka and McClintock demonstrate how the metaphor of the nation-as-family naturalizes gendered conceptions of citizenship, thus foreclosing women's access to the political and public spheres.

The metaphor of the nation-as-family employed in *Notes on the Canadian Family Tree* is a particular mode of recognition whereby a dominant, culturally unmarked segment of society attempts to manage cultural difference, naturalize and dehistoricize the nation, and fix divisions of power in Canada. While the metaphor purports to *describe* the nation, it is in fact an act of recognition which constitutes that which it claims to describe. The metaphor of the nation as family is, in Foucault's terms, an expression of "power-knowledge relations" (*Discipline* 27) insofar as the inscription of knowledge of Canada's increasingly ethnic composition is simultaneously an operation of power in describing, cataloguing, positioning, and managing that ethnicity as external to Canadian heritage. Therefore the critique of both the family and the nation resists the desired homogeneity and repression of difference that both models of community promote. Against the metaphor of the nation-as-family that imagines a particular notion of Canada, *Out of My Skin* rewrites the nation as a dispersed space that is continually rewritten by its diasporic inhabitants, thus locating diasporic double-consciousness within the nation.

Out of My Skin repeatedly returns to the fantasies of heritage and origins implicit in the metaphor of the nation-as-family. In one of the most significant passages in the novel, the narrator describes how

> Daphne moved around to the side window facing the narrow driveway and peered into the bedroom … She pressed her face against the glass to see the source of the light she had seen from the street … On the left wall hung a different kind of photograph, a portrait of a big family. It was the kind of family which was full, bursting over, generation into generation of the same faces. Sisters … so many. Their faces varied, but each had something that connected it to the others: a line of the chin or a fold over the eye. Daphne lifted her forehead from the pane and moved down the alley toward the next window. "*Est-ce que je peux vous aider?*" She leapt, bruising her shoulders as she flattened her back against the wall. (75; italics and ellipses in original)

Daphne is overwhelmed by the image of the "family which was full, bursting over, generation into generation of the same faces," thus rendering material this fantasy of familial homogeneity. She finds the scene both fascinating and disturbing, as if the family "bursting over" is in danger of effacing and absorbing her otherness into its overflowing homogeneity. The phrase "bursting over" foreshadows the passage describing the Chateauguay riots while inverting the "flood of immigrants" trope to describe the family portrait as a flood of genetic and filial homogeneity. The ellipsis in "Sisters … so many" suggests abundance rather than lack, underscoring Daphne's position outside the home looking in on a family that both compels and repulses her. Finally, the interruption of her gazing by a question posed to her in French disrupts the homogeneity of the Canadian family by recalling the presence of Quebec.[4] This question, asked by Daphne's friend Michel, is the first French spoken in the novel and suggests the manner in which English-Canadian fantasies of national unity repress Francophone presences, further indicating the necessary exclusions at work in the family-nation metaphor.

In Gerald's diaries the family tree is transposed onto the colonial relation. He writes, "*The gift of civilization is like the gift of life, and a man does not turn his back on his father after he has learned to copulate*" (107). He continues, "*Today they're all talking about politics and independence – fools. I can't bear to listen…the son who rejects the authority of his father will blister and swell in the sun like a rotting carcass; that will be this country without Britain*" (126; italics in original). Gerald imagines the colonial order as a family romance and his position (perhaps an act of colonial mimicry) as the perfectly subjugated colonized subject leads him to imagine Guyana as the upstart son who rejects paternal authority. The colonial relation is seen in light of Oedipal strife; thus, his incestuous act can be interpreted as an expression of the sexual dynamics of colonialism. The novel suggests that there is an implicit violence and erasure of difference in both the structures of the family and the history of the nation that this metaphor attempts to obscure.

The Government of Canada's repeated statement in the *Canadian Multiculturalism Act* to "recognize the existence of communities whose members share a common origin" takes on new meaning when located within the metaphor of the family. Indeed, this metaphor constitutes an act of recognition that "recognize[s] and promote[s]" racial difference within a manageable structure. Charles Taylor has famously argued that these acts of recognition are an important mode of political address in liberal democracy. Yet Taylor's argument does not consider the forms of identity that are excluded or marginalized within these acts of recognition, particularly when recognition depends on the logic of race. *Out Of My Skin* reveals how recognition relies on the metonymic function of skin as the signifier of racial authenticity. Gerald's abjection is absolute, but Daphne's hyphenation is no less pernicious for being bound up with the discourse of tolerance which must recognize otherness in order to suffer its existence.

Charles Taylor's "The Politics of Recognition" is an attempt to address the democratic racism and structures of white invisibility that Henry and Tator identify in liberal discourse by insisting that multicultural societies must recognize the diverse identities of their citizens. Taylor's argument addresses the question through a consideration of "the supposed links between recognition and identity, where identity designates something like an understanding of who we are, of our fundamental defining characteristics as human beings" (225). Taylor's use of qualifiers indicates his own scepticism towards the connection between recognition and identity, and what he sees as the philosophical blurriness of identity politics. Yet Taylor is cognizant of the link between misrecognition and political exclusion, writing that "our identity is partly shaped by the recognition of its absence, often by the *mis*recognition of others, and so a person or group of people can suffer real damage, real distortion, if the people or society around them mirror back a confining or demeaning or contemptible picture of themselves" (225). Taylor's telling phrase "the recognition of [identity's] absence" evokes the absented identities of Brand's and Clarke's characters, and Daphne's expression of her identity as nothing. Indeed, Taylor cites Fanon as one of the first to articulate the danger of misrecognition and understand a "major weapon of the colonizers was the imposition of their image of the colonized on the subjugated people" (251). Taylor argues that in order to avoid this act of misrecognition and to ensure the equal political participation of all members of a society, liberal societies must practise "The Politics of Recognition," by which he means a mode of political address in which society recognizes subjects as worthy of political consideration and agency despite diverse backgrounds, ethnicities, and cultures, and despite conflicting conceptions of how society ought to be organized. Taylor is also aware that the criteria of these acts of recognition can be biased towards reflecting the ideological and political perspective of the dominant group that is engaged in the act of recognition. As such he advocates, with Hans-Georg Gadamer, for a "fusion of horizons" (252) between recognizer and recognized, such that the framework of recognition is composed by both parties and not simply by the recognizer.

Taylor argues that identity politics emerge from both "the collapse of social hierarchies, which used to be the basis for honor," and "the development of the modern notion of identity, [which] has given rise to a politics of difference" (233). He writes that "against this notion of honor, we have the modern notion of dignity" and where honour was bestowed only on the (allegedly) honourable, now "we talk of the inherent 'dignity of the human being' ... The underlying premise here is that everyone shares in it" (226). It is as a result of this replacement of honour with dignity that "the forms of equal recognition" are rendered "essential to democratic culture" (227). Taylor links dignity to individual identity by arguing that the modern notion of a subject's dignity requires the subject exist in a manner that is *true for them*, that they articulate and live according to their own authentic identity; a condition he describes as "the ideal of authenticity" (229). He argues, borrowing from Johann Herder, that for contemporary conceptions of identity, "There is a certain way of being human that is *my* way. I am called upon to live my life in this way, and not in imitation of anyone else's life. But this notion gives a new importance to being true to myself. If I am not, I miss the point of my life; I miss what being human is for *me*" (228; italics in original). The dignity at the heart of recognition depends on the subject living their life in their own particular authentic way. This element of recognition relies on a notion of the authentic subject, the subject that is true to themselves. There is a tension, however, between this authentic self and what Taylor sees as the fundamentally dialogical quality of identity. He writes, "We define our identity always in dialogue with, sometimes in struggle against, the things our significant others want to see in us" (230). He goes on to state, in stronger terms, that "This crucial feature of human life is its fundamentally *dialogical* character" (230; italics in original). It is unclear how Taylor reconciles this idea of "being human that is *my* way" with the "fundamentally *dialogical* character" of human identity: if human identity is fundamentally dialogical, then there is no identity or way of living that is unequivocally "*my way*" or unshaped by dialogical process. This problem is further compounded when the perspective of the recognizing other imposes an egregious misrecognition of the self. *Out of My Skin* exploits this tension between the authentic and the dialogical in its critique of recognition, particularly the manner in which the politics of recognition tends to fix and polarize identity and difference.

One major critique of Taylor's politics of recognition is his inadequate attention to the manner in which race structures the act of recognition (Appiah 1994). The challenges posed to liberalism's discourse of equality by the language and politics of race are only an implicit consideration in his argument that "misrecognition shows not just a lack of due respect. It can inflict a grievous wound, saddling its victims with a crippling self-hatred" (226). Indeed, Taylor's narrative of the emergence of the modern subject depicts it as emerging strictly from a European context and not at all dialogically. Furthermore, he inadequately considers the manner in which discourses of otherness and racial exclusion are produced within liberal discourses of tolerance and equality to shape the contours of recognition. David Theo Goldberg observes that not only is "*Race* one of the central conceptual inventions of modernity," but "The more explicit universal modernity's commitments, the more open it is to and the more determined it is by the likes of racial specificity and racist exclusivity ... The way in which racial characterizations are articulated in and through, and so come in part to define liberalism, will thus serve to locate the paradox at the center of the modern project" (4; italics in original). Taylor's inattention to race is exposed by Goldberg's insistence on the relationship between liberalism's claim to universality alongside continued racial exclusion. Furthermore, Taylor's argument does not attend to the uneven distribution of civility and dignity, particularly the manner in which black subjects have been and continue to be denied basic dignity through acts of misrecognition. Even if there is an inherent "dignity of the human being," critics such as

Sylvia Wynter, Paul Gilroy, and Cecil Foster have demonstrated the manner in which blackness has signified the borders or outright exclusion from that category of the civil. The analysis of the Albert Johnson case offers a recent Canadian example of how the misrecognition of black people results in the denial of their dignity as human beings. Johnson's depiction in the media reveals the forms of "authentic" blackness that these acts of recognition can discover or project when confronted with a black subject.

In *Blackness and Modernity* (2007), Cecil Foster describes the misrecognition of blackness in Taylor's terms:

> For a specific group of humans, however, the black colour of their skin is rationally and objectively associated … with the undesirable and inferior … skin colour is recognized as a visible approximation of inner qualities and virtues, or it is coupled with specific stereotypes and virtues that are uniformly common and basic to all members of this specific and inferior group … and is used as a means or rationale for exclusion. (10)

Black skin is treated as a "visible approximation of inner qualities and virtues," which Taylor describes as the "inner being or essence" of the subject. Foster also indicates the manner in which the category of "black" in liberal societies is constructed according to "what is projected onto the black body discursively or what is read into the body, rather that [*sic*] what meaning the body or consciousness offers up on its own" (xxi). In his analysis of the meaning of blackness in Canada, Foster argues that it is primarily an effect of the "appearance or the somatic [qualities of the subject], based racially and genetically on the colour of the epidermal skin layer that is perceived to be encoded with values that signify good or evil. This has become the predominant way for discerning who is black in modern society" (94). Foster's argument that blackness is linked to the "appearance or the somatic" qualities of the subject recasts Taylor's recognition, revealing how blackness often depends on a particular reading of skin. The act of recognition treats black skin as signifying an authentic, immutable kernel of blackness. This is precisely the mode of recognition that Gerald in *Out of My Skin* is subjected to when his belief that he is white is not shared by his society. Taylor's inattention to race leads to his overestimating the capacity of recognition to afford a space of agency and self-definition to black subjects. In making the skin the irrefutable proof of blackness, the discourse of recognition consigns multiple, diverse subjects to the category of "essential, and unchangeable" blackness, what Fanon describes as being "Sealed into that crushing objecthood."

Richard Day offers another critique, arguing that "the recognition that Taylor speaks of is not equal, reciprocal, and freely given, but a partial and grudgingly bestowed *gift* from a canonical Self group to a series of problematic Others" (217; italics in original). Day argues that the positions of recognizer and recognized (which he links to the Hegelian positions of Master and Slave) remain undisturbed in Taylor's conception of recognition, and that it is the dominant and unmarked "Self" who is in the position to recognize the "problematic Others." Day's language of recognition as a gift recalls Gerald's description of the colonial order as akin to a "*gift of civilization*" and "*the gift of life*" (107; italics in original), and perhaps these are the gifts bestowed by the racialized gaze. Day also challenges Taylor's reliance on authentic identity, arguing that "recognition for Taylor ultimately depends upon correct outward perception of a pre-existing inner being or essence. It is, in this sense, in keeping with modern essentialist theories of identity" (35). Taylor's recognition reads the "certain way of being human that is *my* way" by validating, recognizing, and solidifying the "inner being or essence" of a group or individual identity. When confronted with a racialized subject, this "inner being or essence" depends on skin as a metonymic signifier of authentic identity. Indeed, Foster argues that authentic, black identity relies on "Seeing ... [as the] privileged ... act of knowing; ... what was seen was considered to be the real or ... genuine, the essential, and unchangeable" (132). Foster's claim develops Day's critique that recognition relies on the "correct outward perception of a pre-existing inner being or essence" to reveal how black skin comes to signify an internal core of racial identity.

Out of My Skin stages the act of recognition in order to show how the emphasis on identity as authenticity produces immobilizing and confining racial identities. Daphne's repeated failure to identify her own "inner being or essence" reveals the limitations of such conceptions of identity and indeed the very title of the novel reveals this thematic concern of separating identity from skin. Taylor's argument that there is, for all subjects, a "certain way of being human that is *my way*" recalls a schoolteacher's exasperated insistence to Daphne that "people are certain things, like Japanese, Chinese ... things like that" (16). Both Taylor and the teacher insist that "people are certain things" and that there is a "certain way of being human that is *my way*." After reading the word "Negro" in a story, the teacher asks, "Well, does anyone know what a Negro is" to which Daphne's classmate responds "Yeah, Daphne ... 'Oh no, no, not Daphne,' the teacher corrected. 'No that's different. Quite different.' ... The teacher paused before addressing her, 'What are you, anyway, Daphne?'" (16). It is the mention of blackness – particularly the uncomfortable politeness of the word "Negro" – which leads to this act of recognition, revealing how the racialized body is read as a metonym for a particular racial identity. The exasperated "anyway" in the teacher's question expresses the frustration of the liberal confronted with an unrecognizable subject. Further, the teacher's repetition of "no, no, not Daphne... No that's different" indicates at once the devaluing of blackness in the structure of recognition and also the uncertainty and anxiety that the teacher feels in Daphne's apparently negative-identity, and her inability to place Daphne's "Quite different" appearance. Daphne's response to the teacher's inquiry expresses the confusion and anxiety raised by such a probing interrogation: "Daphne sat mute, her cheek beginning to quiver, her eyes to water. She'd never before considered the question ... *They are? What things*? Daphne folded her arms on the desk and cradled her head in them" (16; italics in original). Daphne possesses no authentic identity to recognize or wield in response to the teacher's question. As such, the discourses of otherness and tolerance operate in tandem to silence her.

These acts of recognition fail because they rely on an internally consistent identity that the recognizer aims to discover in order to locate the subject within one of the discrete categories of identity employed by *Notes on the Canadian Family Tree* and by the Royal Commission on Bilingualism and Biculturalism. In another section of the novel Sheila asks Daphne what she tells people when they ask where she is from. Daphne responds, "Nothing" (81), which invokes her absented origins while also discrediting the "fundamentally dialogic" quality of recognition. Throughout *Out of My Skin* there are multiple failed attempts to recognize the inner essence or kernel of Daphne's identity, and indeed the bulk of the narrative is concerned with her resistance to these attempts to discover what "certain things" Daphne could be. Daphne's struggle to assert her identity at once contends with the logic of recognition, the absented heritage of her birth, her adoption, and Gerald's madness. This forces one to question the meaning of heritage for Daphne who knew "Nothing" about her heritage or identity for most of her life, as well as the true recognizable identity of black diasporic people whose heritage is described by Brand as one of collective loss, forgotten pasts, and absented histories.

Out of My Skin's critique of authentic identity is represented in the repeated undermining of demarcations of inside and outside. The text's depictions of inside and outside connote the abjection of black people from the nation, and also suggest the manner in which Taylor's recognition relies on the outside to bespeak the inside. Indeed the stable identities of individual and nation require a policing of the borders between inside and outside: an accurate reflection of the inner kernel on the outer surface. Judith Butler deconstructs the positions of inside and outside, insisting that both "remain linguistic terms that facilitate and articulate a set of fantasies, fears and desires. 'Inner' and 'outer' make sense only with reference to a mediating boundary that strives for stability" (*Gender Trouble* 182). This concern with the inside, outside and "mediating boundary" of subjectivity, identity, and community pervades *Out of My Skin* both in the explicit references to these spatial configurations, and in the representations of the body which undermine this stark demarcation. As the novel begins, Daphne is hiding in the bushes of a garden, secretly gazing into a house, and the narrator explains that "Up close it was all disappointing" (1). This opening sentence indicates the importance of visuality to the novel, and to structuring the division between inside and outside as Daphne's gaze cannot access the inside of the authentic familial scene. As she looks through the window of the home she tries to reach into the room but is "surprised when her hand hit the glass ... she remembered she was on the outside" (2). This division between inside and outside is reinforced in the surfaces, glass windows, mirrors, and pools of water that litter the narrative, all of which are dependent for their meaning on the fragmented and elusive point of view. The novel routinely undermines these divisions, either breaking down the relationship between the two or thematizing them in such a way as to demonstrate the constructedness of border between them. This exploration and critique of the categories of inside and outside are one of the central ways that the novel critiques the concepts of national and familial belonging, of being on the inside of the community, and of having a true identity lodged inside the subject.

Taylor's conception of recognition relies on a visual composition of the body that reads the outside of skin as signifying an inside of authentic identity. The relationship between visuality and authentic identity pervades liberal theories of the subject and citizen, and visual

8 CONTRAST May 30, 1980

Seen the
typical Canadian
lately?

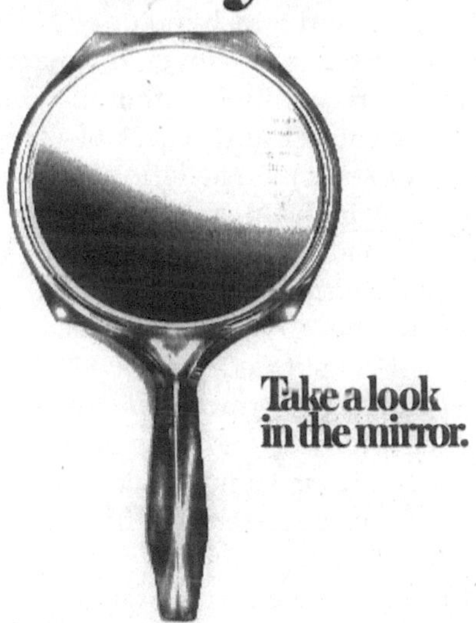

Take a look
in the mirror.

Multiculturalism/The Canadian Experience.

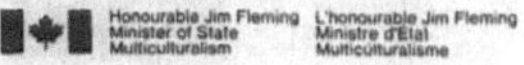

Canada

"Seen the Typical Canadian Lately," Advertisement by the Canadian Ministry of Multiculturalism appearing in *Contrast*, May 1980.

representations of diversity are regularly employed to bolster discourses of equality in liberal societies. This is rendered explicit in the advertisement from the Canadian Ministry of Multiculturalism which appeared in the May 1980 edition of *Contrast*. The advertisement engages in an act of recognition by sustaining the visual register in which it operates. The looking glass that the Canadian is invited to peer into suggests that all Canadians, regardless of ethnic, cultural, or racial distinction, are "the typical Canadian." The advertisement reaffirms the link between phenotypic difference, state recognition, and the field of visuality, suggesting that "the typical Canadian" does not necessarily look like anything in particular but rather is both diverse and innumerable. In one sense the message of the advertisement is that past conceptions of what it means to be a typical Canadian are being replaced by this new act of recognition which includes cultural, ethnic, and racial difference. In another sense, however, the metaphorical use of the mirror situates this act of recognition within the field of visuality such that the positions of the subject and object of recognition remain undisturbed. The voice of state interpellation which hails the multicultural subject to "Take a look in the mirror" at once welcomes that subject into the new inclusive Canadian identity, but does so by recognizing, "enhancing" (*Canadian Multiculturalism Act* 3.1[d]), and crystallizing that subject's difference. This advertisement recalls Foucault's dual notion of the subject as self-constituted yet constituted through subjection to power and regulation. Furthermore, the visual metaphor of the mirror sustains the borders of inside and outside, suggesting that the outside appearance of skin reflects some stable inside identity of the subject. This metaphor does not indicate the "fusion of horizons" Taylor calls for, but rather interpellates subjects so that their difference is constructed as an unchangeable kernel of their identity, and is signified by their physical and epidermal appearance. These tropes of visuality that pervade Canadian multicultural interpellations of ethnic subjects affirm Taylor's concept of recognition while constructing racial, ethnic, and cultural difference as authentic, crystallized, and permanent.

The spatial and visual renderings of inside and outside find thematic parallels in the intertextual moments of *Out of My Skin*, particularly in Daphne's multiple acts of reading. When Daphne learns that her biological family name is Eyre she begins reading *Jane Eyre*. There are a number of links between Jane and Daphne, both of whom are orphans searching for their true identity, and both of whom engage in acts of forgiveness at the conclusion of their narratives. Yet Daphne is never able to fully integrate her own narrative with that of *Jane Eyre*, and her reading of the novel is repeatedly interrupted by outside forces. For instance, when she opens the novel, she finds, "*It's a very strange sensation to inexperienced youth to feel itself quite alone in the world: cut adrift from every connection, uncertain whether the port to which it is bound can be reached … Well, looka who dat is here … yu tink she mind if we read about she?* The bouncy accent of her mother invaded again. Daphne looked around, expecting a presence over her shoulder" (33–4; italics in original). The first-person narrative voice of *Jane Eyre* originates from within Jane's own consciousness and this structural interiority parallels her desire to protect the hallowed interiority of her identity. The intrusion of Daphne's mother's voice into Jane's thoughts and Daphne's reading disrupts these discrete positions of interiority and exteriority, suggesting that this interiority is not possible in *Out of My Skin*. Where *Jane Eyre*'s first-person narrative stresses a one-to-one relationship between Jane's interiority and the text's representation of her experience, *Out of My Skin*'s third-person omniscient narrative voice is at once inside and outside of Daphne's subjectivity. *Jane Eyre* employs a synchronous narrative temporality that mirrors the development of Jane's identity; on the contrary, analepsis and intertextuality contribute to a far less synchronous narrative and to a denaturalized emergence of Daphne's identity in *Out of My Skin*. Jane imagines herself "*cut adrift from every connection*," further stressing the interiority of her narrative. Daphne, however, cannot escape the connections of her past, as her thoughts are repeatedly interrupted by her mother's voice, suggesting that even the interior space of her identity is permeated by other presences.

The difference between Daphne's life and *Jane Eyre* is also evident in Daphne's refusal to borrow a copy of *Jane Eyre* out of the library, instead always reading the novel within the library walls. Daphne enjoys the "cold air that blasted through the library with a vengeance, battling the humidity [outside] that threatened to curl pages" (34). This contrast between the cool and quiet library and the humid summer weather outside marks the difference between the neat, ordered world of text and the complicated lives of Daphne, Surefoot, and the other residents of Montreal. Daphne's retreat into the world of the library can only offer temporary relief from the humid, political, and antagonistic world outside her reading experience. The difference between the ordered, air-conditioned space of the library and the humid and noisy outside parallel the differences between the ordered world of authentic selves and the disordered identities of the novel. The mode of narrative interiority constructed in *Jane Eyre* parallels a true (in Taylor's sense) interiority of the subject, and *Out of My Skin*'s abandonment of that interiority indicates the manner in which subjects in the novel do not possess such a secure sense of belonging and identity.

If *Jane Eyre* is associated with the ordered space of the library, Gerald's diary is linked with the humid and messy spaces of Montreal. The diary supplements *Jane Eyre* in both content and form as it provides a detailed account of the madness of racism and a far more troubled narrative of a lack of identity. Taylor's description of the "grevious wound" of "misrecognition" (226) is palpable in Gerald's diaries because he feels that his society has misrecognized him as black. Gerald shares a number of similarities with Bertha Mason, and his diaries give voice to the madness of race and colonialism which structure both of their identities. The categories of inside and outside that mediate *Jane Eyre* dissolve in Gerald's diaries to the extent that the alleged inner core of his identity is destroyed first by racism and then by electroshock treatment. The form of *Jane Eyre* posits narration as integral to the assertion of one's true identity, while the form of the diaries is often cryptic, temporally disjointed, and sometimes completely incoherent, thus reflecting the madness of the racialized identity into which Gerald has been forced. Unlike the temporal continuity that distinguishes Jane's Bildungsroman, Gerald's diaries often skip days, and he repeatedly feels as though he is losing his sense of time. Further, as his identity is dissolved by the electroshock treatment, the form of his writing parallels the dissolution of his subjectivity. In a later entry, Gerald depicts his interaction with a nurse in the hospital:

> *October 16, 1959*
> SHE SAYS: *"Here now, Gerald, why so sad today?"*
> HE SAYS: *nothing*
> SHE SAYS: *"We'll have to get the doctor to come to talk to you; perhaps he can cheer you up a bit."*
> HE SAYS: *nothing*
> SHE SAYS: *"Now look here, why don't you come for a walk with me down to the common room and you can have a bit of tea with the others."*
> HE SAYS: *nothing* (105; italics in original)

This passage depicts the slow erasure of Gerald's subjectivity in his refusal to identify himself by a name or to speak to the nurse. Both

Daphne and Gerald respond with "nothing" to these acts of recognition, suggesting that Daphne's encounter with structures of recognition is akin to Gerald's encounter with the madness of race. In Taylor's terms, Gerald is recognized by his society as one-dimensionally black and Gerald's silence marks his resistance to this recognition. Gerald's diaries trace the gradual dissolution of his identity while Jane's is stable, discrete, and knowable. The narrative form of *Out of My Skin* is caught between the two narrative modes, at once unable to follow the textual model of *Jane Eyre* and unwilling to completely surrender identity to dissolution.

Despite being a record of her father's descent into madness, Gerald's diaries also provide Daphne with an unexpected language for conceiving of identity beyond the logic of authenticity. In reading about the erasure of Gerald's identity, Daphne paradoxically discovers a meaningful language for writing her own presence beyond the immobilizing logic of internally consistent identity signified by skin. Certainly the form of *Out of My Skin* mirrors this breaking down of inside versus outside, as Daphne feels that the reality of Gerald's diary leaks into her reality in Montreal and she begins to experience the same sensations and feelings that Gerald describes. Furthermore, while the diary is initially separate from the main plot, the climax occurs when the Oka resistance reaches its conclusion and Daphne learns the truth behind her incestuous birth. At this point, the divisions between the main narrative and Gerald's narrative break down, and passages from the diary are interspersed with passages in Montreal. Thus the narrative's dissolving of spatial, intertextual, and formal representations of "inside" indicate the text's broader concern to deconstruct the inside of identity.

As Daphne reads *Jane Eyre*, she thinks "The words were like keys that gradually unshackled Jane from her predicament in a century uneasy with freedom" (33). Jane's words might operate like keys that unlock her identity and her freedom, but for Daphne and Gerald, words carry no such power, failing to unshackle them from the madness of race or the absence of identity. This metaphor of the liberating power of language is inappropriate to Daphne and Gerald for whom the only recourse to resist racism is often to say "Nothing." The model of language employed in *Out of My Skin* is, instead, found in the first passage of Gerald's diary that Daphne reads: "*Telephones, like gossamers, connect me to dead voices*" (84; italics in original). After reading this entry, Daphne thinks "Words were conspiring again … *like fat hides bone* … She tried to concentrate on the images, but they dissolved into the fine strands of the word *gossamers*, which kept surfacing in her mind" (84; italics in original). Gerald's words work like gossamers, "conspiring" to connect Daphne to the dead voice of her Mother, grandfather, and her absented history in the black diaspora. Daphne's Aunt Sheila Eyre tells her, as she gives Daphne her grandfather's diaries, to remember that "Some words hide truth just like fat hides bone" (82). Daphne's linking of the two statements from Gerald and Sheila indicates the connection between language, skin, and heritage that pervades the novel. Furthermore, the image of gossamers – cobweb-like strands that make imperceptible connections between things – provide a metaphor for the manner in which narrative and language connect Daphne to her history, and for the networks of difference that structure Daphne's identity. Gossamers undermine the logic of inside and outside, instead suggesting dispersed networks connecting memory, narrative, history, and politics. Gossamers also offer an image of a more complicated notion of historical emergence than the idea of heritage promoted by the metaphor of the national family tree, replacing the logic of authenticity with a notion of identity in difference.

Throughout the narrative Daphne struggles with expressing her identity not as a single, discrete thing but as constituted in difference. As she stares at herself in a mirror, she thinks, "Her real mother had probably been part Chinese, part white, and part black. She touched her cheek and drifted in and out of the ingredient colours of her mother's skin: yellow, white, black. *Yellow, white, black* – it reminded her of the game with the variable winner: *scissors, stone, paper* … her mind sticking on *black*, on *paper*, and wondering how it ever won" (15; italics in original). Daphne's mother's unknown origins and the swirling mix "of the ingredient colours of her mother's skin" indicate the tenuous link between surface and core, skin, and identity. Her identity shifts between the multiple threads of "*Yellow, white, black*." Daphne's focus on "*black* … and wondering how it ever won" indicates her awareness that within this visual field of recognition and identity, black is the devalued term. Yet Daphne's imagining of race as a game also suggests that she can alter its rules to make black win. Furthermore, the link between "*black*" and "*paper*" reveals the textuality of race and the body that informs the novel's conception of identity. Rather than recognizing herself as authentically black, Daphne increasingly conceives of her identity and her body as transformable signifiers of identity constituted through difference. Her transformation of her body employs the link between skin and identity to resist the logic of recognition and instead treats blackness as malleable.

The novel's treatment of skin, colour, and physiognomy recodes the values that signify blackness as authentic essence. This is particularly evident in the visual representation of the black body. Daphne refuses the state injunction to "Take a look in the mirror," as she is aware of the manner in which visual representations of inside and outside enforce a notion of authentic identity that misrecognizes her. The narrator explains that Daphne "kept few mirrors in the house – a casual, early morning encounter with a likeness of herself was startling. Shiny appliances were to be avoided whenever possible; she had painted her kettle red, her toaster matte white. Everything in her apartment had been dulled and muted, safe from reflection" (4). The mirror does not represent Daphne authentically, but rather constructs her "likeness" within a "startling" regime of visuality. Her distrust of mirrors reveals both her anxieties about her appearance and her awareness of the false premise of authenticity that imagines a tangible link between appearance and identity. When Daphne eventually confronts her likeness in the mirror she is described as

> bracing herself momentarily at the door before confronting the mirror. The first thing that came into view was the nose: large, wide, and fleshy, nostrils asymmetrical, one an imperfect oval, the other circular. Her grape-coloured lips were full and perfectly pleated – almost beautiful … Her skin was brown, not a permanent, wealthy tan, but rather copper-coloured in the summer and sickly olive by February. She was small-boned but had a bouncing, high-rumped gait. A trace of Africa. (4–5)

The asymmetry of Daphne's nostrils suggests a parallel between her body and her own sense of her multiple origins. Also, the shifting tones of her "tan," "copper," and "brown" skin indicate that black is a misnomer. It is significant that the focalization of this passage shifts from Daphne to an unspecified, anonymous, third-party observer for whom "The first thing that came into view was the nose." Is it this gaze or Daphne's that identifies her body as lacking, "almost beautiful," and "not a permanent, wealthy tan?" Does the observation that Daphne's body signifies "A trace of Africa" originate from Daphne, the narrator, or is this the implied reading of her body from a third perspective? This shift in focalization indicates the manner in which the gaze always occupies the space of the Other.

The link between visuality and race continues throughout the text not only in the specific instances of recognition, but also in the recurring themes of visibility and invisibility. Daphne attempts to resist this visual framing through what she calls her "Invisible trick" whereby she imagines herself as invisible at work and in public spaces. While her coworkers Joanne and Daniel argue about the Oka resistance, Daphne tunes out the debate, with the narrator explaining that "It had happened again: the *click* – something hyper-aural – that always pulled Daphne out of events into a protected dreamspace ... She would swirl above the day's events as if in a dream" (40–1; italics in original). Frustrated at Daphne's behaviour, Joanne accuses her of walking "around the shop as if you're in some kind of daze half the time. Like you float through concrete or something. Think we can't see you? that you're invisible? Is that it? Some black guy said that to me once; I told him he was full of shit" (197). Joanne insists that Daphne can be seen, that her body is there and that she cannot disappear. Joanne's question, posed from the perspective of a white, Canadian, invisible "we," indicates the extent to which Joanne actually *cannot* see Daphne, as she has imagined her as different and outside the "we" that Joanne claims to speak for. Joanne's provocative question, "Think that we can't see you? that you're invisible?" is a real world invocation of the politics of recognition, demanding that the racialized subject appear as a consistent and known racial identity before the white gaze. Her recognition that it was a "black guy" who accused her of not seeing him confirms his accusation and makes explicit the racialized gaze of recognition. Joanne's incessant questioning and anxiety about Daphne's identity reveals the white anxiety that motivates these moments of recognition, securing the white hegemonic position by requiring that Daphne reflect a stable racial identity. McKittrick's unvisibility is palpable in these sections where Daphne's invisibility is a response to the manner in which she is rendered (un)visible by Joanne's gaze. Gerald refers to a similar type of invisibility in his diaries when he describes reading *"a new book by an invisible man"* (135; italics in original) which he later explicitly identifies as Ralph Ellison's *Invisible Man* (1952).

Against this logic of recognition, authenticity, and unvisibility, Daphne disrupts the visual reading of skin in order to transform and reframe the relationship between skin and identity. These transformations resist the logic of visuality as capable of revealing the authentic, inner identity of the subject and instead conceive of the body as text to be rewritten. For instance, while working at the printing press *Copie Copie* (a name which suggests the novel's deep suspicion of claims of cultural authenticity), Daphne photocopies parts of her body in order to distort the representation of her body and skin. The narrator explains that "She tried her hand first, reducing it to 75% of the original. Then she put her finger on the glass and enlarged it to 150%. Next she bent over and stared into the light as the flash copied her nose onto the paper that shot out of the machine ... She set the machine to 25% and again pressed her nose against the glass. It was this copy that she would pin up beside the bathroom mirror" (32). Daphne transforms the visual representation of her body, resizing and reframing the image such that her body signifies differently. This photocopying of her body is an act of anamorphosis, a visual transformation akin to metamorphosis that keeps the subject intact yet distorts its shape and form. Sylvia Söderlind describes anamorphosis as a form of visual representation marked by "a monstrous projection; or a representation of some image, either on a plane or curved surface, deformed and distorted; which at a certain distance shall appear regular and in proportion" (*Margin/Alias* 35). She argues that the "monstrosity alluded to in the definition points to its affinity with metamorphosis and the uncanny," and indeed Daphne's recreation of this image of herself, distorted by the zooming function of the photocopier, disrupts the visual logic of authentic interiority by creating an uncanny representation of her body. Daphne's act of anamorphosis undermines the link between a visual reading of the body and the recognition of an authentic identity. Indeed, photocopying the body has the effect of rendering racial characteristics unintelligible, as the photocopier renders black and white bodies through a racially-ambivalent spectrum of grey. This reproduction recreates a "likeness" of her body that transforms both the image of her body and the visual frame of recognition. Furthermore, placing this anamorphic representation of her body alongside the mirror juxtaposes the "monstrous projection" with the allegedly neutral image of the mirror such that the very frame of gazing is "deformed and distorted." Daphne's representation shows how the gaze of recognition is racially structured and these anamorphic distortions of her body present, in fact, a more accurate representation of her subjectivity. The anamorphic quality of Daphne's image is also evident in the photographs of Surefoot that Daphne stumbles upon in an adoption clinic: "Skin. Photographs of skin upon skin. Glossy, pocked-grey close-ups of an arm, a leg, a torso, all of which had been scarred from burning or tearing" (12). The glossy surfaces of the photographs and the skin itself reinforce the structures of inside and outside that recognition depends upon. Yet the close-ups of the burnt, torn, and scarred skin render these images a "monstrous projection" that undermines the connection between skin and identity. Indeed, the image of Surefoot's damaged skin suggests the presence of depth and something buried beneath the surface.

In place of this visual logic of recognition, the narrative repeatedly disrupts the metonymic link between skin and identity and conceives of identity and the body in spatial, rather than visual, terms. Like gossamers which contain multiple points of connection, the spatiality and depth of the body foregrounds the multiple connections, influences, fragments, and differences that comprise embodiedness. The visual emphasis on skin reifies heritage, while the spatial imagination of the body shows multiple points of connection, difference, and disjuncture within that heritage. This is evident in a passage of the novel where Daphne attends a protest in support of the Mohawk warriors at Oka and sees Surefoot on the other side of the police barricades:

> She saw the corpulence of Surefoot … Surefoot's round, jiggling face was tempered and sober, yet something undermined authority. Something cracked the certainty. Her body rooted and abundant, seemed at the same time ready to cleave. Something subterranean, existing in the infinite memory of the granite, in the cleft between vegetable and rock, seeped from her … Her whole elbow, Daphne noticed, was a scab … Far away in her thoughts, Surefoot raised her hand to the scab on the elbow. The injury was many days old and the crust that had formed over the wound was dry and dark brown. She began to pick away at the scab. A few small pieces flew off into the air. Then she … calmly, purposefully, tore off the dried blood and skin until the scab was gone; underneath the revealed pink flesh, blood welled up to pour again. Each fragment of old skin was tossed onto the pavement of the bridge. (148–9)

Daphne's observation of "the corpulence of Surefoot" along with Surefoot's tossing of "old skin … onto the pavement of the bridge" links Surefoot's body and identity with the land itself. Surefoot's picking at her scab suggests that while she yearns to shed her skin and the trauma of her childhood, her old wounds "welled up to pour again." Surefoot's repeated wounding recalls Taylor's "grevious wound" (226) of misrecognition, but also the wounding implicit in the act of recognition itself, particularly as skin is interpreted as a metonym for identity. Like Gerald, Surefoot wants to escape her skin and transform her identity;

however, her recognition and resistance of her misrecognition repeatedly reopens the wound of her identity and heritage. This continually swelling scab suggests that this wound is part of that belonging. The reference to "Something [that] cracked the certainty" recalls Daphne's own lack of identity as a kind of "falling between cracks," and is present in Daphne's observation that while Surefoot's body is "rooted and abundant" it also "seemed at the same time ready to cleave." Thus the depth of Surefoot's wounding and the cracks in her identity undermine any stable connection between recognition, skin, and identity.

This shift from the depiction of the skin as the surface of authentic identity to a conception of the body as containing depth, layers, and fissures indicates the multiple gaps, points of conflict, and fragments that make up Daphne's, Gerald's, and Surefoot's identities. Their heritage is one of absence, scarring, wounding, and loss, and the text's shift to spatial representations of the body tries to reveal this "subterranean" absence, the moment when identity seems "about to cleave." The spatial conception of the body offers a genealogy of identity, indicating the multiple connections, losses, and breaks that compose the subject in surprising and unexpected ways. Foucault, in "Nietzsche, Genealogy, History" (1977) uses the same metaphors of depth, archaeology, tectonics, and fissures that *Out of My Skin* does in order to articulate his concept of genealogy. Foucault's genealogical project "opposes itself to the search for 'origins'" and "rejects the metahistorical deployment of ideal significations and indefinite teleologies" (77). Genealogy shows that "What is found at the historical beginning of things is not the inviolable identity of their origin; it is the dissension of other things. It is disparity" (79). This genealogical disavowal of origins reads like a summation of the conclusion of *Out of My Skin*, particularly Daphne's abandoning of her desire for her own "inviolable identity," along with the text's turn towards archaeological metaphors. These all point to the text's project to show not an "inviolable identity" of blackness or nation, but rather the "dissension of other things" and the "subterranean" "cleav[ing]" and "disparity" between national and individual identity. Contrary to the discourse of recognition that reads the surface of the skin as an "ideal signification" of race, identity, and national belonging, these spatial and depth metaphors of the body instead indicate the genealogical emergence of the subject made up of multiple fragmentary sources. Indeed, *Out of My Skin* all but explicitly indicates its move towards a Foucauldian genealogical conception of identity and heritage when, in a conversation with Michel where he asks about her family, Daphne thinks, "Michel was direct, digging with an archaeological skill she was unable to sidestep" (89).

These spatial metaphors of the body increase as the novel progresses and are present in Gerald's diaries in which he writes about his childhood relationship with a boy named Manny. They play a game called "*High man and Low Man*" in which the Low Man masturbates the High Man and then they "*bathe in the pool and before drying off would roll our entire bodies in the red brown mud we dug from the side of the pool. The sun dried it into an armour of mud and we couldn't smile or scratch without it cracking and falling off*" (108). The "*armour of mud*" that Gerald and Manny cake onto their bodies signifies an outer skin and thematizes their desire to conceal and dance out of their skin and engage in a corporeal transformation. The physical immobility that they experience in their transformation recalls Clarke's and Fanon's articulation of the psychic immobilities of race. Further, conceiving of his body as layered and containing depth allows Gerald to imagine his skin as something he can shed in the hope that the civility beneath will be revealed. Later in his diaries, he writes that "*These nurses are making my bowels back up ... This morning my guts exploded into the toilet on their way to hell ... It's the last of the blackness, the last of the stifling servitude ... I am a white man*" (130). Gerald's multiple references to shedding skin, masking his skin, and evacuating his body of some inner blackness is a gesture of transformation that reveals his desire to be liberated from the madness of the racial-epidermal schema.

Daphne sees, in Gerald's diaries, both the tragedy of his succumbing to the Manichean logic of race and a sense of hope and possibility in his desire to dance out of his skin. Daphne attempts to honour his desire for transformation with her own act of transformation in the shower:

> Rubbing hard on her arms, legs, and face, she showered under a cold spray, trying to peel off a layer of something that had begun to grow on her. Real and imagined smells ... She reached back into his words, just barely able to imagine the regular throbbing and then, nothing ... the treatment and the slow and deliberate eradication of memory. The annihilation of personality. After a few minutes she felt drowned under the obliterating spray. She was tempted to stay there, to disappear inside the crack that had opened wider, but she forced her hand to the tap and turned it

> off, just barely able to catch her breath ... Lying on the rim of the tub was a cosmetic facial mask – a green gel, glutinous and cohesive – which she squeezed from its container onto her fingers and spread over her face. It started to dry immediately, pulling the skin of her nose tighter to her cheek, her chin tighter to her neck. It dried into a plastic mould ... staring into the mirror at the shining, impermeable face. Peeling off the mask, she felt the tingling of opened pores underneath, and the green sheath, this second skin, came off in one long unconnected layer – a reptilian moulting. (127–8)

Gerald's words physically affect Daphne as she imagines his narrative as "a layer of something that had begun to grow on her." They mark a connection between their lives such that the obliterating spray of the shower is akin to the obliteration of Gerald's memory and identity in the electroshock treatment. Daphne finds "the annihilation of personality" that Gerald experiences as a result of the electroshock therapy desirable because it connotes an erasure of memory and her troubled heritage. Yet in place of an annihilation of her past, Daphne instead repeats Gerald's gesture of transformation in her application of the facial mask. Daphne's recreation of shedding her mask is a "reptilian moulting," and Gerald alludes to this image of the lizard's transformation multiple times in his diary. Daphne, like Gerald, aims to transform her body through this moulting which makes her skin signify something other than a confining singular identity. Surefoot's scab, Gerald's armour of mud, and Daphne's facial mask are all forms of moulting that aim to transform the signification of skin and articulate identity beyond the logic of recognition and the madness of race. Unlike the stable correspondence between skin and authenticity that the politics of recognition promotes, Surefoot's, Daphne's, and Gerald's acts of "reptilian moulting" evince the genealogical qualities of identity and embrace metamorphosis as the principle of their existence.

Daphne repeats Gerald's action to dance out of her skin in an act of liberation. Gerald, however, sought to do so to discover the whiteness beneath, ironically imprisoning himself in the lure of skin. Towards the end of the novel, the narrator describes how Daphne returns to *Copie Copie* with one of Gerald's diaries and transforms the meaning of her skin, her identity, and her heritage by marking herself with the words therein.

> [Daphne] took the diaries out of her bag and looked through them, searching for the right page. Finally she found the word, just a single word in Gerald's scrawl. She adjusted the size button to 150% and placed the journal on the glass. The handwriting shot out enlarged. She cut the word out, placed it back on the glass, blew it up again. Finally, CHAMELEON shot out of the machine, almost the size of the thing itself. She took the scissors and cut around it in the shape of a lizard. Then with some clear tape she fastened it to her triceps. Patting it and smoothing it down, she was content with her new tattoo. (179)

The phrase that Daphne photocopies from the diary reads "*I, chameleon, now belong*" (111; italics in original). That she selects the word "CHAMELEON" from the sentence indicates that moulting rather than belonging animates the "I" that she is becoming rather than is. More importantly, Daphne's taping of the word to her triceps makes her skin signify transformation, rebirth, and moulting rather than racial authenticity, foreign heritage, or a stable identity. Her tattoo makes her body signify in a manner that undermines recognition and the disabling aspects of blackening, insisting that she be recognized by others as not one thing but as multiple, transforming identities. Daphne, Surefoot, and Gerald are "creatures that made sense only in the imagination" (148) and her tattoo signifies that act of imagination and re-invention, just as it undermines any organic unity or link between skin and identity. Furthermore, the tattoo is an appropriation of Gerald's words in the interests of preserving and honouring some element of her grandfather's struggle against racism. Her anamorphic transformation of Gerald's "scrawl" makes her heritage signify something other than loss, trauma, and absence.

At the end of the novel, Daphne attempts to affirm this new conception of her identity as one that has "to be invented" (149). Her final act of self-construction at the end of the text occurs when she travels out of the city and into northern Quebec. Outside the city, she retreats into the bush and has an epiphany concerning her self-constituted identity, her absent heritage, her desire to find a place in her biological family, and what she must to do to lay her history to rest. Reflecting on the lives of Surefoot, her mother, and Gerald, she declares,

> All of the others ... had disobeyed the inevitable, had tried to reverse the current of their circumstances. Her mother had walked into the water to cleanse shame and had never walked out, but perhaps there she'd found

> the mercy she'd needed. Even in jail, Surefoot would continue her conversation with the pine trees, and belonging would drip from her like blood from a pierced palm. Then there was Gerald … he had been alive enough to reinvent himself. She wanted to preserve this act of his, this triumph of the will in the pit of insanity, and it was then that she knew what to do with the diaries. A bow to memory. To let the snow and rain work on them until they became a place in which her own body could eventually be laid to rest. To have paper petrify and fill the cleft between vegetable and rock, the words silent and grinning in the earth. (202)

Daphne testifies to the manner in which her mother, Surefoot, and Gerald all struggle with history, a lack of identity, and the disabling logic of recognition and race. Daphne's mother surrendered to her shame by drowning herself, and Surefoot asserts her belonging out of her ongoing wounding. Yet Daphne aligns herself with Gerald whose desire to "reinvent himself" is read as his "triumph of the will in the pit of insanity" (202). As part of her desire to "preserve this act" she buries his diaries in the wilderness. The description of Gerald's diaries "silent and grinning in the earth," while evoking skeletal remains, also communicates that she is at peace with her destructive past. Also, Daphne's description of the paper that will "fill the cleft between vegetable and rock" is a return to the archaeological and spatial metaphors of the text; her "bow to memory" in burying the diaries fills the crack that pervades her identity and creates a "place in which her own body could … be laid to rest." The act of burial transforms both familial and national heritage, as she inserts Gerald's memories into the land while marking her desire to bury her history, engage in a "bow to memory," and plant a "seed of forgiveness" (203). She creatively converts the violence of her birth, the absences of her heritage, and her grandfather's tragedy into a "seed of forgiveness." This act of burial is not a repression or disavowal of her history, but an embrace of her history in all its ugliness.

Daphne's burial of the diaries places Gerald's history and the history of colonialism and the black diaspora within Canada, and thus insists that Daphne's absented heritage and the traumas of colonialism and slavery are part of Canada's multicultural heritage. She thus rewrites these categories of belonging, heritage, and recognition on her own terms. Sharon Morgan Beckford argues that black Canadian women writers "must of necessity come to terms with the language of the land" (479) in order to "*re*map the land in their own terms and reinscribe images of themselves into the Canadian geographical imagination in which they are often rendered invisible" (465). Daphne makes the language of the land come to terms with her – particularly the language of heritage and recognition – by insisting that Canada recognize her and Surefoot's history as part of this national heritage. It is through the process of rewriting the land that Daphne is able to transform her identity and heritage on her own terms. Placing the diaries deep within the land, in "the cleft between vegetable and rock," employs metaphors of depth to insist that Gerald's history has a place within Canada itself. Gerald's diaries are not buried and forgotten, but are layered, palimpsestically, into the land, becoming part of the tectonic core of the nation. Thus the primordial symbol of Canadianness is rendered chameleonic and textual. This is a profound transformation of the very referents of belonging that may be drawn upon to exclude Gerald's life and Daphne's heritage from Canadian multicultural heritage. In this sense the act of burial rewrites Canadian history as a palimpsest, making Gerald's diaries part of the genealogy of Canadian heritage. This is reflected in the cover of the novel which shows an image of Montreal as palimpsest where Gerald's writing is inscribed on the city alongside an image of a manta ray (Gerald repeatedly imagines himself as a manta ray, a "fish that should have been a bird" [192]). Daphne's burial of the diaries constitutes a remapping of land and nation from a black diasporic perspective by layering Gerald's narratives and memories into the history and "language of the land" (479). She insists that the language of recognition and heritage must go further and recognize Gerald, colonialism, slavery, and the Middle Passage as part of this Canadian heritage.

It is after this final act of burial that Daphne emerges from the wilderness and hitchhikes "home" to Montreal. The novel concludes with the narrator describing Michel having "caught sight of Daphne, who held his gaze for the first time. She walked toward him, the sentence forming easily, spontaneously, as she pursed her flush lips. In a small but firm voice she uttered two brittle words. 'I'm here.' Slender words, but sharp as a deep cut exposing bone" (208). Daphne's articulation of her presence indicates the manner in which she has, through her acts of reading, interpretation, and transformation, been able to articulate an identity of her own and create a place for herself in Canada. That she is able to hold Michel's gaze for the first time suggests that she has undermined the gaze of recognition. She no longer hides from the truth of her violated past or yearns for the world on the other side of the window pane. Instead, Daphne's reconciled self is both brittle and sharp, and finally, recognizable to *herself*.

In place of the surface readings of skin as a metonymic link between identity and corporeality, the narrative conceives of identity genealogically, and Daphne struggles to make her body signify in the manner of her choosing. Daphne's discovery that she is the incestuous offspring of her grandfather and his daughter undermines the "fantasy of unity" proposed by the nation-as-family metaphor. Furthermore, the text's depictions of the Oka resistance and the struggle of Francophone Canadians to find a place in the nation undermines the fantasies of familial and national unity through shared national heritage. Thus diasporic memories, in the form of Gerald's diaries, blacken the nation, rewriting the meaning of national heritage. The structures of recognition cannot account for characters like Daphne, Surefoot, and Gerald whose existence makes "sense only in the imagination" and whose claim on the nation unravels the neat categories that struggle to contain them. Yet the narrative transforms Daphne's alleged absence of identity into an expression of different forms of individual and national identities. *Out of My Skin* deploys the decentered and genealogical metaphor of gossamers to define identity in and through difference, transformation, and dissension.

Daphne's final statement of identity, "I'm here," marks a difference between the conclusion of *Out of My Skin* and the conclusion of the other texts in this study. It is impossible to imagine any of the characters from Brand's or Clarke's oeuvre making such an uncompromising statement of presence and identity in Canada. Brand describes Alan as a "slender lacuna" (II), and depicts the absented-presence of the Door of No Return as pervading black diasporic life. The figures in her poetry are never completely "here"; their "here" is always structured and inflected by other places and times. Similarly, Clarke depicts his characters "sliding," "shifting," and "uncontrollable," thus undermining their stable presence in Canada with the contradictory feeling of corporeal mobility and psychic immobility. The image at the beginning of *The Origin of Waves* of Tim and John emerging from the blizzard and recalling the events of their lives evokes Cho's conception of diasporic subjectivity as "a complex process of memory and emergence." The importance of memory is given further weight in Idora's and Brand's memories of Albert Johnson as they oppose the erasure of Johnson's presence from the Canadian historical record. Similarly, the actual killing of Johnson and the public discourse concerning his death show that this sense of abjection is not merely affective or imagined but real. Brand's and Clarke's texts and their narrating of Albert Johnson's history repeatedly depict black people abjected from the nation, and their double-consciousness emerges from this absented presence and unvisibility. The narration of memory in each of the texts is a critical site of their double-consciousness, as they transform their memories of loss and absence of origins into an expression of a different kind of presence in the nation. As such, Daphne's final statement "I'm here" marks a difference between this repeated abjection of black people from Canada, or a doubly-conscious presence of black people in the nation, and a hopeful gesture that black people can now announce themselves "here" within the nation. Indeed, Daphne's statement of presence reads like a response to Frye's (in)famous question, "Where is here" (220)? For Daphne, as Frye knew, enunciation is an effect of (dis)location.

Yet Daphne's doubleness remains, and her expression of identity is inflected by a sense of wounding as the narrator describes her statement composed of "Slender words, but sharp as a deep cut exposing bone" (208). Thus her statement retains the doubleness and vigilance of double-consciousness by coupling her presence in the nation alongside the "deep cut" and wounding that comes with her proclamation of identity. McWatt's critique of recognition insists that the wound of identity, the lost memories, and absented histories of diasporic life along with the buried and forgotten histories of the nation must be kept in view in this expression of palimpsestic presence within Canada. She keeps these losses in view with her turn to spatial and genealogical metaphors, by which the wounds of Daphne's identity are not buried but transformed into an integral part of her being. Furthermore, McWatt does not turn away from the language of double-consciousness; the conclusion of the novel shows that recognition must function doubly, recognizing diasporic subjects' presence and identity as it is defined through the doubleness of diasporic life, the pain of hyphenation and the wound of an identity composed out of absence, forgotten histories and inexpressible losses. The narrator's description of the "deep cut exposing bone" evokes this doubleness of recognition where Daphne's assertion of her identity and her place in the nation are inextricable from the wound of her origins. Skin gives way to the depth of the cut in a way that makes visible how Daphne remains "torn asunder," and her exhibition of the fragmentary and painful tearing reconceives of that tearing as part of her assertion of belonging. Like Johnson's "slender lacuna," Daphne's "Slender words" do not merely gesture towards absence, but evince the manner in which the very articulation of black diasporic presence in Canada is always-already inflected with absence.

Doubleness thus irradiates the poetics and prose of these texts at both the formal and thematic levels. As such, Daphne's final statement of identity does not signal a resolution of double-consciousness in Canada or a reconciling of blackness with nation such that the historical and contemporary abjections of black people in Canada are finally resolved. Instead, McWatt continues the project of blackening, transforming the abjection of black people into an inscription of the doubleness of black diasporic life in Canada. McWatt imagines this doubleness as the wound of identity, a dual exhibition of absented-presence, an expression of identity and belonging that is "torn by the ambivalence of mourning losses that are both your own and yet not quite your own" (Cho 21). Daphne is able to declare her presence, but like Gerald and Surefoot, her identity is not merely marked by – but emerges from – mourning, loss, and absence. While Daphne may be able to dance out of her skin, the wounding of race and the loss of her origins remain critical elements of her identity. *Out of My Skin* heals the wounds of misrecognition, but insists that the wounds that others in the national fabric bear and survive grant them dignity.

Chapter Five

Concluding

The multiple gossamer threads of McWatt's novel demonstrate how her text reinvigorates Canadian multiculturalism and the blackening of Canada by uniquely writing black diasporic life within the terms of Canadian multiculturalism. The varied connections of gossamers explode the bilingual framework that Daniel and others cling to, revealing the gaps and fissures in monolithic notions of Francophone and Anglophone identities, while also locating the voices of others – Surefoot, Gerald, and Daphne – within Montreal and Canada. *Out of My Skin* is concerned with the absences of diasporic history, the relationship between memory and history, Canada's buried colonial past, and the way in which that history and the primordial symbols of nationhood continue to structure contemporary notions of race, recognition, and belonging. Each of these narrative threads is linked to the representation of skin as it justifies the abjection of Gerald and Daphne from their respective societies. The threads of connection between Gerald's explicitly racist society and Daphne's subtly and invisibly racist society rewrite notions of Canadian heritage and identity to include colonialism, slavery, and the Middle Passage. The connecting threads between colonial Guyana and multicultural Montreal do not merely indicate similarities between the two spaces, but remap Montreal and Canada in order to bow to the memory not only of Gerald and his kin, but to the stigmata of Surefoot's pierced palm and bleeding belonging. Surefoot and Daphne's absented belongings and stolen origins offer an imaginative vocabulary that enables a rewriting of national heritage. Similarly, the hyphen of Daphne's identity is not transformed into an ampersand or imagined as a badge of exclusion, but rather brandished as a sign of the doubleness and "cut" of her history and identity.

McWatt's project, to superimpose the metaphors, images, histories, memories, and struggles of the black diaspora onto Canada and reimagine the nation as anamorphic, has been a constant theme of this study. Brand, Clarke, and McWatt reveal how the histories of slavery and the Middle Passage inflect notions of race and citizenship in Canada. The narration of memory is one of the critical ways in which these authors locate the absences and histories of the black diaspora within Canada. McWatt adds to this project with her depiction of history as genealogy and her insistence that diasporic memory and heritage must honour the acts of dispossession that create diasporic communities. Together, these authors comprise a chorus of voices that engage in a blackening of Canada by writing the continuities between the memories and histories of the black diaspora and contemporary Canada. The metaphor of gossamers, then, is appropriate to this project of blackening and to black diasporic writing in Canada more generally. Gossamers provide a spatial metaphor for the disparate sites and connections that pervade these texts, and for the crossing and hybridizing of forms that these authors practise. Furthermore, gossamers offer a metaphor for the multiple terms that each of these authors generates in their lexicon of diasporic life in Canada. The numerous geographies, routes, histories, identities, languages, idioms, desires, memories, and dreams of this field of writing all link together in surprising and often barely-detectable ways as part of a broader project of blackening Canada.

In *Out of My Skin,* Daphne pulls together the multiple threads of gossamers through her acts of memory, reading, and interpretation. The novel's assertion of black diasporic identity is mediated through Daphne's multiple acts of reading that bring together the narratives of *Jane Eyre,* Gerald's diaries, the public discourse concerning Oka, the Mohawk communiqués, political pamphlets, and the discourses of identity and nation. Similarly, Brand's and Clarke's narrations of blackening are concerned with transforming the memories and losses of the black diaspora into a different kind of assertion of identity that employs the double-consciousness of the diaspora as a means of blackening the nation. Brand's observation of the Door of No Return in quotidian life and Clarke's use of memory to undermine psychic immobility do not merely express the absent histories and lost origins that form the substrate of black diasporic life: their depiction of memory transforms that absence into a critique of origins and structures of belonging. The memory of loss enables a doubleness that undermines national and individual identities, revealing Bhabha's "minus in the origin" of national identity and Canadian multiculturalism. This project continues in their narrative recollection of Albert Johnson where the narration of memory stands in opposition to historical erasure, and transforms historical narratives of black silence, abjection, and death into a blackening of the nation. Johnson is not merely remembered; Brand's and Clarke's emplotment of their characters' (and their own) memories of Johnson rewrite his death and make it signify something other than absence, loss, and trauma. Idora's preservation of the newspaper article concerning Johnson's death is an act of historical work that she creatively reshapes through her memory. Idora mis-remembers the details of Johnson's life and death in a manner that renders them relevant to her own life and transforms his individual trauma into a surprising narrative of collective black life in Canada. Similarly, Brand recasts his death through the memories of her speaker, Chloe, and Julia. These narrative acts of remembering dispute the erasure of black histories, smearing the nation rather than blackness.

Out of My Skin further complicates the importance of the narration of memory to the project of blackening Canada. Daphne has no memory of her biological familial origins or heritage, and this heritage of absence leads to her pervasive feeling that she is "Nothing." Daphne repeatedly returns to her childhood recollections to understand her feeling of nothingness but finds no comfort in memories of a life that do not seem to fit her. Gerald's diaries seem to offer Daphne the refuge of origins, but reading it brings her no closer to the truth. Rather, she finds that the truth of her origins and the violence of her heritage are more immobilizing and debilitating than the absence of those origins. Daphne thus transforms Gerald's diaries – and her own origins – by burying the diaries in Canada. Her "bow to memory" signals the shift from her role as interpreter to that of the author of her own tale, allowing her to transform Gerald's writing and her own memory of absence, loss, and trauma into an expression of her presence beyond the logic of origins, heritage, or hyphenated belonging. Daphne's bow to memory writes Gerald's narrative palimpsestically onto the nation in a way that transforms the meaning of her absented origins in the diaspora and her current place in Canada. Foucault explains that "Genealogy...operates on a field of entangled and confused parchments, on documents that have been scratched and recopied many times" (76). This conception of genealogy makes Daphne's anamorphic image of herself, her chameleon tattoo, and Gerald's buried diaries (that are also her buried selves) the grounds of her being.

Each author narrates the painful memories of the diaspora in a manner that signifies something other than black abjection, silence, and trauma. As with Daphne's doubly-inflected statement of presence, these authors at once long to redress black abjection from Canada while also keeping the absences of memory and the irrecoverability of origins in view as part of their critique of nation as a stable form of belonging. The struggle to blacken Canada is a struggle to transform absences and aporias into an openness of identity and form that can critique and transform the nation by locating the themes, motifs, and metaphors of the black diaspora in Canada. Thus, perhaps the critical site of blackening for McWatt, Brand, and Clarke are the acts of reading, writing and narration that their characters engage in, particularly as these creative acts open a space of black expression in the nation and mediate diasporic memory and identity. As Imre Szeman notes, "every interpretation or reading is a kind of translation mechanism," and these texts conceive of reading as a kind of translation while also insisting "that it is best to acknowledge rather than to hide the workings of" (812) that translation. The acts of narration in each of these texts translate the black diaspora into Canada, and thus show how the "complex process of memory and emergence" renders Canada diasporic. Daphne's acts of reading, writing, and translation articulate the gossamer threads of her identity as a common "language of the land." The acts of reading and narration in each of the texts are linked to the struggle to remember one's past even when that past is forgotten, absent, or erased. If, as Szeman suggests, the mechanics of translation must be acknowledged, then these texts at once attempt to translate the absented origins of black diasporic life into Canada while keeping the wound of that absence visible. As such, the doubleness of double-consciousness reframes this "complex process of memory and emergence" in a way that renders palpable the absences and losses of the past, while also translating that absence into a different kind of presence in Canada.

Each author's attention to narrative, reading, and writing insists that theories of black diasporic subjectivity cannot be isolated from these acts of narration. These narratives do not simply illustrate or embody theories of black diasporic subjectivity, but are a form of blackening unto themselves. It is through Brand's acts of narration that she is able to render palpable that which is invisible or unspeakable within Walcott's framework of blackening. The unspoken yearnings, longings, gestures, and inflections of diasporic life are made visible in Brand's poetic, fictive, and critical narratives. It is through her acts of narration that the "romance with the past tense" (XX) that she observes in diasporic life is rewritten as a hopeful, enabling form of betweenness and doubleness. Indeed, the repetitions that Brand observes in the diaspora are rewritten in her poetry such that they exhibit a kind of grace and a longing for something to come rather than for something to return. "Water More Than Flour" shows how the grace of a phrase can offer hope in bleak material circumstances. Similarly, the speaker in *thirsty* must narrate the history that Chloe, Julia, and the daughter cannot. The silence of the unnamed daughter suggests the hope for stories that have yet to be written and that are not Brad's to tell. Through her narrative Brand transforms their loss and Alan's absence into a kind of doubled presence. As such, her poetry interrupts national temporality with diasporic becoming.

Austin Clarke's texts are equally concerned with narrative as a form of blackening, and his characters tell stories in order to make sense of their acts of migration and movement. Clarke's narratives do not merely offer instances of Fanon's depiction of psychic immobility, but rather show how the narration of that immobility constitutes a form of psychic mobility unto itself. Tim, John, Idora, and Mary-Mathilda all narrate the events of their lives to both understand their diasporic movement and to render the absent histories and psychic immobilities of the diaspora less disabling. In addition to these explicit acts of narration, Clarke's texts repeatedly employ multiple frame narratives that foreground the act of telling a story, and in which the person hearing the story describes being transported through the act of storytelling. As Sargeant Percy listens to Mary-Mathilda's narrative throughout *The Polished Hoe*, the narrator describes how "He has been travelling along with her story of personal history, over that landscape, observing the chapters of the journey" (276), and he thinks of Mary-Mathilda's narrative as a kind of "Travelling over life, and over land" (324). For Clarke, narrative is a form of mobility that undercuts the psychic immobility of race, slavery, and colonialism while also remapping national space as diasporic and unfamiliar. As Mary-Mathilda gives her statement to Percy and they walk in the dungeons beneath the plantation house, the narrator observes,

> The story that duplicates this strange underground journey Sargeant is being made to take causes him to feel he is a foreigner, a stranger in a land in which he thought he had a straight course, but which he now knows is winding, if not circuitous; something like the alienation, the hopelessness and the invisibility Manny told him he felt, when he lived in Georgia and in Florida and in Philadelphia. (342)

Percy's feeling of being a foreigner and a stranger in his own country indicates how Mary-Mathilda's narrative has estranged him from a once familiar place. The language of "hopelessness and ... invisibility" recalls the feelings of invisibility that pervade *More*, *The Origin of Waves* and "Sometimes, A Motherless Child"; narrative thus bespeaks and transforms these forms of social invisibility through a diasporic inscription of place. Percy originally sets himself on a "straight course" but Mary-Mathilda alters his sense of place such that he now feels "something like ... alienation." For Clarke, the story is itself the "winding, if not circuitous route" that his characters travel. Tim in *The Origin of Waves* observes a similar connection between narrative, mobility, and blackening when John reacts to his story "as if he himself is going through the exertion of the narrative, as if he himself has endured the details of my journey over the landscape of the story" (85). Tim and John's narratives not only rewrite the meaning of Canada but also resist the social and psychic immobility to which they are otherwise confined. Similarly, while Idora's narration of her life does not undo her social immobility, it does constitute a kind of psychic mobility and a blackening of Canada. Clarke's texts demonstrate how the acts of migration, displacement, and "crossing" are acts of imagination, and the felt effects of immobility, unvisibility, and outright racism are tempered through these diasporic narratives. These narratives are one means of resisting this enforced immobility, allaying the contradictions of migration and transnational existence, and rendering Canada diasporic through a blackening of the nation.

Brand's, Clarke's, and McWatt's narratives do not merely describe the conditions of being black in Canada but transform those conditions from one of absence to an assertion of the doubleness of black diasporic identity. The absent memories, heritage, and origins of diasporic life depicted in the authors' texts are transformed through these acts of narration. Mary-Mathilda explains "all that we possess to hand-down is love. And bitterness. And blood. And anger. And all four, wrap-up in one narrative" (354). Narrative does not replace or fill in the absented origins and memories of black diasporic life, but transforms those absences into something other than black silence and abjection. It is this narration of black identity in Canada as at once present and paradoxically attuned to the presence of absence that constitutes the double-consciousness of these narratives. Gerald's narrative is his only means of writing against the madness of racism, and his narrative of love, bitterness, blood, and anger is Daphne's troubled inheritance. Daphne transforms Gerald's narrative from signifying origins as absence and trauma to offering a different expression of blackness. It is through her re-narration of Gerald's narratives, her acts of anamorphosis, and her palimpsestic layering of Gerald's diaries within Canada that Daphne is able to transform her heritage, engage in a blackening of Canada, and assert and recognize her own presence. Blackening is not merely expressed in these narratives but *is* a kind of narrative which intervenes in the narration of nation. Blackening therefore, remaps the "language of the land" (479) such that black people can articulate their presence in – and affinity with – the nation in a manner that renders the vigilance and "cut" of double-consciousness a structuring principle of that presence.

The project of blackening and of inscribing diasporic double-consciousness within the nation is particularly suited to Canada where the presence of "multicultural heritage" and the lack of stable national origins, homogeneous identity, one national language, or a definitive national historical genesis leaves opens the conditions of possibility for intervening in the narration of nation and rewriting it from the position of the black diaspora. The narrative of Canada is particularly open to transformation and reinterpretation, and these authors seize upon that thematic and formal openness to offer a deeper language of difference and multiculturalism. Numerous Canadians are, in Jonathan Kertzer's words, engaging in a practise of *Worrying the Nation* (1998), whereby the lack of a stable Canadian identity or history generates the anxiety that "The object of theoretical inquiry in Canadian literary studies – Canada – no longer functions as it once did" (3). The worry that things in Canada are not what they used to be is seemingly as old as Canadian writing itself. This worrying which is present in the endless cycle of crises concerning multiculturalism, race, and immigration, signals, perhaps, the end of a stable narrative of Canada – if one ever existed. Indeed, George Grant's *Lament for a Nation* (1965) marked the end of a dominant Canadian narration of nation just as it ushered in a new narrative of national lamentation of lost origins, eroding traditions, and forgotten national memories. Thus Canada's own absences enable these new forms of presence. In other words, what is for some a source of worry over this reduction of the Canadian nation is, for others, cause for celebration and a sign of Canada's timeliness as the first post-national nation. Davey's *Post-National Arguments* (1993) is the first in a long series of critical texts that announce "the arrival of the post-national state" and "suggest a world and a nation in which social structures no longer link regions or communities" (266). Söderlind critiques this celebration of Canadian post-nationalism as a "'Canada first' movement" ("Ghost-National" 675), which "emphasizes the perpetual 'newness' of Canada" (690) and repeatedly shows how Canada was always-already post-national, post-colonial, transnational, and diasporic. Söderlind insists that these critics transform "the lamentations over Canada's belatedness that characterized the nationalist 1970s into a millennial celebration of Canada's – belatedly discovered – firstness" (674). Canada's lack of stable identity, national genesis, and collective ghosts are not a sign of its lack of national unity, but rather a sign of it being "first past the post of the outdated notion of nation" (674). Canada's lack of identity becomes the very basis of its firstness, uniqueness, and timeliness within the emerging transnational world.

The validity or "preposterous" (Söderlind 674) quality of these post-national arguments is beyond the scope of this project. What is relevant to the question of blackening is the manner in which the shared lack of origins and the feeling of lost history connects the narrations of the black diaspora with the narratives of Canada.[1] Black people in Canada are often cited as evidence of Canada's increasing post-nationalism, as the cause for worrying the nation, and as being responsible for the loss of a coherent national narrative. These authors turn such accusations into the means by which they can insist on a shared experience of loss, and provoke Canada into recognizing their and its legitimacy. Du Bois concludes *The Souls of Black Folk* with an assessment of African-American "Sorrow Songs," explaining that "Through all the sorrow of the Sorrow Songs there breathes a hope" (162) and asking "Would America have been America without her Negro people" (163)? Thus the question with which Du Bois begins his study, "How does it feel to be a problem," is transformed into the question of how African-Americans have transformed and blackened America. The writers in this study do not undo the meaning of Canada, but rather render it diasporic through their narratives of black diasporic life in Canada. They turn the question of "Where you from" back on their interlocutors to insist upon the imagined origins of the nation itself. It is precisely this openness of Canada's national narrative and lack of a stable history or collective identity that enables these writers to write Canada within the black diaspora. Like the diasporic figures in these texts, Canada has no identifiable origins or stable heritage by which to justify boundaries between true Canadian heritage and the heritage of others. Rather, these narratives translate the losses and absences of stable identity in the black diaspora into forms of Canadianness in order to render Canada diasporic. These authors do not abandon Canada or surrender it to the "global soup of neo-conservatism" (Bentley 19–20), but rewrite the nation from a black diasporic perspective. George Elliott Clarke's assertion that "*blackness* possesses a Canadian dimension that is recognized by engaging with black cultural works located here" (*Odysseys* 10; italics in original) is rewritten by these authors as a diasporic practice that mutually reshapes the meaning of blackness and Canada.

In one sense these writers reveal the uneven and contradictory effects of multiculturalism. While multicultural policy purports that "No citizen or group of citizens is other than Canadian, and all should be treated fairly" (Trudeau), it often lacks a means of identifying and addressing racism or notions of accumulated advantage, and in its disavowal of historical injustices, reaffirms the dominant position of white Anglo Canadians within the national history and present. Sunera Thobani is correct, for instance, in her argument that Canadian multiculturalism produces "exalted subjects" and that "the historical exaltation of the national subject has ennobled this subject's humanity and sanctioned the elevation of its rights over and above that of the Aboriginal and the immigrant" (9). Furthermore, her arguments that multiculturalism "helped stabilize white supremacy by transforming its mode of articulation" (146) and that Canadian multiculturalism "has thus come to attest to the enduring superiority of whiteness, of its ability to transform and accommodate itself to changing times and new opportunities" (155) are supported by each of the texts in this study. But that is just one story, and it is not the whole story as Brand, Clarke, and McWatt reveal in their insistence on moving beyond critique. Their work wrests multiculturalism from its liberal origins, infusing it with a much more potent and critical language of anti-racism in order to imagine history, identity, and nation differently. What multiculturalism offers these writers and diasporic people in Canada is a different vocabulary for imagining the nation. Canada's stated cultural openness, its assertion that it has "no official culture," and the hope that the expressions and political demands of "various cultures and ethnic groups ... give structure and vitality to our society" (Trudeau) all provide an alternate vocabulary for different Canadian stories. This enables these authors to rewrite the signifiers of belonging, heritage, tolerance, origins, and nation itself from a black diasporic perspective. Indeed it is this capacity of multiculturalism to effect an imaginative transformation of the nation that is missing from strictly sociological or empirical accounts of multiculturalism. Thus Rinaldo Walcott accurately argues that "Canadian multiculturalism has been a useful instrument in the unfolding of neo-liberalism" ("Disgraceful" 20) and stresses that "multicultural policy ... is in no way a challenge to the national myth of Canada as a white nation-space or a raceless state" ("Disgraceful" 23). Yet multiculturalism is not strictly policy but also a vocabulary for imagining and narrating diasporic and national subjects. These texts reveal what empirical and sociological studies of multiculturalism often to fail to recognize: despite the many shortcomings and criticisms of multiculturalism, they reveal how "everyday Canadians – make multiculturalism work for them" (Clarke, "Multi-cultural, multi-faith" 52). Thobani argues that "There prevails in Canada a master narrative of the nation, which takes as its point of departure the essentially law-abiding character of its enterprising nationals, who are presented ... as responsible citizens, compassionate, caring, and committed to the values of diversity and multiculturalism" (4). Yet this "master narrative" is continually being cut apart, detoured, and re-narrated by Brand, Clarke, McWatt and others *through* their re-coding of the language of multiculturalism. These writers engage in "seizing the value-coding" (Bhabha 344) of multiculturalism, and while their blackening of nation is primarily at the narrative level, it has implications beyond the stories Canadians tell themselves about their nation. Thus Brand's interpolation, Clarke's crossing, and McWatt's chameleon identities provide an imaginative vocabulary for bespeaking the nation anew.

These authors give critical meaning to notions of recognition, national belonging, and "the multicultural heritage of Canadians." If there is a multicultural heritage of Canadians, it is a heritage that remains open, caesuric, and is continually inflected by the "complicated process of memory and emergence" that renders diaspora vital. At a time when the language of multiculturalism rings so hollow that it is synonymous with the reduction of "the Canadian nation to bite-sized chunks" and the *Globe and Mail* insists that Canadians "Strike multiculturalism from the national vocabulary," these authors reinvigorate the language and politics of Canadian multiculturalism. They write in the gaps of Canada's lack of national unity, ghosts, traumas, and collective identity in order to take possession of the openness and thereby locate blackness *here*. These narratives do not aim to fill in the absences produced by narrations of nation and diaspora, but rather to engage in productive acts of crossing, rewriting, and blackening that locate both the possibilities and pain of double-consciousness within, across, and at odds with narrations of nation.

Chapter Six

Re-Beginning: "Blah, Blah, Blah." Emergent Critical Multiculturalism in Brampton, Ontario

All roads lead to Brampton

Official Slogan for the City of Brampton, Ontario

This project raises the "tired" question of multiculturalism with renewed urgency and purpose, and in the voices of black diasporic writers and critics in Canada. For these figures, as it was for their African-American counterparts and forebears, national belonging and exclusion are contained in and signified by the hyphen and the ampersand. These writers describe their inscription within the frames and protocols of nation formation, blackening the space of the nation in order to inhabit it on their own terms. This journey is both painful and incomplete; the question "Where you from?" encapsulates diasporic double-consciousness, posing the "problem" of race within the cosy confines of nation and tearing the black self apart.

However, "Where you from," is also open to reclamation, as the comedian Russell Peters points out in the same *Globe and Mail* series on multiculturalism discussed at the outset. In Peter Scowen's interview with Peters and three other non-white comedians in Canada, Scowen finds it "refreshing to see someone being so unabashed about asking people what their ethnic background is" ("Four Comics"). Peters responds,

> I think it's the way I grew up. My dad would always do that. We'd almost play that game, wherever we'd go [imitates father], "You see that guy? I bet he's blah blah blah." We'd walk by and he'd ask, Where are you from? "I'm Polish." [imitates father again] "I told you!"

...

I find everyone is sensitive. It's actually funny when people get weird about it. 'What are you?" "What do you mean? I'm a human!" You're a dumb-ass, is what you are. ("Four Comics")

Is Peters right? Are these writers just whiners and dumb-asses (again, the hyphen!) or is Peters's consideration of the hyphen more complicated than it initially appears? Perhaps Peters is simply responding to Scowen's dare to demonstrate how "unabashed" he is about ethnicity. Yet what is particularly interesting about his response is his claiming of the question, and the right to interrogate identity as his own. He conceives of the question not as a means by which white Canada marginalizes others, but as a question that can be asked by a non-white interrogator of a white person. Unlike the writers in this study who are always on the receiving end of the question, always placed outside of the imaginative community by virtue of their blackness, Peters insists that he can be the one asking the question. Peters reimagines the question of "where you from" as a sort of game through which he and his family lay claim to the space of Brampton, Ontario and to Canadian identity. His response, like his comedy, conceives of ethnicity as a free-floating signifier. Peters's comedic inscription of cross-cultural hybridity turns racism and white liberal guilt simultaneously into sources of hilarity and grounds for outrage. The actual meaning of racial or cultural identity is irrelevant for Peters, as it is replaced by "blah blah blah"; he is more interested in the multicultural comedy that arises between ethnic identities and in the way that those identities are assumed or performed by Canadians.

Peters is obviously different from the writers in this study in that he is not black and is of a younger generation than Brand, Clarke, Bissoondath, and McWatt. While he is certainly diasporic, the double-consciousness that structures these authors' negotiation of nation and blackness is not present in Peters's work. Yet, his response is indicative of the shifting way in which questions of race and citizenship are being conceived of in Canada. Peters's appropriation of the question operates as a hopeful gesture of inclusion and as a different and emergent form of multiculturalism. For instance, he begins his autobiography, *Call Me Russell* (2010), thus:

I'm never just a comic. No matter how people describe me, there's always something before my name or my profession. There's always that

> hyphen: South-Asian comic, Indo-Canadian comic, South-Asian-Canadian comic, Canadian-born-Indian comic, Brampton-raised stand-up comic … To my friends and family, though, there's no hyphen. They just call me Russell. To me, I'm just a comedian who happens to be Indian … or wait, Canadian … or Indo-Canadian … Anglo-Indian, South-Asian, South-Asian Canadian? Jeez, even I'm confused. (9; ellipses in original)

For all his criticism of the sensitivity towards questions of origin, Peters reveals his own uncertainty and amusement when he comments on the politics of the hyphen and his struggle against his own hyphenation. Peters describes learning to cope with the interrogation of the hyphen from his father's struggle to answer the question of, "'Where are you from?' 'I'm from India,' Dad would say to whoever was asking. 'But if you're from India, then why do you speak such good English? Where did you learn?' 'On the plane ride over,' Dad would answer sharply" (19). His father's hilarious response, as well as Peters's own enumeration of this baffling array of identities along with the ellipses in this passage, recall Daphne's expression of "Nothing." Like Daphne, Peters worries that the hyphen renders him a cliché, a species of emerging Canadian exotica, or simply "Nothing," effacing the presence of "Russell" himself.

While I find Peters's attitude towards the hyphen compelling, I am particularly interested in the origins of that stance. He insists that his nonchalance towards and curiosity about the question of "Where you from" emerges from "the way I grew up," and perhaps also the place in which Peters grew up: Brampton, Ontario. Like Peters, I grew up in Brampton and the genesis of this inquiry is certainly located in Brampton's strange project of isolated and segmented suburban space and ongoing and exciting mix of cultures. I share Peters's unshakeable fascination with cultural difference, with the hilarity, sadness, and possibility that emerge between cultures, and with a healthy scepticism towards the capacity of official multiculturalism to model the experience of people caught between cultures and within the logic of the hyphen. Having moved from England to Canada at a young age, I lived in Niagara Falls and Toronto before my family settled in the newly-laid suburbs of Brampton. One of my first memories of Brampton life is of when my parents sent a copy of my class photograph to my family in England. They were shocked, in their distinctly Northern-English way, at the visible lack of white students in my class. This was not the colony they had signed up for. The contradictory belief that I should not be surrounded by (visible) immigrants in a country in which I was an immigrant was apparent to neither myself nor my relatives at the time. Indeed, up until this time the meaning of race and cultural differences for me had more to do with food, music, and learning to swear in other languages than with an understanding of white privilege, racism, or cultural segmentation. Yet it seems clear to me now that growing up in Brampton provided an undeniable "public pedagogy" (Giroux [1981]) in multiculturalism and race.

Multiculturalism in Brampton is not simply government policy, but is everyday reality in a way that it is not always elsewhere in Canada. Certainly there is the prescriptive multiculturalism of the classroom and workplace that so many people in Brampton mockingly describe as "sensitivity" or "ethnic" training. There is also a long and relatively unknown history of racism in the city ranging from the early persecution of Irish Catholics by members of the Brampton and Orangeville Orange Order, to the 1992 shooting of Michael Wade Lawson by the Peel Regional Police (the officers were acquitted). Yet, despite the undeniable and persistent racism in Brampton, there is also something occurring in the city that suggests a far more interesting and exciting critical kind of multiculturalism emerging from the its combination of suburban space and mélange of peoples. There are forms of cultural production and citizenship emerging that demonstrate awareness of being part of an unplanned project of cultural mixing, a transferral of cultural meaning, and of what it means to be part of a broader multicultural experiment. This is particularly true of young people who possess something like a critical awareness of multiculturalism as a state-sponsored, watered down substitute for anti-racism, and also as a lived reality and a source of new and exciting possibilities. This is a different notion of doubled awareness evident in the ironic dismissal and embrace of multiculturalism in Brampton. It seems evident that the residents' awareness of the unique forms of cross-cultural interaction that occur in Brampton displays a critical multiculturalism that possesses a vibrancy and dynamism, and is far closer to Brand's sense of "interpolation," Clarke's crossing, and Daphne's "chameleon" identity than state multiculturalism. Indeed, this critical multiculturalism emerges from the experience of everyday interpolation combined with seeing that daily experience modelled and theorized so poorly in the banal celebrations and "sedative politics" (Kamboureli *Scandalous* 82) of CultureFest and CaraBram. This sophisticated way of thinking about multiculturalism arises from the tension between a lived reality of identity as difference, and the liberal state's representation of that reality: identity as sacred object and multiculturalism as a kind of museum of identities. This is akin to a critical reading practice that is aware of the contradictions of multicultural life and of the notion of identity within multiculturalism.

Russell Peters's comedy, business names such as Khalsa Gas, Liberation Lounge, and Heritage Fish and Chips give some sense of the unpredictable and inadvertent hybrid identities and multicultural vibrancy that I observe emerging in Brampton. There is a closeness between people of all cultures in Brampton that makes a self-conscious multiculturalism virtually impossible to avoid. I can vividly remember the images of the aftermath of Operation Bluestar that were circulated around my classroom in local Sikh newspapers, and I struggled to understand their relevance to my life in Brampton. The closeness between people in Brampton overrides, in some ways, the segmentation and atomization of suburban life. Whereas Clarke depicts the racially-managed "periphractic space" that Idora occupies in downtown Toronto, Brampton seems to offer a different kind of space that puts "self" and "other" into interaction with one another such that those categories of identity lose their polarity and oppositional quality. I have often wondered whether it is this closeness that led Rohinton Mistry from Toronto to Brampton. I wonder, too, if Mistry gets as annoyed as I when critics attempt to juxtapose his hurried, hybrid, and exciting life in Bombay with what they assume must be a dreary, monastic, and isolated life in the hinterlands of Brampton. They don't consider that perhaps not all political and multicultural life happens south of Bloor Street in Toronto. Similarly, when Brand describes Brampton (and other suburbs) as a place where immigrants go to forget their pasts and escape other immigrants, she misses a great deal of the excitement that happens in these places despite themselves.

This project certainly has its roots in Brampton where there is a constant awareness of cultural difference, race, and of how this ongoing interpolation may be leading to different cultural formations and conceptions of citizenship. There are parlances, postures, gestures, and affectations that are emerging from the city's unique mix of immigrants. In place of state multiculturalism, there is something akin to what Henry A. Giroux describes as critical or "insurgent multiculturalism" (326) that conceives of identity as non-essential, interested, conjunctural, and discursive. Giroux argues that critical or insurgent multiculturalism aims to "bring a wider variety of cultures into dialogue with each other, to theorize about cultures in the plural, within rather than outside 'antagonistic relations of domination and subordination'" (337). This is opposed to the state multiculturalism that aims to contain these antagonistic relations by trafficking in identity as a prized possession, and promises to "protect and preserve" the inner kernel of cultural identity. When Peters replaces the inner, privileged marker of ethnic identity with "blah blah blah," he engages in just such a critical multiculturalism that imagines identity as textual and produced through difference. This is the kind of interpolation that Brand describes and longs for throughout her corpus. Indeed, in *Map to the Door of No Return*, Brand quotes Chantal Mouffe's argument (from "For a Politics of Nomadic Identity" [1994]) that "Every identity is irremediably destabilized by its 'exterior'" (109). Brand cites Mouffe's argument as part of her critique of origins and what it might mean to conceive of the "interior" of identity as "something purely contingent" (109). Mouffe argues that "Inasmuch as objectivity always depends on an absent otherness, it is always necessarily echoed and contaminated by this otherness" (109–10), and that "What we commonly call 'cultural identity' is both the scene and the object of political struggles. The social existence of the group is always constructed through conflict" (110). There is, within Brampton, an ongoing and continuous process of being "contaminated by … otherness" and this is a productive kind of contamination that produces the simultaneously wounded and incomplete, yet also hopeful, identities of a more critical form of multiculturalism. Peters's comedy investigates what it means to be "both the scene and object of political struggles" in his translation of authentic identity into "blah blah blah." In Peters's work and in the forms of insurgent multiculturalism that I identify in Brampton, identity is no longer something one discovers but becomes, as Daphne learns, a continuous act of transformation and inscription that is "continuously contaminated by … otherness." These are, in Szeman's terms, acts of translation that keep the ongoing process of translation in view, such that the dialogue and conflict between identities comes to take the place of authentic identity. The shift from the banal forms of multiculturalism that these authors critique to a more critical multiculturalism involves abandoning claims to authentic identity and instead conceiving of identity in difference, in dialogue, and as "both the scene and object of political struggles."

This struggle over the meaning of identity and nation is evident in the responses to Kyla Pawis's infamous Youtube video entitled "Brampton Problems." In the video Pawis complains about the presence of brown people (by which she means people of South Asian descent) in Brampton, making a number of outrageous racist comments. Pawis, who professes her whiteness throughout the video, speaks in a decidedly Brampton patois infused by the very languages she disparages and repeatedly kisses her teeth in her frustration at the presence of cultural others. The notion of a white person hoping that we "get some more white people" in Brampton while simultaneously engaging in the Caribbean practice of kissing one's teeth (also called struups) to express frustration demonstrates not only the absurdity of her remarks but the very forms of interpolation and crossing that Clarke and Brand call for. Identity in Brampton is continually "destabilized by its 'exterior'" and is "contaminated by ... otherness" such that discrete identities are rendered less and less comprehensible. Even in the expression of her own fear of this contamination, Pawis reveals the inescapable interpolation of her own identity.

If Pawis's rant suggests the dystopian breakdown of Canadian multiculturalism that many critics have predicted, the responses to her video are far closer to Brand's observation of the gestures towards utopia that emerge at the crossroads of identities. While many of the outraged responses to Pawis express sadness over her racism or attack her appearance, others offer a sustained critical analysis of her statements. These critical respondents invoke the language of multiculturalism and a transformed conception of nation to critique Pawis's comments, her absurd notion of cultural difference, and her conception of "belonging." Youtube user Superwoman insists that Pawis's racism is not "a brown issue but more of a human issue" and that "It's sad to see that in such a multicultural country ... there are people who are still unaware." She then advises people who are "enraged and angry" by racists to "smile when they least expect it." LandonProductions responds to Pawis's request that brown people "go back to your own country" by saying, "I'm brown ... and I'm in my own friggin country. Where the fuck do you want me to go? ... You think white people own Canada? I don't think so, it was the natives that founded this land and you just happen to live here. Why can't you accept all other people?" He then jokingly predicts what will happen if "brown people" were to fulfill Pawis's request to leave Canada: "when you go to the bargain store, and you want a deal with that brown guy, you're not going to get it because that brown guy is no longer in Canada. You want your taxes done? No problem: do it yourself ... you want your ... computer fixed? Too friggin bad because we're not going to do it!" Similarly, poster

ItszMiszDattu parodies Pawis's depiction of South Asian people by staging a conversation between her mother and herself where she explains that "Mom I know what I want to be when I grow up … a terrorist" to which her mother replies, "I'm so proud of you!" Poster ThatIndianG inverts Pawis's criticisms by suggesting Pawis herself "go back to Toronto or wherever you came from," and that "if you're tired of seeing brown people … move to Antarctica where it's all white." xtheWitnessx begins his response with "Ahhh … racism in the morning is so refreshing." He then uses her rant as context to his own experience of being attacked by racists and then critiques the notion of race altogether, stressing that ignorance of race within Canada "is the issue."

Like Peters, each respondent employs a combination of humour and an awareness of the language and history of Canadian multiculturalism to rebuke Pawis's racist statements and express their own notions of identity and belonging in Brampton. The quick denunciation of her views and the articulation of different conceptions of identity suggest that multiculturalism has provided Bramptonians with a critical vocabulary for enunciating the nation and locality differently. In a twist, however, they claim the local space within the nation to transform diasporic and local notions of belonging. These responses affirm Pheng Cheah's observation that "*the unevenness of political and economic globalization* makes the nation-state necessary" and renders "national formation through negative identification both historically unavoidable and ethically imperative" (300; italics in original). While Cheah is describing the citizens of global South who return to the nation as a defence against "the shortfalls of neocolonial capitalist global restructuring" (300), his description of responses to global capitalism as a type of "aporetic nationalism" describes the local responses of Brampton citizens to Pawis's statement. This is not merely a cosmopolitan celebration of difference, but a transformation of national narratives and signifiers in pursuit of a different articulation of the local and national. These expressions of community and identity link Canadian multicultural discourse to critical race analysis in such a manner that does not allow white identity to go unmarked, and renders all identity unstable. Where Brand, Clarke, and McWatt adapt multicultural discourse into an imaginative vocabulary for reimagining the nation, the respondents to the video provide evidence of an emerging critical imaginative vocabulary that bespeaks the nation anew. Their responses make evident Brown et al.'s observation that "race is a relationship, not a set of characteristics one can ascribe to one group or another" (228). Furthermore, these young people in Brampton transform the relationship between race and citizen by employing the language of multiculturalism to make their own claims on Canada.

This is not to suggest, of course, that Bramptonians somehow, between their day jobs and lengthy commutes, have solved the multicultural riddle and are now basking in the flux of non-essential and radically democratic identities. Rather, there is a continuous and difficult awareness in everyday Brampton life that increasingly acknowledges the destabilizing of any interior space of identity. This goes beyond the plethora of flags attached to cars during the World Cup or the cultural displays of the Peel Heritage Complex.[1] In place of these reifications or subsumptions of difference and social division is a form of interaction organized around the differential nature of identity. In Laclau and Mouffe's terms, if state-sponsored multiculturalism performs a hegemonic function that aims to suture social space and identities, then there is, within this critical multiculturalism, an awareness and pronouncement of the antagonism at the heart of Canadian multiculturalism.

I end with this discussion of the meaning of race and cultural difference in Brampton not to engage in an assessment of my own politics of location or to force my own biography into this project. Rather, I want to suggest the ways that my own critical work takes up some of the same questions that these authors have engaged in their texts. Each author is concerned with how black diasporic subjects in Canada negotiate nation, and the complex ways multicultural Canada engages black subjects through oscillating techniques of erasure and presence. Furthermore, these authors' projects of blackening and of becoming diasporic inscribe a space for the antagonisms of race and diaspora in Canada. They respond to the question of "Where you from" through their inscription of diasporic double-consciousness, and their depiction of the feeling of being "torn asunder" by the antagonisms and contradictions of what it means to be black and diasporic in Canada. While I do not want to try and generalize black diasporic double-consciousness to apply to all diasporic people or migrants, I do want to suggest that the kind of longing, affectations, postures, and antagonisms of diasporic life that these authors observe are present in Brampton public life. Certainly the comedy of Russell Peters is a far cry from the torrid history of slavery, the haunting figure of the Door of No Return, or the brutal state violence committed against Albert Johnson. Yet I do suggest that in Brampton there is an emerging process of "becoming diasporic" that eclipses organized forms of multiculturalism. This "becoming diasporic" is far closer to the kind of subjectivities, citizens, and politics that these authors desire than state multiculturalism.

Throughout this project I have detailed the way in which these writers conceive of narrative as not just giving texture to black diasporic life, but also as a structuring element of that life. The narrative acts that accompany diasporic life are ways of making sense of the experience of migration and of writing against the confines and limits of the question "Where you from?" Like the authors in this study and like Peters, my acts of criticism constitute a means by which I am attempting to understand, disentangle, and perhaps resolve the contradictory elements of multicultural Canada. My critical readings constitute, in Szeman's terms, acts of translation and writing, thus becoming narrative acts of their own, reinscribing the contradictions and antagonisms among identity, nation, and race that these texts identify.

These acts of narration constitute a public intervention that links the semiotic with the discursive and gives voice to the kind of critical multiculturalism which these authors are advocating. Peters's comedic narratives do not merely retell his diasporic family romance, but intervene in a public discourse of ethnicity and race to reveal, register, and laugh at the antagonisms of that discourse. The same is true of the authors in this study who, in their acts of narration, reinvent the romance and horror of the slave past to blacken their Canadian present. Finally, my own acts of criticism engage in a type of narration that rewrites, as palimpsest, the texts that I read in order to foreground their aporias and their transformation of Canada. I regard this project as an act of citizenship and public intervention that discerns the antagonisms of the social and revels in the coming undone of both nation and narration.

Notes

Introduction

1 Kamboureli's analysis of multiculturalism fatigue focuses on Gina Mallet's 1997 article in the *Globe and Mail* entitled "Multiculturalism: Has diversity gone too far?"

2 Day distinguishes between "three prevalent usages of 'multiculturalism': to *describe* (construct) a sociological *fact* of Canadian diversity; to *prescribe* a social ideal; and to *describe and prescribe* a government policy or *act* as a response to the fact and an implementation of the ideal" (6; italics in original).

3 For instance, Frances Henry and Carol Tator define democratic racism in Canada as an ideology in which "two conflicting sets of values are made congruent with each other. Democratic principles such as equality, fairness, and justice conflict with, but also … coexist with, racist attitudes and behaviours" (228). While their analysis is invaluable, they acknowledge that the contradictory and invisible nature of democratic racism makes it "an elusive concept" (228). This elusiveness is evident in their vague claim that democratic racism advances "negative feelings about minority groups and differential treatment of them." In a different context, Kymlicka's theory of minority rights within a liberal framework is unable to contend with the particular forms of racism that black people experience in Canada, and the argument that "anti-black racism is qualitatively different from that suffered by other visible minorities." (Banting and Kymlicka 64). His discussion of minority rights concedes that "Blacks in Canada, particularly immigrants from the Caribbean, face many barriers to integration not faced by other immigrants, including non-white immigrants" (*Vernacular* 178). Kymlicka goes on to suggest that many immigrants have become successful "precisely by gaining some distance from 'blacks'. They have come to be seen as

'respectable', like whites, in contrast to the 'unruly' Blacks. They are seen as decent, hard-working and law-abiding citizens, as opposed to the promiscuous, lazy, and criminal Blacks" (*Vernacular* 189). Despite the strength of Kymlicka's analysis he concludes with the vague and generalized statement that given the particularly pernicious form of racism that black people experience in Canada, "prejudice against 'blacks' may prove very difficult to dispel" (*Vernacular* 191). In one sense perhaps Kymlicka's weak conclusion merely reveals the limitations of his framework of the "liberal multicultural hypothesis" ("Symposium" 1). The authors in this study are well aware of these limitations, particularly as multiculturalism transforms race into ethnicity, has no vocabulary for linking historical racism to the present forms of discrimination, and does little to unsettle the notions of race that inform categories of nation and citizen. Despite their invaluable philosophical and sociological analysis of Canadian multiculturalism, Henry, Tator, Kymlicka, and others repeatedly offer vague and weak summations of the persistence of racism and the affective experience of racism within liberal democracy.

4 Marlene Nourbese Philip (1992) describes this split of double-consciousness when she describes herself "arguing out of both sides of my mouth" (*Frontiers* 20), and when she insists that "The only way the African artist could be in this world ... was to give voice to this split i-mage of voice silence. Ways to transcend that contradiction had to and still have to be developed" (*She tries* 16). Philip provides a vivid image of her own double-consciousness in her depiction of the two oppositional imaginary figures that she imagines guide her writing. The first is "Male, white and oxford-educated, he stands over my right shoulder; [the second]...is old, Black and wise and stands over my left shoulder – two archetypal figures symbolizing the two traditions that permeate my work" (*Frontiers* 26). Philip's position between these figures and mediating their voices expresses the split that marks her poetic voice. Clarke claims to have found a voice that is both "black – *and* Canadian – like me," but Philip's work speaks from the split "i-mage of voice silence" that emerges from the contradictions of black life in Canada. While Philip may long for the transcendence that George Elliott Clarke claims to have achieved, her poetic voice dwells in and speaks from that split of double-consciousness. She provides a vivid image for her own double-consciousness in her depiction of the two oppositional imaginary figures that she imagines guiding her writing. The first is "Male, white and oxford-educated, he stands over my right shoulder; [the second] ... is old, Black and wise and stands over my left shoulder – two archetypal figures symbolizing the two traditions that permeate my work" (*Frontiers* 26). Philip's position expresses the split that marks her own poetic voice. This

split speaks to the contradictions of being black in Canada, to the "voice silence" of living the hyphen as a minus sign, and of being rendered "Nothing." The writers in this study repeatedly frame the difficulty of being "black – *and* Canadian" in terms of the question, "How does it feel to be a problem?"

5 The difference between Walcott's and Clarke's positions on blackness and nation is evident in the titles of their respective collections. Walcott's *Black Like Who? Writing. Black. Canada.* (1997) poses blackness as a question and refuses to make any organic link between "Writing," "Black" and "Canada" (the isolation of each term can be read as a disruption of Jonathan Kertzer's formulation of his reading practice that links "national + literary + history"). In contrast, Clarke's *Odysseys Home: Mapping African-Canadian Literature* posits Canada as the site of arrival and "Home" and the terms Home, Mapping, and African-Canadian signifies certitude anchored by the secure position of the African-Canadian subject in the nation.

6 Cho's and Walcott's conceptions of diasporic identity foreground the affective and experiential dimensions of diaspora over the "checklist approach" (Butler Kim 193) of diaspora theorists such as Robin Cohen (1997) and Nicholas Van Hear (1998), who define the black diaspora through qualities such as a "common history of forcible dispersion through the slave trade" (Cohen 144) or "The deployment of skin colour … as a signifier of status, power and opportunity" (Cohen 144). Where Armstrong describes as diasporic any "ethnic collectivity which lacks a territorial base within a given polity" (393), thus stressing lack and absence as defining features of diaspora, Cho and Walcott instead stress the contradictory overlap of absence and presence within diasporic imaginaries.

7 His reading of Brand's *A Map to the Door of No Return* argues that her "gesture of inclusion for immigrant blacks … excludes the history of indigenous African Canadians" ("Treason"). Similarly, his critique of Walcott's *Black Like Who* asks whether "African Canadians are always and only marginals and transients" ("Treason") or if they can ever be part of the nation proper.

8 Clarke himself, in his broad assessment of Africadian literature, employs religious terminology that echoes Du Bois's double-consciousness. In his introduction to the first volume of *Fire on the Water*, Clarke argues that the Africadian community is a "community of believers" and that "The religious foundation of Africadian culture cannot be overlooked in any responsible examination of its literature" (20). The belief in community, against the forces of historical erasure and uprooting, and of Africadians as a chosen people are expressed in the language of hymns, sermons, and spirituals. Even history, in these works, "becomes a secular bible which

furnishes illustrations of the assertion of Black identity and the attainment of spiritual liberty despite oppression" (12–13). Africadian literature, Clarke writes, "has two broad themes: 1) the achievement of a liberatory identity and 2) the denial and destruction of identity. The first theme can be called *messianic*; the second *apocalyptic*" (22; italics in original). Clarke argues that where "The messianic work stresses *revolution* – the appearance of the world as it ought to be; the apocalyptic work stresses *revelation* – the appearance of the world as it is" (22). While Clarke's argument stresses the recurring religious vocabulary of this literature, the doubly-inflected theme of an "achievement of a liberatory identity" alongside the "denial and destruction of identity" recalls Du Bois's expression of the self "torn asunder" and of Walcott's articulation of blackening Canada.

9 Kara Keeling (2006) argues that "'black females' entry into the feminine is marked over time by struggles to 'reconstruct womanhood' in a way that could accommodate visibly black and female bodies" (83). *All the Women Are White, All the Blacks Are Men, but Some of Us Are Brave* marks a break in that attempt to reconstruct womanhood, and instead challenges the conception of woman both within white patriarchy and within the black power movement. See particularly Michelle Wallace's "A Black Feminist's Search for Sisterhood" (1982) and Barbara Smith's "Toward a Black Feminist Criticism" (1985).

10 Certainly early black feminist criticism is diverse and offers a varied and complicated depiction of the black female body. Indeed, while Andre Lorde's phrase "our blood's telling" (*Sister Outsider* 152) is concerned with the materiality of the body and the history of blood, it is also attuned to the act of telling and the narrating of that body and history. Brand's work aligns with those writers and critics who are equally concerned with the materiality itself of the body and with the varied and multiple ways in which the act of telling can transform the signification of the body. Barbara Smith, for instance, in "Toward a Black Feminist Criticism" (1985) explains some early black feminists' reluctance to discuss sexual differences: "Heterosexual privilege is usually the only privilege that Black women have. None of us have racial or sexual privilege, almost none of us have class privilege, maintaining 'straightness' is our last resort" (171). While reluctant to abandon the position of straight altogether, Smith, like Brand, practices a black feminism that is at once "constituted around the problematic of 'race'," while it simultaneously and "performatively defies confines of the boundaries of its constitution" (Brah 114). Patricia Hill Collins reiterates Smith's position in *Black Feminist Thought* (2000), arguing that "Black lesbian relationships are not only threatening to intersecting

systems of oppression, they can be highly threatening to heterosexual African-American women's already assaulted sense of self" (167).

11 Brand's conception of the grammar of the body differs from that of June Jordan (1988) who insists, "Our language devolves from a culture that abhors all abstraction, or anything tending to obscure or delete the fact of the human being who is here and now/the truth of the person who is speaking or listening" (129). Audre Lorde (1984) declares, "We are African women and we know, in our blood's telling, the tenderness with which our foremothers held each other. It is that connection which we are seeking. We have the stories of Black women who healed each other's wounds" (*Sister Outsider* 152). Brand is more sceptical of the authenticity of blood, tenderness, truth, or healing. For her, speaking and listening irrevocably alter black women's relationships to their bodies and each other just as they constitute and exceed the knowledge of embodiment.

1 Dionne Brand's *thirsty*

1 Clarke further clarifies his position in a later interview, explaining, "We can't just take a handful of texts and say, 'They are written by Black people, therefore they are against racism.' They might be, but that's not enough. I am tired of reading reviews simply saying Dionne Brand is against racism and homophobia, Marlene Nourbese Philip is against sexism and regionalism … I am sick of that! How does such criticism advance us" (Dominguez 2001)?

2 Clarke's views are affirmed by the major thread of Brand criticism which is primarily concerned with Brand's representation of cultural difference, otherness, shifting identity categories, and her writing's capacity to conceive of identity in an anti-essentialist manner. Clarke's criticism of the tedious and sociological qualities of much Brand criticism is true of these critics who analyze the representation of difference, otherness, and hyphenated identities in Brand's work. For instance, Heather Smyth's argument that "Brand offers an urban, cosmopolitan vision of a politics of difference that transcends the limits of multicultural discourse" (272) is typical of this kind of reading which celebrates a vague sense of difference, yet has little to say about Brand's formal poetics. Emily Johansen argues that in Brand's *What We All Long For* (2005), "the identity of diasporic characters … continually oscillates between belonging and non-belonging" and "members of diasporic communities … must move between different social, ethnic, and gendered areas in the city. These material places are sites of complex social relationships which offer varying and unstable

levels of permeability based on class, gender, ethnicity, and a host of other axes of identification" (48). Johansen focuses on plot, valorizes identities that "continually oscillate between belonging and non-belonging," resorts to axes of identification without content, and ignores how these themes emerge out of Brand's poetics. Indeed, Johansen's contention that characters "continually oscillate between belonging and non-belonging" treats this oscillation as an existential condition rather than as historically produced, effacing distinctions between different diasporic subjects. For instance, a central character in *What We All Long For*, Carla, is described as "slipping through the city on light" (30) and as "liquid and jittery and out of control" (101). Oscillation is quite different from slipping and jitteriness, and the liquidity of Carla's movement suggests a connection between this contemporary form of movement and the forced movement of the Middle Passage. Similarly, Diana Brydon's argues that Brand's *Inventory* "may be read as performing an affective citizenship that calls her readers to do the same" ("Global Intimacies" 1001–2). Brydon's argument would be enriched by attending to the poem's repeated combination of S and SH sounds as in "the sunset in Cheyenne" (3) and in the repetition of words like "sugars" (33), "glacial" (4) and "surreptitious" (3). These S and SH sounds mimic the "irregular susurrus" (49) of the world, evoking in sound what words cannot communicate. Brydon intuits Brand's intimate and affective conception of citizenship, but abstracts this intuition from its performance in conspiratorial, clandestine, and whispering sounds.

3 Louise Fabiani's review of *Land To Light On* (1997) is exemplary of this kind of criticism, complaining that the speaker's "choleric voice is full of anger and anger's sorry cousin, self-pity… Brand alienates by being in your face about racism, male chauvinism, and classism" (167). Fabiani does not indicate who Brand alienates or why alienation and anger are not effective poetic techniques.

4 See Johanna X.K. Garvey (2003), Krishna Sarbadhikary (1996), and Joanne Saul (2004).

5 Brand's work is also inadequately contextualized within the fields of Caribbean poetry and black diasporic writing. Indeed, within these fields, Brand's work is typically marginalized or ignored outright. In numerous analyses of "Caribbean Women's Writing," Brand's work is often seen as falling outside the critical or generic paradigms that constitute Caribbean writing or black diasporic writing. The organizers of the first International Conference of Caribbean Women Writers did not include Brand's contribution to the conference, "Madam Alaird's Breasts," or her critical response to the conference, "This Body for Itself," in their collection of works from the

conference. Similarly, Denise deCaires Narain's *Contemporary Caribbean Women's Poetry: Making Style* (2002) creates a critical framework of structural, thematic, and generic "in-betweenness" that "offers a suitable model for the reading of Caribbean women's writing" (244). Despite the inclusion of other Caribbean women poets in diaspora (Grace Nichols) and Canada (Marlene Nourbese Philip), Narain's only discussion of Brand occurs at the very conclusion of her text where she briefly addresses Brand's exclusion from the published collection of the Conference of Caribbean Women Writers. Brand is mentioned at the very end of the final chapter, "Playing the field: anthologizing, canonizing and problematizing Caribbean women's writing," and Narain invokes Brand when she gestures towards "problematizing" the field of "Contemporary Caribbean Women's Poetry" (213) that she has outlined in her argument. Narain's argument that Caribbean Women's poetry is marked by an "indeterminacy of all kinds of identities, whether of geography, culture, race, class, sexuality or gender" (244) seems particularly suited to Brand's work, yet Brand is noticeably absent from Narain's analysis. Indeed, the relegation of Brand to the very end of the text suggests that Brand's indeterminacy is somehow too indeterminate for Narain's framework. In another context, Peter Dickinson's *Here is Queer: Nationalisms, Sexualities, and the Literatures of Canada* (1999) includes a very brief chapter on Brand's *In Another Place, Not Here* (1997) which primarily discusses Brand's ill fit within the field of queer Canadian writing. Dickinson vaguely insists that "a more fluid definition of the 'politics of location' is required before beginning any study of Brand's work" (157).

6 Clarke argues that "The *essential* trouble here is that Brand writes out of willful hypocrisy: she skewers the 'romantic' nationalisms … but Brand never queries her own essentialist posture, namely, that all black people … are disturbed, disfigured – by the experience of slavery and thus yearn for some form of re-collection" (*Review* 557; italics in original). Clarke's review unfairly suggests that Brand insists that all black people are "disfigured – by the experience of slavery." Rather Brand suggests that the losses and absences of slavery and the Middle Passage continue to inflect everyday black diasporic life. She does not insist that all black people "yearn for … re-collection," but rather writes a grammar to express the absences, longing, and yearning that she observes in the diaspora.

7 Mason's argument that the figures in the poem are haunted by history needs to contend more effectively with the speaker's claim in *thirsty* that what happens in the poem "isn't a haunting. That would be too fabulous. / It happened and what happened, happened" (XXIX). My concern is that the language of haunting slips too easily into reading history and trauma in

Brand's texts through the frame of psychoanalysis, particularly the return of the repressed, which may efface the historical and material realities of slavery and colonialism. Furthermore, the language of trauma can relegate racism and racial thinking to a past which must be reckoned with rather than as aspects of the lives of Brand's characters that appear in new and more virulent guises.

8 Mason points out that *thirsty* is inspired by the real case of Albert Johnson who was killed by the Toronto police in 1979.

9 Sandra Djwa takes issue with a great deal of Kamboureli's argument, especially her relegation of E.J. Pratt to the margins of the development of the Canadian long poem. Against Kamboureli's assertion, Djwa insists on "Pratt's centrality to the development of the Canadian long poem; indeed, it is doubtful if the long poem would have emerged as a distinctive Canadian genre without Pratt's example" (65). Djwa then proceeds to dispute Kamboureli's claim that Pratt's "idiosyncratic originality" led to his marginalization within the development of the genre by demonstrating Pratt's influences over subsequent poets such as Atwood, Reaney, and Ondaatje. In his review of *Bolder Flights*, Tracy Ware tempers the critique of Kamboureli, explaining that "Kamboureli is a fine critic when she deals with the postmodern writing to which she is sympathetic. *On the Edge of Genre* would be a better book without its opening attempt at a historical survey, which a good editor would have removed" (46). For perhaps the strongest criticism of Kamboureli's argument, see Manina Jones (1992). I agree with Djwa that Kamboureli's text glosses over Pratt's undeniable importance to Canadian long poetry. I also agree with Ware that Kamboureli's historical survey is inadequate; Bentley's "A General History" of the early Canadian long poem in *Mimic Fires: Accounts of Early Long Poems On Canada* (1994) offers a far more nuanced and accurate account of the genre. Yet these criticisms do not take away from the importance of Kamboureli's theorizing of the destabilization of national genre alongside the destabilization of the nation. Kamboureli's general thesis that the Canadian long poem "is produced within ... the very generic and cultural fissures it observes ... between its colonial predecessors and postcolonial instances" (204) marks a unique intervention into reading the Canadian long poem that productively situates debates concerning national literary forms within concerns about the eroding stability of the nation.

10 In some respects Kamboureli's argument relies on a concept of genre as stable textual "monism" which she then demonstrates is disrupted by the long poem. Surely there is a similar "ambivalent positioning" within seemingly more stable genres of writing, and genres are far more flexible

and versatile than Kamboureli suggests. Indeed, are the borders of genres not defined by the exemplary works which disrupt generic patterns and break the "generic laws of [their] species?"

11 Brand's representation of the process of becoming diasporic through temporalities of delay and prolongation differentiate her poetry from Brathwaite's tidalectics which conceives of history as cyclical and palimpsestic. Wayde Compton explains that tidalectics "describes a way of seeing history as a palimpsest where generations overlap generations, and eras wash over eras … There is change, but the changes arise out of slight misduplications of the pattern rather than from essential antagonisms. In a European framework, the past is something to be gotten over, something to be improved upon; in tidalectics, we do not *improve upon* the past, but are ourselves *versions* of the past" (17; italics in original). Brand's poetry does not depict the ceaseless return or repetition of the past, but rather represents diasporic subjectivity as a complicated prolongation of the past and delay of the future.

12 Bhabha's focus on discourse and sites of enunciation within post-colonial agency has been critiqued by Benita Parry, and others, as lacking necessary attention to the material structures of colonial and post-colonial societies. Parry notes that "Bhabha's affiliation with a critical practice which undertakes to reveal how the instability of textual meaning is produced/undermined as permutations on a chain of signification" ("Signs" 6) require that his "elaborations dispense with the notion of conflict – a concept which certainly does infer antagonism, but contra Bhabha, does not posit a simplistically unitary and closed structure to the adversarial forces" (6). She critiques Bhabha for representing "colonialism and transactional rather than conflictual" (12), arguing that "When language is taken as a paradigm of all meaning-creating or signifying systems, and human practice is consequently perceived as mimicking Writing, the definitive disparities between construing the structure of language and explaining the forms of social and cultural practice are collapsed" (10). Similarly, Arif Dirlik accuses Bhabha of "a reduction of social and political problems to psychological ones, and of the substitution of post structuralist linguistic manipulation for historical and social explanation" (333), and Pheng Cheah argues that Bhabha "inflates hybridity into a wellspring for the political contestation of all forms of cultural symbolization and the general articulation of marginal political identities by extending this definition of cultural authority to over all hegemonic forms" (294). While these critiques (as well as criticisms made by Parry and others concerning Bhabha's mis-reading of Fanon) are valid, Bhabha's work remains a rich source for interpreting

insurgent and subaltern transformations of colonial and national discourse. Indeed, Brand's use of the image of caesura to indicate not only the gap and ambivalence in Canada's national discourse but also the violence done against Alan's material body indicates her poetic attempt to supplement this "seizing the value coding" with a simultaneous attention to the material effects of power on those who attempt to rewrite and transform that Writing. Brand's poetics, in a sense, engage in this palimpsestic rewriting without jettisoning the material, class, and racial dimensions of power and struggle in the manner that Bhabha's critics accuse him of.

13 This is particularly clear in Bhabha's use of "sublated" to describe this "problem of the not-one, the minus in the origin … in a doubling that will not be sublated into a similitude." Bhabha's use of "sublated" surely alludes to Hegel's use of Aufhebung (roughly translated as "sublation") to describe the interactions between thesis and antithesis within a dialectic. The impossibility of sublating this repetition of cultural signs into a sign of cultural similitude (as a dialectical movement would require) indicates that the processes of the dialectic cannot function here and that this impossibility articulates contradiction rather than synthesis.

2 Austin Clarke's Recent Fiction

1 One can trace Idora's route on a map as she moves through Moss Park and through Toronto to the Cathedral. One error in Idora's route is that Clarke seems to confuse "Barton" with "Britain St." which is the actual street that Idora would cross according to her route. Clarke lives in this neighbourhood and knows it well, so perhaps his erasure of "Britain" from Idora's route is more an anti-colonial joke than cartographic error.

2 See, for instance, Michael Bucknor (2005) and Heike Härting (2004).

3 Michael Bucknor makes this point about early readers of Clarke's work, arguing that "the history of early Clarke criticism exposes a critical enterprise limited to representationalist assumptions of mimeticism and aestheticism … generally Clarke's work has been limited to readings addressing the authenticity of representation in it" (141). Bucknor's comments on early Clarke scholarship continue to be true of much contemporary Clarke criticism which is largely interested in the manner in which Clarke represents Canadian multicultural realities before they were enshrined in Canadian law and cultural mythos.

4 Gilroy justifies his decision thus: "There are also obvious omissions [in his text]. I have said virtually nothing about the lives, theorists, and political activities of Frantz Fanon and C.L.R. James, the two best-known black

Atlantic thinkers. Their lives fit readily into the pattern or movement, transformation, and relocation that I have described. But they are already well known if not as widely read as they should be and other people have begun the labour of introducing their writings into contemporary critical theory" (xi). One could also add Marcus Garvey to the list of black thinkers for whom movement is centrally important.

5 Despite Gilroy's reading of Delany, he is criticized by George Elliott Clarke for his broader erasure of Canada from the map of the Black Atlantic. George Elliott Clarke writes that within Gilroy's theory, "Canada, as a subject space, is patently absent. [Gilroy] never registers it as a site of New World African enslavement, immigration, emigration, anti-racist struggle, and cultural imagination … Hence his *Black Atlantic* is really a vast Bermuda Triangle into which Canada – read as British North America or Nouvelle-France or even as an American satellite – vanishes" (*Odysseys* 9).

6 Clarke originally planned to title the novel "Where Are The Men" (private interview). This title comes from Bill Cosby's famous rant about the absence of black fathers in African-American families and is part of a long history of critiquing the allegedly fatherless, African-American family.

7 One of the limitations of Clarke's texts is the attention he pays to the vulnerability of black male bodies at the expense of the vulnerability of black women's bodies. Throughout Clarke's narratives, black women fear that they will lose their identity, their decency, and their dignity whereas black men are faced with far more corporeal threats. In this instance, Idora imagines herself as trapped by the forces of class, spatial configurations of race, and structural racism, but she worries that her son will be the victim of a far more explicit and corporeal form of violence by the police or other black men.

8 It is this kind of prose, pervasive throughout Austin Clarke's writing, that leads George Elliott Clarke to playfully suggest that "Perusing Austin Chesterfield Clarke's short stories, one catches, now and then, the distinctive odour of the entertaining *and* tawdry James Bond spy adventures … both authors stud their pages with references to pricey autos and shapely women … Conceivably, if Fleming were still alive, he would make an apt partner for Clarke in one of those racially two-toned, 'buddy' films that Hollywood insists we must have" (*Odysseys* 238).

9 The title of the story is surely a reference to the repeated claim that black men from the Caribbean (and other immigrants) are not suited to working in Canada because they lack "Canadian experience." As Idora explains, "She was sure that when they say 'You do not have Canadian Experience,' they were using the code word for 'You black'" (13).

10 Clarke describes, in *Growing Up Stupid Under the Union Jack*, the influence of the plantation house in his own village: "And I saw that the first man in the village, dependent as the entire village was dependent on the plantation, which was our symbol in the many ways of our lives and our ambition, this first man must have looked as I was looking now, out into that first morning, after he had accumulated two boards and a half-pound of nails and a sheet of galvanize to build this one-roofed chattel house, and then has *seen the similarity*! ... And that is why the chattel house is merely a section of the plantation house – that part clearly visible in the morning sunlight. It was his only model. And it was the blueprint of his perspective, drawn in the hazy distance of many evenings of dreams and many mornings of blinding ambition" (150). The plantation house of Clarke's youth dominates the physical and imaginative landscape of his village, constituting a symbol of not merely economic dependence, but a "blueprint" of "perspective."

11 This is one of a number of links between the plantation of *The Polished Hoe* and the plantation in *The Survivors of the Crossing*. As in Mary-Mathilda's story, characters in *Survivors* demand higher wages for their work and are subsequently attacked by the plantation owners.

3 Representation of Albert Johnson

1 This public sphere approximates but is not equivalent to Jürgen Habermas's description of the eighteenth-century European public sphere as "a realm of our social life in which something approaching public opinion can be formed" (350). This conception of the public sphere must be modified, however, as both Habermas and John Keane argue that "The ideal of a unified public sphere and its corresponding vision of a territorially bounded republic of citizens striving to live up to their definition of the public good are obsolete" (Keane 366). This is not to say that the public sphere no longer exists, but rather that it takes new fragmented and diverse forms as conceptions of the public, private, and nation are transformed. If Habermas is right in suggesting that there is an increasing "'refeudalization' of the public sphere" whereby "large organizations strive for political compromises with the state and with each other" (354) outside the public realm, then perhaps white Canada constitutes just such an organization that delimits access to that public sphere along racial lines.

2 They describe their methodology as follows: "A discourse is a way of referring to or constructing knowledge about a particular topic or practice: a cluster or formation of ideas, images, and practices that provide ways of

talking about forms of knowledge and conduct associated with a particular topic, social activity, or institutional site in society. A *discursive formation* defines what is and is not appropriate in our formulation of, and our practices in relation to, a particular subject or site of social activity; what knowledge is considered useful, relevant and true in that context; and what sorts of persons or subjects embody its characteristics. *Discursive* has become the general term used to refer to any approach in which meaning, representation, and culture are considered to be constitutive" (26; italics in original).

3 Razack argues that one of the major problems facing opponents of democratic racism is "not simply the failure of collective rights advocates to present their failings within liberalism but the way in which the discussion is already regulated to obscure relations of domination" (33). Each of these critics indicates the specific ways in which democratic racism operates through the discourse of liberalism, and the manner in which invisible white privilege "obscure[s] relations of domination" and accumulated advantages. These critics argue that liberalism's privileging of the individual subject, its colour-blindness, and its discourse of individual equality render it unable to contend with claims of systemic oppression, racism, and discrimination in ways that do not make claims according to a discourse of equality. Criticisms of these positions insist that they posit an inflexible and archaic version of liberalism, and that modern liberalism has responded to these challenges through programs such as affirmative action, minority rights, and recognition of systemic discrimination. Defenders of liberalism such as Will Kymlicka and Charles Taylor have attempted to demonstrate the flexibility of liberalism in Canada in responding to these challenges. Kymlicka, for instance, argues that these criticisms of liberalism often posit a deeply conservative notion of liberalism, or pose a false dichotomy between liberalism's notion of individual rights and concepts of collective or minority rights. Disavowing the language or "collective rights," Kymlicka argues "that minority rights are not only consistent with individual freedom, but can actually promote it" (75), and he critiques the argument that liberal theories of individual rights reflect an "atomistic, materialistic, instrumental, or conflictual view of human relationships," arguing instead that "individual rights can be … used to sustain a wide range of social relationships" (26). Yet in Kymlicka's defence of liberalism, the specific forms that minority rights will take under liberalism remain vague. For instance, he argues against group "internal restrictions … where the basic civil and political liberties of group members are being restricted," but in favour of "External protections" where "the ethnic or national group may seek to protect its distinct existence and identity by limiting the impact of the decisions of the

larger society" (36). However, the difference between internal restrictions and external protections may only be a matter of perspective, and external protections may conflict with liberal notions of individual rights. Indeed, while an "ethnic or national group" may seek external protection, it may be interpreted by members of the group who do not seek that protection as a form of internal restriction (this issue is raised in *Out of My Skin* in the conflicts *within* the Quebecois community). Multiculturalism itself can be simultaneously interpreted as a form of internal restriction and external protection. Kymlicka's defense of liberalism argues that liberalism is not as inflexible as its critics allege, while also demonstrating that many of the criticisms of liberal notions of rights remain unresolved.

4 The reason for Johnson losing his job is also under dispute. The police defence insisted that his mental breakdowns began to affect his work, as reported in *Contrast*: "Buckley, president of Industrial Tire Ltd, a Mississauga tire plant where Johnson worked said that he fired Johnson in May 1979 as the outbursts became more frequent and often. This was five months before the shooting" ("Cop Changed Statement, Johnson Trial Told"). Johnson's supporters claim that he was beaten by police which led to him being dismissed for no longer being physically capable of completing his work. Yet the *Globe and Mail*'s reporting of Buckley's testimony explains Johnson's dismissal: *Globe* reporter Vivienne Carriere writes that Buckley "told the jury that Mr. Johnson's behavior became strange and erratic after an incident in March, 1979, when immigration officials and members of the Royal Canadian Mounted Police raided the plant and took away four workers who were in the country illegally ... One of the workers was Mr. Johnson's nephew, Mr. Buckley said, and although Mr. Johnson was not there at the time of the raid, he became very upset about it afterward" (Carriere, "Witnesses for Constables Testify Police Were at Johnson's at Least Twice Before," 5).

5 The *Toronto Star* routinely describes Johnson as an immigrant and a Jamaican immigrant, but never indicates whether he was a landed immigrant or a naturalized citizen.

6 This depiction of Johnson and the scene inside the Johnson home directly conflicts with the testimony of other witnesses, including neighbours and Johnson's sister who testified that the house was "quiet and calm until Inglis and Cargnelli broke into the kitchen" (Blatchford, "Police Feared 'Berserk' Man Would Hurt Family," A2).

7 'The Johnson Trial' is the mainstream media's title for the officers' trial. This nomenclature reveals precisely who is really on trial within public discourse.

8 Mbembe, building on the work of Giorgio Agamben and others, argues that contemporary forms of sovereignty are "expressed predominantly as the

right to kill" (16). To apply Mbembe's analysis to Canada runs the risk of levelling the differences between the various modes of sovereignty in the slavery plantation system, colonies, and a contemporary liberal democracy like Canada. There are certainly differences, of kind and degree, between each of these realms of the necropolitical. Yet the notion that white civility relies on the production of docile and killable racialized bodies indicates the continuities between the way in which subjects are marked and managed according to their race in each of these regimes. Mbembe argues that necropolitics is an extension of Foucault's concept of biopower as a mode of control that "presupposes the distribution of human species into groups, the subdivision of the population into subgroups, and the establishment of a biological caesura between the ones and the others. This is what Foucault labels ... *racism*" (17; italics in original). In this sense, Coleman's white civility can be supplemented with an account of how power regulates, manages, confines, and kills the bodies on which it operates.

9 Miller must not have read the *Toronto Star* article written eleven days after Johnson's death, headlined "Drunk who aimed rifle at police gets 2 months." Gary Oakes reports, "An alcoholic who pointed a loaded rifle at a Metro police officer and fired a shot into the ceiling has been sentenced to two months in jail for possessing a dangerous weapon." Police "ordered Markham to come out and he then pointed the rifle at Constable William Campbell. Campbell and the other officers told him to drop the weapon but Markham went back into the bedroom. The officers eventually talked Markham into giving up. Crown Attorney Bruce Young said the officers in the case 'are to be commended for their actions – nobody got hurt.' Trotter said it was 'most fortunate' no one was shot" (Oakes A3). Apparently the circumstances would have been much different for Johnson if he were white.

10 Blatchford never mentions the death of Albert Johnson in her coverage of the Just Desserts killings nor in her history of violence in Toronto. This indicates that this discourse that links race and crime and is employed by the *Toronto Star* and others to solidify a sense of white civility and black criminality is selective in deciding which incidents to remember and resurrect, and which incidents to forget and consign to historical irrelevance.

11 McKittrick has shown the history of black people's exclusion from Canada by virtue of the inhospitable weather. She explains that "Louis XIV gave limited approval to institute slavery in New France. In his statement sanctioning the institution, the monarch also commented that the project of slavery may fail in Canada – black slaves, he suggested, coming from such a different climate might perish due to the cold Canadian weather. That

New France might be an uninhabitable site for blackness collapses biocentric categories and geographic categories ... the monarch's comments did affirm a discourse through which black in/and Canada could be imagined – as unacceptably impossible or geographically inappropriate" (*Demonic Grounds* 136).

12 Hallam Street is the next street from Albert Johnson's residence on Manchester Avenue. His confrontation with the police began in the alleyway between Hallam and Manchester.

13 This is also true of Brand's earliest poetic reference to Albert Johnson in her collection *Primitive Offensive* (1981) which is a long poem broken up into Cantos. In Canto XI she writes "we die badly / always / public and graceless ... / in our houses / on Sunday mornings / in Toronto / if the police say we're wielding / machetes" (50). In this poem Brand links Johnson's death to other violence committed against black people in Africa and the Caribbean without specifically mentioning Johnson's name.

4 Tessa McWatt's *Out of My Skin*

1 The title, "Citizens Plus," comes from the 1966 Hawthorne Report which states that "Indians should be regarded as 'citizens plus': in addition to the normal rights and duties of citizenship, Indians possess certain additional rights as charter members of the Canadian community" (13).

2 Gerald's madness, his belief that he is white (he has white ancestors), and his constant desire to shed his skin all link his diaries to Fanon's work on the madness of racism and the racial-epidermal schema. Indeed, Gerald's diaries are written in 1959, two years before Fanon published *The Wretched of the Earth* (1961).

3 Black Nationalist Alexander Crummell confirms this mythologizing capacity of the nation-as-family metaphor when he insists that "Races, like families, are the organisms of God; and race feeling, like family feeling, is of divine origin. The extinction of race feeling is just as possible as the extinction of family feeling. Indeed, race *is* a family" (Appiah "Racisms" 11; italics in original).

4 Sylvia Söderlind has argued that Quebec's presence in the nation has been repressed since the national invention of multiculturalism, and that "English-Canadian writing – particularly critical writing – about nation is in a way doubly haunted: on the one hand by the particular role played by Quebec in the country's history, and, on the other – perhaps as a result – by its own inability to acknowledge its indebtedness to Quebec for its self-definition as a nation" ("Ghost-National" 673). While Söderlind's

arguments are complicated and beyond the scope of this chapter, her claim that English-Canadian writing and English-Canadian articulations of nationality are haunted by the presence of Quebec links the interruption of Daphne's gazing with the question that is posed to her in French.

5 Concluding

1 Kamboureli indicates this shared sense of lack between narrations of Canada and narrations of diaspora in her assessment of the field of Canadian Ethnic Anthologies: "The consciousness of no longer belonging to a cultural continuum induces a feeling of lack. Lack is imaged in terms both of a distant originary place and of the subject's lack of sameness vis-à-vis the dominant society. The writing in these anthologies articulates this lack" (*Scandalous* 138). Kamboureli seems to confuse *lack* with *loss* as the experience of "no longer belonging to a cultural continuum" indicates the loss of something that was once possessed. As such, one experiences the loss of a cultural continuum as well as the loss of the "distant originary place" in conjunction with the "lack of sameness vis-à-vis the dominant society." Similarly, Coleman discovers in *Masculine Migrations*, "Loss, as *Masculine Migrations* shows, returns again and again as a masculine theme [in the texts Coleman studies]. As an indication of crisis, loss represents a moment of instability that can be tipped towards either constraint or innovation" (168–9).

6 Re-Beginning

1 The Peel Heritage Complex is the only pseudo-museum in Brampton, and always suggested to me that Peel has something of a heritage complex. The irony that the Heritage Complex was once a jail seems to have been lost on Brampton city officials, although my class trips to the complex often felt like a prison sentence. Huey Newton, when imprisoned in the now Peel Heritage Complex, complained that it was "worse than any jail in Cuba" (Brown, *Behind Bars* 12).

Works Cited

"Abide." *The Oxford English Dictionary*. 2006. Print.

Agamben, Giorgio. *Homo Sacer: Sovereign Power and Bare Life*. Palo Alto: Stanford University Press, 1998. Print.

Alcoff, Linda. "Philosophy and Racial Identity." *Radical Philosophy* 75 (Jan/Feb 1996): 14. Print.

Alexander, Ken and Avis Glaze. *Towards Freedom: The African Canadian Experience*. Toronto: Umbrella Press, 1996. Print.

Alexis, André. *Childhood*. Toronto: McClelland Stewart, 1997. Print.

Algoo-Baksh, Stella. *Austin C. Clarke: A Biography*. Toronto: ECW Press, 1994. Print.

Allen, Lillian. *Women Do This Every Day: Selected Poems of Lillian Allen*. Toronto: Women's Press, 1993. Print.

Anderson, Benedict. *Imagined Communities: Reflection on the Origin and Spread of Nationalism*. London: Verso, 1983. Print.

Antwi, Phanuel. "Rough Play: Reading Black Masculinity in Austin Clarke's 'Sometimes, a Motherless Child' and Dionne Brand's *What We All Long For*." *Studies in Canadian Literature* 34.2 (2009): 194–222. Print.

Appadurai, Arjun. *Modernity at Large: Cultural Dimensions of Globalization*. Minneapolis: University of Minnesota Press, 1996. Print.

Appiah, Kwame Anthony. "Identity, Authenticity, Survival: Multicultural Societies and Social Reproduction." *Multiculturalism*. Ed. Amy Gutman. Princeton, NJ: Princeton University Press, 1994. Print.

– "Racisms." *The Anatomy of Racism*. Ed. David Theo Goldberg. Minneapolis: University of Minnesota Press, 1990. 3–17. Print.

Armstrong, Jeanette C. *Slash*. Penticton, BC: Theytus Books, 2002. Print.

Armstrong, John A. "Mobilized and Proletarian Diasporas." *American Political Science Review* 70 (1976): 393–408.

Atwood, Margaret. *Surfacing*. Toronto: McClelland & Stewart, 1972. Print.

Ball, John Clement. "White City, Black Ancestry: the Immigrant's Toronto in the Stories of Austin Clarke and Dionne Brand." *Open Letter* 8 (Winter 1994): 9–19. Print.

Bannerji, Himani. *Returning the Gaze: Essays on Racism, Feminism, and Politics*. Toronto: Sister Vision Press, 1994. Print.

Banting, Keith and Will Kymlicka. "Canadian Multiculturalism: Global Anxieties and Local Debates." *British Journal of Canadian Studies* 23.1: 43–72. Print.

Barrett, Paul. "Dreaming of the Millions: Austin Clarke's *More*." *Historical Perspectives on Canadian Publishing*. McMaster University. Web. 10 Oct. 2010.

Bauman, Zygmunt. *In Search of Politics*. Stanford: Stanford University Press, 1999. Print.

– *Liquid Life*. London: Polity Press, 2005. Print.

Beckford, Sharon Morgan. "A Geography of Mind: Black Canadian Women Writers as Cartographers of the Canadian Imagination." *Journal of Black Studies* 38.3 (Jan. 2008): 461–83. Print.

Benjamin, Walter. "Theses on the Philosophy of History." *Illuminations*. Ed. Hannah Arendt. New York: Harcourt, Brace & World, 1968. Print.

Bentley, D.M.R. "Colonial Colonizing: An Introductory Survey of the Canadian Long Poem." *Bolder Flights: Essays on the Canadian Long Poem*. Ed. Frank M. Tierney and Angela Robbeson. Ottawa: University of Ottawa Press, 1998. 7–29. Print.

– *Mimic Fires: Accounts of Early Long Poems on Canada*. Montreal: McGill-Queen's University Press, 1994. Print.

Best, Carrie M. "*That Lonesome Road*." Clarke 118–23. Print.

Bhabha, Homi. *Nation and Narration*. London: Routledge, 1990. Print.

– *The Location of Culture*. London: Routledge, 1994. Print.

Bissoondath, Neil. *Selling Illusions: The Cult of Multiculturalism in Canada*. Revised Edition. Toronto: Penguin, 2002. Print.

– *The Innocence of Age*. Toronto: Knopf Canada, 1992. Print.

Blatchford, Christie. "Blacks Cry 'Shame' as Jury Finds Policemen Not Guilty." *Toronto Star* 14 Nov. 1980. A1+. Print.

– "Daughter's Testimony Ruled Unacceptable." *Toronto Star* 13 Nov. 1980: A1+. Print.

– "'I Would Have Shot,' Police Trial Told." *Toronto Star* 30 Oct. 1980: A2. Print.

– "Police Feared 'Berserk' Man Would Hurt Family, Trial Told." *Toronto Star* 7 Nov. 1980: A2. Print.

– "What the Jury Didn't Hear in the Albert Johnson Case." *Toronto Star* 14 Nov. 1980: A10. Print.

Borden, George A. "*Plantation North*." Clarke 162–3. Print.
Bourdieu, Pierre. *Pascalian Meditations*. Palo Alto: Stanford University Press, 2000. Print.
Brah, Avtar. *Cartographies of Diaspora*. New York: Routledge, 1996. Print.
Brand, Dionne. *A Map to the Door of No Return: Notes to Belonging*. Toronto: Vintage Canada, 2002. Print.
– *At the Full and Change of the Moon*. Toronto: Vintage Canada, 1999. Print.
– "Bathurst." *Bread Out of Stone*: 67–82.
– *Bread Out of Stone*. Toronto: Coach House Press, 1994. Print.
– *In Another Place, Not Here*. New York: Grove Press, 1996. Print.
– *Inventory*. Toronto: McClelland & Stewart, 2006. Print.
– *Land to Light On*. Toronto: McClelland & Stewart, 1997. Print.
– *Map to the Door of No Return*. Toronto: Random House Canada, 2002. Print.
– *No Language Is Neutral*. Toronto: McClelland & Stewart, 1998. Print.
– *Ossuaries*. Toronto: McClelland & Stewart, 2010. Print.
– *Primitive Offensive*. Toronto: Williams-Wallace, 1982. Print.
– *thirsty*. Toronto: McClelland & Stewart, 2002. Print.
– "This Body for Itself." *Bread Out of Stone*. 250. Print.
– "Water More Than Flour." *Bread Out of Stone*. 123–30. Print.
– *What We All Long For*. Toronto: Vintage Canada, 2005. Print.
– "'We Weren't Allowed to Go into the Factory until Hitler Started the War': The 1920s to the 1940s." Bristow et al. 171–92. Print.
Bristow, Peggy, et al. *We're Rooted Here and They Can't Pull Us Up*. Toronto: University of Toronto Press, 1994. Print.
Brontë, Charlotte. *Jane Eyre*. 1847. Ed. Margaret Smith. Oxford: Oxford University Press, 1998. Print.
Brown, Ron. *Behind Bars: Inside Ontario's Heritage Gaols*. Toronto: Natural Heritage/National History, 2006. Print.
Brown, Michael K. *Whitewashing Race*. Berkeley: University of California Press, 2003. Print.
Brydon, Diana. "Dionne Brand's Global Intimacies: Practising Affective Citizenship." *University of Toronto Quarterly* 76.3 (2007): 990–1006. Print.
– "Detour Canada: Rerouting the Black Atlantic, Reconfiguring the Postcolonial." *Reconfigurations: Canadian Literatures and Postcolonial Identities*. Ed. Marc Maufort and Franca Bellarsi. Brussels, Belgium: Peter Lang, 2002. 109–21. Print.
Bucknor, Michael. "Voices Under the Window of Representation: Austin Clarke's Poetics of Body Memory in *The Meeting Point*." *Journal of West Indian Literature*. 13.1 – 2 (2005): 141–175. Print.
Butler, Judith. *Bodies That Matter*. London: Routledge, 1993. Print.

– *Gender Trouble*. London: Routledge, 1990. Print.
– *Precarious Life*. New York: Verso Press, 2004. Print.
Butler, Judith, Ernesto Laclau and Slavoj Zizek. *Contingency, Hegemony, Universality*.London: Verso Press, 2000. Print.
Canada. Canadian Citizenship Branch. *Notes on the Canadian Family Tree*. Ottawa: Department of Citizenship and Immigration, 1960. Print.
– Ministry of Indian Affairs and Northern Development. *Statement of the Government of Canada on Indian Policy*. Ottawa: Department of Indian Affairs and Northern Development, 1969. Print.
Canadian Multiculturalism Act. Bill C-93. 21 July 1988. Print.
Carriere, Vianney. "Had 'Nowhere to Go,' Jury Told Feared for His Life, Constable Testifies." *Globe and Mail* [Toronto] 7 Nov. 1980: P.5. Print.
– "Witnesses for Constables Testify Police Were at Johnson's at Least Twice Before." *Globe and Mail* [Toronto] 5 Nov. 1980: P.5. Print.
Carriere, Vianney and Howard Fluxgold. "Two Policemen Are Acquitted by Jury in Johnson Shooting." *Globe and Mail* [Toronto] 14 Nov 1980: P1. Print.
Casas, Maria. "Codes as Identity: The Bilingual Representation of a Fragmented Literary Subject." *Language and Discourse* 2 (1994): 54–61. Print.
– "Orality and the Body in the Poetry of Lillian Allen and Dionne Brand." *Ariel* 33.2 (2002): 7–32. Print.
– "Codes as Identity: The Bilingual Representations of a Fragmented Literary Subject." *Language and Discourse* 2 (1994): 54–61. Print.
Casteel, Sarah. "Experiences of Arrival: Jewishness and Caribbean-Canadian Identity in Austin Clarke's *The Meeting Point*." *The Journal of West Indian Literature*. 14.1 - 2 (2006): 113–40. Print.
Chariandy, David. "'That's What You Want, Isn't It?' Austin Clarke and the Politics of Recognition." *The Journal of West Indian Literature* 14.1–2 (November 2005): 141–61. Print.
– *Soucouyant*. Vancouver: Arsenal Pulp Press, 2007. Print.
Cheah, Pheng. "Given Culture: Rethinking Cosmopolitical Freedom in Translation." *boundary 2* 24.2 (Summer 1997): 157–97. Print.
Cho, Lily. "The Turn to Diaspora." *Topia* 17 (Spring 2007): 11–30. Print.
Christian, Barbara. "What Celie Knows That You Should Know." *Anatomy of Racism*. Ed. David Theo Goldberg. Minneapolis: U of Minnesota Press, 1990. 135–45. Print.
City of Brampton – Directions to Brampton. City of Brampton. 2010. Web. 10xNov. 2010.
Clarke, Austin. "Canadian Experience." *Choosing His Coffin: The Best Stories of Austin Clarke*. Toronto: Thomas Allen, 1996. 23–40. Print.
– "Don't Shoot!" *Callaloo* 29.2 (Spring 2006): 254–63. Print.

– *Growing Up Stupid under the Union Jack*. 1980. Toronto: McClelland and Stewart, 2005. Print.
– "I'm Running for My Life." *Choosing His Coffin: The Best Stories of Austin Clarke*. Toronto: Thomas Allen, 1996. 41–62. Print.
– *In This City*. Toronto: Exile Editions, 1992. Print.
– *More*. Toronto: Thomas Allen, 2008. Print.
– Personal Interview. 24 Mar. 2009.
– *Public Enemies: Police Violence and Black Youth*. Toronto: HarperCollins, 1992. Print.
– "Sometimes, a Motherless Child." *Choosing His Coffin: The Best Stories of Austin Clarke*. Toronto: Thomas Allen, 1996. 327–64. Print.
– *The Survivors of the Crossing*. Toronto: McClelland & Stewart, 1964. Print.
– *The Origin of Waves*. Toronto: McClelland & Stewart, 2003. Print.
– *The Polished Hoe*. Toronto: Thomas Allen, 2003. Print.
– "Why I Call Johnson Killing Murderous" *Contrast* [Toronto] 30 Aug 1979: 12. Print.

Clarke, George Elliott. *Eyeing the North Star: Directions in African-Canadian Literature* Toronto: McClelland and Stewart, 1997. Print.
– "For a Multicultural, Multi-faith, Multiracial Canada: A Manifesto." *Home and Native Land: Unsettling Multiculturalism in Canada*. Ed. May Chazan, et al. Toronto: Between The Lines, 2012. 51–7. Print.
– "Harris, Philip, Brand: Three Authors in Search of Literate Criticism." *Journal of Canadian Studies* 35.1 (2000): 161–89. Print.
– *Odysseys Home: Mapping African Canadian Literature*. Toronto: University of Toronto Press, 2002. Print.
– Rev. of *A Map to the Door of No Return: Notes to Belonging*, by Dionne Brand. *University of Toronto Quarterly* 72.1 (Winter 2002/3): 557–8. Print.
– "Treason of the Black Intellectuals" *Athabasca University: Canadian Writers*. Web. 6 May 2012.

Clarke, George Elliott, ed. *Fire on the Water: An Anthology of Black Nova Scotian Writing*. 2 vols. Porter's Lake, NS: Pottersfield, 1991–1992. Print.

Clegg, Ian. "Workers and Managers in Algeria." *Peasants and Proletarians: The Struggles of Third World Workers Ed.* Robin Cohen, Peter C.W. Gutkind and Phyllis Brazier. New York: Monthly Review Press, 1979. 223–47. Print.

Cohen, Robin. *Global Diasporas: An Introduction*. Washington: University of Washington Press, 1997. Print.

Coleman, Daniel. *Masculine Migrations*. Toronto: University of Toronto Press, 1998. Print.
– *White Civility: The Literary Project of English Canada*. Toronto: University of Toronto Press, 2006. Print.

Collins, Patricia Hill. *Black Feminist Thought*. New York: Routledge, 2000. Print.

Compton, Wayde, ed. *Bluesprint: Black British Columbian Literature and Orature*. Vancouver: Arsenal Pulp Press, 2001. Print.

Coltrane, John. *A Love Supreme*. John Coltrane, Jimmy Garrison, Elvin Jones, McCoy Tyner. Impulse!, 1965. CD.

Cook, Meira. "The Partisan Body: Performance and the Female Body in Dionne Brand's *No Language is Neutral*." *Open Letter* 9.2 (1995): 88–91. Print.

"Cop Changed Statement, Johnson Trial Told." *Contrast* [Toronto] 7 Nov 1980: 3. Print.

Craig, Terence. *Racial Attitudes in English-Canadian Fiction, 1905 – 1980*. Waterloo: Wilfrid Laurier Press, 1984. Print.

Dabydeen, Cyril. *Black Jesus and Other Stories*. Toronto: TSAR Publications, 1997. Print.

Davey, Frank. *Post-National Arguments: The Politics of the Anglophone-Canadian Novel Since 1967*. Toronto: University of Toronto Press, 1993. Print.

– "The Language of the Contemporary Canadian Long Poem" *Surviving the Paraphrase*. Winnipeg: Turnstone, 1983. 184–92. Print.

Davies, Carole Boyce. *Black Women, Writing and Identity: Migrations of the subject*. London: Routledge, 1994. Print.

Davis, Andrea. "Black Canadian Literature as Diaspora Transgression: *The Second Life of Samuel Tyne*" *Topia* 17 (Spring 2007): 31–49. Print.

Day, Richard. *Multiculturalism and the History of Canadian Diversity*. Toronto: University of Toronto Press, 2000. Print.

Delany, Martin. *Blake: Or the Huts of America*. Boston: Beacon Press, 1970. Print.

Dickinson, Peter. *Here Is Queer: Nationalisms, Sexualities, and the Literatures of Canada*. Toronto: University of Toronto Press, 1999. Print.

Dirlik, Arif. "The Postcolonial Aura: Third World Criticism in the Age of Global Capitalism" *Critical Inquiry*. 20.2 (Winter 1994): 328–56. Print.

Djwa, Sandra. "Pratt's Modernism, or Digging in the Strata." *Bolder Flights: Essays on the Canadian Long Poem*. Ed. Angelo Robbeson and Frank M. Tierney. Ottawa: University of Ottawa Press, 1998. 680. Print.

Dobson, Kit. *Transnational Canadas: Anglo-Canadian Literature and Globalization*. Waterloo: Wilfrid Laurier Press, 2009. Print.

Dominguez, Pilar Cuder. "On Black Canadian Writing: In Conversation with George Elliott Clarke." *Atlantis* 23.2 (Dec 2001): 187–200. Print.

Du Bois, William Edward Burghardt. *The Souls of Black Folk*. 1903. Ed. Henry Louis Gates Jr. and Terri Hume Oliver. New York: Norton Critical Edition, 1999. Print.

Dunton, A. Davidson *et al*. *Royal Commission on Bilingualism and Biculturalism: Book I: The Official Languages*. 4 vols. Ottawa: Governor General, 1967. Print.

– *Royal Commission on Bilingualism and Biculturalism.* Volume 4. *The Cultural Contributions of the Other Ethnic Groups.* Ottawa: Governor General, 1969. Print.

Dutton, Don. "Police Gun Down Father of Four Waving Lawn Tool." *Toronto Star* 27 Aug. 1979: A1+. Print.

Dutton, Don and Mietkiewicz. "Albert Johnson 'Needed Help'." *Toronto Star* 29 Aug. 1979: A2. Print.

Dyer, Richard. *White.* London: Routledge, 1997. Print.

Edugyan, Esi. *The Second Life of Samuel Tyne.* Toronto: HarperCollins, 2004. Print.

Ellison, Ralph. *Invisible Man.* New York: Random House, 1952. Print.

Engel, Marian. *Bear.* Toronto: New Canadian Library, 1976. Print.

Fabiani, Louise. Rev. of *Land to Light On,* by Dionne Brand. *Arc* 41 (1998): 66–8. Print.

Fanon, Frantz. *Black Skin, White Masks.* Trans. Charles Lam Markmann. New York: Grove Press, 1952. Print.

– "Racism and Culture."*Towards the African Revolution.* Ed. Francois Maspero. Trans. Haakon Chevalier. New York: Grove Press, 1967. 31–44. Print.

– *The Wretched of the Earth.* Trans. Richard Philcox. New York: Grove Press, 1961. Print.

Fiasco, Lupe. "Kick Push." *Lupe Fiasco's Food & Liquor.* Atlantic, 2006. CD.

– "The Cool."*Lupe Fiasco's Food & Liquor.* Atlantic, 2006. CD.

Firestone, Shulamith. *The Dialectic of Sex.* London: Jonathan Cape Press, 1970. Print.

Forster, Sophia. "'Inventory Is Useless Now but Just to Say': The Politics of Ambivalence in Dionne Brand's *Land to Light On.*" *Studies in Canadian Literature* 27.2 (2002): 160–82. Print.

Foster, Cecil. *A Place Called Heaven: The Meaning of Being Black in Canada.* Toronto: Harper Collins, 1996. Print.

– *Blackness and Modernity: The Colour of Humanity and the Quest for Freedom.* Montreal: McGill-Queen's University Press, 2007. Print.

– *Slammin' Tar.* Toronto: Random House, 1998. Print.

Foucault, Michel. *Discipline and Punish.* Trans. Alan Sheridan. New York: Vintage Books, 1979. Print.

– "Nietzsche, Genealogy, History." *The Foucault Reader.* Ed. Paul Rabinow. Toronto: Random House, 1984. 76–100. Print.

Freire, Paulo. *Pedagogy of the Oppressed.* New York: Continuum International, 1970. Print.

Freiwald, Bina Toledo. "Cartographies of Be/Longing: Dionne Brand's *In Another Place, Not Here.*" *Mapping Canadian Cultural Space: Essays on Canadian Literature.* Ed. Danielle Schaud. Jerusalem: Magnes, 1998. 37–53. Print.

Frye, Northrop. *The Bush Garden: Essays on the Canadian Imagination*. Toronto: House of Anansi Press, 1971. Print.

Gates, Henry Louis. Jr. "Critical Fanonism." *Critical Inquiry*. 17 (Spring 1991): 456–70. Print.

– "Wonders of the African World." Screenwriter and Narrator. Six-part series, BBC/PBS, 1999. DVD.

Garner, Steve. *Whiteness:An Introduction*. New York: Routledge, 2007. Print.

Garvey, Johanna X. K. "The Place She Miss': Exile, Memory, and Resistance InDionne Brand's Fiction." *Callaloo* 26 (2003): 486–503. Print.

Georgis, Dina. "Cultures of Expulsion: Memory, Longing and the Queer Space of Diaspora." *New Dawn: Journal of Black Canadian Studies* 1.1 (2006): n. pag. Web. 10 December 2009.

– "Mother Nations and the Persistence of 'Not Here'." *Canadian Woman Studies* 20.2 (2000): 27–34. Print.

Gilbert, Sandra and Susan Gubar. *The Madwoman in the Attic: The Woman Writer and the Nineteenth-Century Literary Imagination*. New Haven, CT: YaleUP, 1979. Print.

Gilroy, Paul. *Against Race*. Cambridge: Harvard University Press, 2000. Print.

– *Darker Than Blue: On the Moral Economies of Black Atlantic Culture*. Cambridge, MA: Harvard UP, 2010. Print.

– "One Nation Under a Groove: The Cultural Politics of 'Race' and Racism in Great Britain." Ed. David Theo Goldberg. *Multiculturalism: A Critical Reader*. Oxford: Blackwell, 1994. 263–82. Print.

– *The Black Atlantic: Modernity and Double-Consciousness*. Cambridge: Harvard University Press, 1993. Print.

Giroux. Henry A. "Cultural Studies, Public Pedagogy, and the Responsibility of Intellectuals." *Communication and Critical/Cultural Studies*. 1.1 (March 2004): 59–79. Print.

– *Ideology, Culture and the Process of Schooling*. Philadelphia, PA: Temple University Press, 1981. Print.

– "Insurgent Multiculturalism and the Promise of Pedagogy." Ed. David Theo Goldberg. *Multiculturalism: A Critical Reader*. Oxford: Blackwell, 1994. 325–43. Print.

Goldberg, David Theo. *Anatomy of Racism*. Minneapolis: University of Minnesota Press, 1990. Print.

Goldman, Marlene. "Mapping the Door of No Return: Deterritorialization and the Work of Dionne Brand." *Canadian Literature* 182 (2004): 13–28. Print.

Gopinath, Gayatri. *Impossible Desires: Queer Diasporas and South Asian Public Cultures*. Durham, NC: Duke University Press, 2005. Print.

Grange, Hamlin. "Police Told Man to Kneel Then Fired: Daughter." *Contrast* [Toronto] 30 Aug. 1979: 1. Print.

Grant, George. *Lament for a Nation: The Defeat of Canadian Nationalism.* Montreal: McGill-Queen's Press, 1965. Print.

Grewal, Inderpal and Caren Kaplan, ed. *Scattered Hegemonies.* Minneapolis: University of Minnesota Press, 1993. Print.

Griffin, Sarah Jasmine. "Textual Healing: Claiming Black Women's Bodies, the Erotic and Resistance in Contemporary Novels of Slavery." *Callaloo* 19.2 (1996): 519–536. Print.

Gubar, Susan. "What Ails Feminist Criticism?" *Critical Inquiry* 24 (Summer 1998): 878–902. Print.

Habermas, Jürgen. "The Public Sphere." *The Information Society Reader.* Ed. Frank Webster and Raimo Blom. London: Routledge, 2004. 350–6. Print.

Hall, Stuart. "Cultural Identity and Diaspora." *Theorizing Diaspora: A Reader.* Ed. Jane Evans Braziel and Anita Mannur. Oxford: Blackwell Publishing, 2003. 233–46. Print.

– "Encoding/Decoding." *Culture, Media, Language.* Ed. Stuart Hall, Dorothy Hobson, Andrew Lowe, and Paul Willis. New York: Routledge, 1980. 117–27. Print.

– "New Ethnicities." *Stuart Hall: Critical Dialogues in Cultural Studies.* Ed. David Morley and Kuan-Hsing Chen. New York: Routledge, 1996. 441–9. Print.

– *Representations: Cultural Representations and Signifying Practices.* London: The Open University, 1997. Print.

– "The Whites of Their Eyes: Racist Ideologies and the Media." *Gender, Race, and Class in Media.* Ed. Gail Dinec and Jean M. Humez. New Delhi: SAGE, 2011. 81–4. Print.

– "What Is This 'Black' in Popular Culture?" *Stuart Hall: Critical Dialogues in Cultural Studies.* Ed. David Morley and Kuan-Hsing Chen. New York: Routledge, 1996. 4675. Print.

Hamilton, Sylvia. *"In My Neighbourhood."* Clarke 95. Print.

Haque, Eve. *Multiculturalism within a Bilingual Framework: Language, Race, and Belonging in Canada.* Toronto: University of Toronto Press, 2012. Print.

Haraway, Donna. *Primate Visions: Gender, Race and Nature in the World of Modern Science.* New York: Routledge, 1990. Print.

Harewood, John. "Learning from the Johnson Killing." *Contrast* [Toronto] 27 Sept. 1979: 9. Print.

Harris, Claire. *Drawing Down a Daughter.* Fredericton, New Brunswick: Goose Lane Editions, 1992. Print.

Hartigan, John. *Odd Tribes: Towards a Cultural Analysis of White People.* Durham, NC: Duke UP, 2005. Print.

Härting, Heike. "Performative Metaphors in Austin Clarke's *The Origin of Waves." Adjacencies: Minority Writing in Canada.* Toronto: Guernica Editions, 2004. 103–27. Print.

Hartman, Saidiya. *Lose Your Mother: A Journey along the Atlantic Slave Route.* New York: Farrar, Straus and Giroux, 2007. Print.

Haslett, Tim. "Hortense Spillers Interviewed by Tim Haslett for the Black Cultural Studies Web Site Collective." *Black Cultural Studies.* 4 Feb. 1998: n. pag. Web. 10 Aug 2010.

Hawthorne, Harry B. *A Survey of the Contemporary Indians of Canada: A Report on Economic, Political, Educational Needs and Policies in Two Volumes.* Ottawa: Indian Affairs Branch, 1966. Print.

Henderson, Carol. *Scarring the Black Body: Race and Representation in African American Literature.* Columbia, Missouri: University of Missouri Press, 2002. Print.

Henry, Frances and Carol Tator. *Discourses of Domination: Racial Bias in the English-Language Press.* Toronto: University of Toronto Press, 2002. Print.

Henry, V. "'Outraged' at Shooting Headline." Letter. *Toronto Star* 3 Sept. 1979: A9. Print.

"Heritage." *The Oxford English Dictionary.* 2006. Print.

Hluchy, Patricia. "Angry Jamaicans Shout at Slaying Probe Team." *Toronto Star* 30 Aug. 1979: A3. Print.

Hogg, Peter W. *Canada Act 1982 Annotated.* Toronto: Carswell Company, 1982. Print.

hooks, bell. *Yearning: Race, Gender, and Cultural Politics.* Toronto: Between the Lines, 1990. Print.

Howard-Pitney, David. *The African American Jeremiad: Appeals for Justice in America.* Philadelphia, PA: Temple University Press, 2005. Print.

Hull, Gloria T., Patricia Bell Scott, and Barbara Smith, eds. *All the Women Are White, All the Blacks Are Men, but Some of Us Are Brave.* New York: The Feminist Press, 1982. Print.

Hunter, Lynette. "After Modernism: Alternative Voices in the Writings of Dionne Brand, Claire Harris and Marlene Philip." *University of Toronto Quarterly* 62.2 (1992/1993): 256–281. Print.

Hunter, Patrick. "Johnson May Be the Start of Something Big." *Contrast* [Toronto] 20 Sept. 1979: 9. Print.

Hutcheon, Linda. *The Canadian Postmodern: A Study of Contemporary Canadian Fiction.* Oxford: Oxford University Press, 1988. Print.

Indian Chiefs of Alberta. "Citizens Plus." *Aboriginal Policy Studies.* 1.1 (2011): 188–281. Print.

ItszMiszDattu. "I Smell Like Curry & I'm a Terrorist." *Youtube.* Web. 15 May 2012.

Jacobs, Harriet. *Incidents in the Life of a Slave Girl, Written By Herself.* Boston, 1861. Print.

JanMohamed, Abdul R., and David Lloyd, ed. *The Nature and Context of Minority Discourse*. London: Oxford University Press, 1990. Print.

The Jerusalem Bible. Alexander Jones, Gen. Ed. New York: Doubleday, 1966. Print.

Johansen, Emily. "'Streets Are the Dwelling Place of the Collective': Public Space and Cosmopolitan Citizenship in Dionne Brand's *What We All Long For*." *Canadian Literature* 196 (Spring 2008): 48–62. Print.

Johnson, Erica L. "Unforgetting Trauma: Dionne Brand's Haunted Histories." *Anthurium* 2.1 (Spring 2004): n. pag. *LION*. Web. 5 Sept. 2010.

Jones, Manina. "The Language of Paradox." Rev. of *On the Edge of Genre: The Contemporary Canadian Long Poem*, by Smaro Kamboureli. *Canadian Poetry* 31 (Fall/Winter 1992): 104–16. Print.

Jordan, June. "Nobody Mean More to Me Than You and the Future Life of Willie Jordan." *Harvard Educational Review* 58.3 (Aug 2008): 363–74. Print.

Joseph. Maia. "Wondering into Country: Dionne Brand's *A Map to the Door of No Return*." *Canadian Literature* 193 (2007): 792. Print.

Kamboureli, Smaro. *On the Edge of Genre: The Contemporary Canadian Long Poem*. Toronto: University of Toronto Press, 1991. Print.

– *Scandalous Bodies: Diasporic Literature in English Canada*. Oxford: Oxford University Press, 2000. Print.

Kamboureli, Smaro, and Roy Miki, ed. *Trans.Can.Lit: Resituating the Study of Canadian Literature*. Waterloo, Ont: Wilfred Laurier Press, 2007. Print.

Keane, John. "Structural Transformations of the Public Sphere." *The Information Society Reader*. Ed. Frank Webster and Raimo Blom. London: Routledge, 2004. 350–356. Print.

Keeling, Kara. *The Witch's Flight: The Cinematic, The Black Femme, and The Image of Common Sense*. Durham, NC: Duke University Press, 2006. Print.

Kertzer, Jonathan. *Worrying the Nation: Imagining a National Literature in Canada*. Toronto: University of Toronto Press, 1998. Print.

King, Thomas. *Green Grass, Running Water*. Toronto: Houghton Mifflin, 1993. Print.

Kroetsch, Robert. "For Play and Entrance: The Contemporary Canadian Long Poem." *The Lovely Treachery of Words*. Toronto: Oxford University Press, 1989. 11134. Print.

Kymlicka, Will. *Liberalism, Community and Culture*. Oxford: Oxford University Press, 1989. Print.

– *Multicultural Citizenship*. Oxford: Oxford University Press, 1995. Print.

– *Politics in the Vernacular: Nationalism, Multiculturalism and Citizenship*. Oxford: Oxford University Press, 2001. Print.

– "Invited Symposium: New Directions and Issues for the Study of Ethnicity, Nationalism, and Multiculturalism: Multiculturalism in Normative Theory and Social Science." *Ethnicities* 11(1) 5–11. Print.

Laclau Ernesto, and Chantal Mouffe. *Hegemony and Socialist Strategy: Towards a Radical Democratic Politics*. New York: Verso Press, 2001. Print.

Laferrière, Dany. *Comment faire l'amour avec un nègre sans se fatiguer*. Montreal: Typo, 1985. Print.

LandonProductions. "Racist White Girl HATES Brown People?!" *Youtube*. Web. 20 June 2012.

Lazarus, Neil. "Disavowing Decolonization: Fanon, Nationalism, and the Question of Representation in Postcolonial Theory." *Frantz Fanon: Critical Perspectives*. Ed. Anthony Alessandrini. London: Routledge, 1999. 161–94. Print.

Lewis, Stephen. *Report to the Premier on Racism in Ontario*. (Summer 1992). Print.

Littman, Sol. "Assessing the Effects of the Johnson Case." *Toronto Star* 6 Dec. 1980: B1+. Print.

Lorde, Audre. "Good Mirrors Are Not Cheap." *The Collected Poems of Audre Lorde*. New York: W.W. Norton, 1997. 67. Print.

– *Sister Outsider: Essays and Speeches*. Trumansburg, NY: The Crossing Press, 1984. Print.

Mackey, Eva. *The House of Difference: Cultural Politics and National Identity in Canada*. London: Routledge, 1999. Print.

Mallet, Gina. "Multiculturalism: Has Diversity Gone Too Far." *Globe and Mail* [Toronto] 15 Mar. 1997: D.1. Print.

Mason, Jody. "Searching for the Door*way*: Dionne Brand's *thirsty*." *University of Toronto Quarterly*. 75.2 (Spring 2006): 784–800. Print.

Mayr, Suzette. *Venous Hum*. Vancouver: Arsenal Pulp Press, 2004. Print.

Mbembe, Achille. "Necropolitcs" *Public Culture* 15.1 (2003): 11–40. Print.

McCallum, Pamela and Christian Olbey. "Written in the Scars: History, Genre and Materiality in Dionne Brand's *In Another Place, Not Here*." *Essays on Canadian Writing* 68 (1999): 159–82. Print.

McClintock, Anne. *Imperial Leather: Race, Gender, and Sexuality in the Colonial Context*. New York: Routledge, 1995. Print.

McClintock, Anne, Aamir Mufti, and Ella Shohat. *Dangerous Liaisons: Gender, Nation Postcolonial Perspectives*. Minneapolis: University of Minnesota Press, 1997. Print.

McKay, Albert. "'Where Would We Be without the Police?'" Letter. *Toronto Star* 5 Sept. 1979: A9. Print.

McKibbin, Molly. "The Possibilities of Home." *Journal of Black Studies* 38 (2008): 502–18. Print.

McKittrick, Katherine. *Demonic Grounds: Black Women and the Cartographies of Struggle*. Minneapolis: University of Minnesota Press, 2006. Print.

– "'Their Blood Is There and They Can't Throw It Out:' Honouring Black Geographies." *Topia* 7 (Spring 2002): 27–37. Print.

McWatt, Tessa. *Out of My Skin*. Toronto: Riverbank, 1998. Print.

Mercer, Kobena. "Diaspora Culture and the Dialogic Imagination: The Aesthetics of Black Independent Film in Britain." *Theorizing Diaspora: A Reader*. Ed. Jane Evans Braziel and Anita Mannur. Oxford: Blackwell Publishing, 2003. 247–60. Print.

Meyer, Susan L. "Colonialism and the Figurative Strategy of *Jane Eyre*." *Victorian Studies*. 33.2 (Winter, 1990): 247–68. Print.

Miller, Pearl. "'Sick and Tired of Cries of Racism' in Police Shooting, Reader Complains." Letter. *Toronto Star* 5 Sept. 1979: A9. Print.

Mills, Charles. "Racial Exploitation and the Wages of Whiteness." *What White Looks Like: African-American Philosophers on the Whiteness Question*. Ed. George Yancy. New York: Routledge, 2004. 25–54. Print.

Mironowicz, Margaret and Yves Lavigne. "Man Fatally Shot inside His Home by Police Officer." *Globe and Mail* [Toronto] 27 Aug. 1979: P.1. Print.

Mohanty, Chandra Talpade, Ann Russo, and Lourdes Torres, Ed. *Third World Women and the Politics of Feminism*. Bloomington, Indiana: Indiana University Press, 1991. Print.

Moodie, Susanna. *Roughing It in the Bush*. London: Richard Bentley, 1852. Print.

Mootoo, Shani. *Cereus Blooms at Night*. Toronto: McClelland & Stewart, 1996. Print.

Morrison, Toni. *Beloved*. New York: Random House, 1987. Print.

– *Playing in the Dark: Whiteness and the Literary Imagination*. New York: Vintage, 1993. Print.

Moses, Wilson. *Black Messiahs and Uncle Toms: Social and Literary Manipulations of a Religious Myth*. University Park, PA: Penn State Press. 1993. Print.

Mouffe, Chantal. "For a Politics of Nomadic Identity."*Traveller's Tales: Narratives of Home and Displacement*. Ed. George Robertson et al. New York: Routledge, 1994. 105–13. Print.

Mukherjee, Arun Prabha. *Oppositional Aesthetics: Readings from a Hyphenated Space*. Toronto: TSAR Publications, 1994. Print.

Narain, Denise de Caires. *Contemporary Caribbean Women's Poetry: Making Style*. New York: Routledge, 2004. Print.

Oakes, Gary. "Drunk Who Aimed Rifle at Police Gets Two Months." *Toronto Star* 7 Sept. 1979: A3. Print.

Olbey, Christian. "Dionne Brand in Conversation." *Ariel* 33.2 (2002): 87–102. Print.

Ong, Aihwa. *Neoliberalism as Exception: Mutations in Citizenship and Sovereignty*. Durham, NC: Duke University Press, 2006. Print.

– *Flexible Citizenship*. Durham, NC: Duke University Press, 1999. Print.
Parry, Benita. "Problems in Current Theories of Colonial Discourse." *Oxford Literary Review* 9 (1987): 27–58. Print.
– "Signs of Our Times: Discussion of Homi Bhabha's *The Location of Culture*." *Third Text* 8.28–29 (1994): 5–24. Print.
Pawis, Kyla. "Brampton Problems." *Youtube*. Web. 6 June 2012.
Peters, Russell. *Call Me Russell*. Toronto: Doubleday Canada, 2010. Print.
Philip, Marlene Nourbese. *Frontiers: Essays and Writings on Racism and Culture*. Toronto: Mercury Press, 1992. Print.
– *She Tries Her Tongue, Her Silence Softly Breaks*. Toronto: Ragweed, 1989. Print.
Plumwood, Valerie. *Feminism and the Mastery of Nature*. London: Routledge, 1993. Print.
Razack, Sherene. *Looking White People in the Eye*. Toronto: University of Toronto Press, 1998. Print.
– *Casting Out: The Eviction of Muslims from Western Law and Politics*. Toronto: University of Toronto Press, 2008. Print.
Renk, Kathleen J. "Her Words Are Like Fire': The Storytelling Magic of Dionne Brand." *Ariel* 27 (1996): 97–111. Print.
Rich, Adrienne. "Notes toward a Politics of Location." *Blood Bread and Poetry: Selected Prose, 1979 – 1985*. New York: W.W. Norton, 1986. 239–56. Print.
Roach, Maureen. "Albert Was 'Victim of Harassment' Says Family." *Contrast* [Toronto] 30 Aug. 1979: 9. Print.
Sarbadhikary, Krishna. "Recovering History: The Poems of Dionne Brand." *Intersexions: Issues of Race and Gender in Canadian Women's Writing*. Ed. Coomi S. Vevaina and Barbara Godard. New Delhi: Creative, 1996. 116–130. Print.
Saul, Joanne. "'In the Middle of Becoming': Dionne Brand's Historical Vision." *Canadian Woman Studies* 23.2 (2004): 59–63. Print.
Scarry, Elaine. *The Body in Pain: The Making and Unmaking of the World*. London: Oxford University Press, 1985. Print.
Schuller, Malini Johar. *Locating Race: Global Sites of Post-Colonial Citizenship*. Albany: State University of New York Press, 2009. Print.
Scott, David. *Conscripts of Modernity: The Tragedy of Colonial Enlightenment*. Durham, NC: Duke UP, 2004. Print.
Scowen, Peter. "Four Comics Walk into a Breakfast Bar." *Globe and Mail* [Toronto] 30 Oct. 2010: Web. 20 Nov. 2010.
"Seen the Typical Canadian Lately." Advertisement. *Contrast* [Toronto] May 1980. Print.
Selvon, Sam. *The Lonely Londoners*. London: Alan Wingate, 1956. Print.
Sharpe, Christina. *Monstrous Intimacies: Making Post-Slavery Subjects*. Durham, NC: Duke UP, 2010. Print.

Shulman, Morton. "Our police deserve praise." *Contrast* [Toronto] 13 Sept. 1979: 3. Print.
Silvera, Makeda. *The Heart Does Not Bend*. Toronto: Vintage Canada, 2003. Print.
Smith, Barbara. "Toward a Black Feminist Criticism." *The New Feminist Criticism*. Ed. Elaine Showalter. New York: Pantheon, 1985. 168–85. Print.
Smith, Robert. "Jamaica Shouldn't Get Involved." Letter. *Toronto Star* 5 Sept. 1979: A9. Print.
Smyth, Heather. "'The Being Together of Strangers': Dionne Brand's Politics of Difference and the Limits of Multicultural Discourse." *Studies in Canadian Literature/Études en literature canadienne* 33.1 (2008): 272–90. Print.
Söderlind, Sylvia. "Ghost-National Arguments." *University of Toronto Quarterly* 75.2 (Spring 2006): 673–92. Print.
– *Margin/alias: Language and colonization in Canadian and Québécois Fiction*. Toronto: University of Toronto Press, 1991. Print.
Spillers, Hortense. "All the Things You Could Be by Now, If Sigmund Freud's Wife Was Your Mother: Psychoanalysis and Race." *boundary 2* 23.3 (Autumn 1996): 75–141. Print.
– "Mama's Baby, Papa's Maybe. An American Grammar Book." *Diacritics* 17.2 (Summer 1987): 249–61. Print.
– "Whatcha Gonna Do?: Revisiting 'Mama's Baby, Papa's Maybe: An American Grammar Book': A Conversation with Hortense Spillers, Saidiya Hartman, Farah Jasmine Griffin, Shelly Eversley & Jennifer Morgan."*Women's Studies Quarterly* 35.1/2 (Spring – Summer 2007): 299–309. Print.
Sturgess, Charlotte. "Dionne Brand: Writing the Margins." *Caribbean Women Writers: Fiction in English*. Ed. Mary Condé and Thorunn Lonsdale. London: Palgrave, 1999. 202–216. Print.
"Strike Multiculturalism From the National Vocabulary." Editorial. *Globe and Mail* [Toronto] 8 October 2010. Web. 5 Nov. 2010.
Sullivan, Shannon. *Revealing Whiteness: The Unconscious Habits of Racial Privilege*. Bloomington, IN: Indiana UP, 2006. Print.
Superwoman. "Response to Racist Brampton Girl." *Youtube*. Web. 25 June 2012.
Szeman, Imre. *Zones of Instability: Literature, Postcolonialism, and the Nation*. Baltimore: The John Hopkins University Press, 2003. Print.
Taylor, Charles. "The Politics of Recognition." *Philosophical Arguments*. Cambridge, MA: Harvard University Press, 1995. 225–56. Print.
ThatIndianG. "Racist White Girl Hates Brown People?!?!" *Youtube*. Web. 10 July 2012.
Thobani, Sunera. *Exalted Subjects: Studies in the Making of Race and Nation in Canada*. Toronto: University of Toronto Press, 2007. Print.

Thomson Jr., Kenneth. "'Put Yourself in Officer's Situation.'" Letter. *Toronto Star* 3 Sept. 1979: A9. Print.

Tölölyan, Khachig. "Rethinking Diaspora(s): Stateless Power in the Transnational Moment." *Diaspora*. 5.1 (1996): 3–35. Print.

Townshend, Errol. "Abuse of Power the Issue in Johnson Killing." *Contrast* [Toronto] 20 Sept. 1979: 9. Print.

Trudeau, Pierre Elliott. "Canadian Culture: Announcement of Implementation of Policy of Multiculturalism within Bilingual Framework." In Canada. Parliament. House of Commons. *Debates*. 28th Parliament. Vol. 9 (8 Oct. 1971). 8545. Print.

Van Hear, Nicholas. *New Diasporas: The Mass Exodus, Dispersal and Regrouping of Migrant Communities.* London: University College London Press, 1998. Print.

Vassanji, M.G. *The Gunny Sack*. Toronto: Anchor Press, 2005. Print.

– *The In-Between World of Vikram Lall*. Toronto: Knopf, 2004. Print.

– *No New Land*. Toronto: McClelland & Stewart Ltd, 1991. Print.

Walcott, Derek. "The Muse of History." *The Routledge Reader in Caribbean Literature*. Ed. Alison Donnell and Sarah Lawson Welsh. London: Routledge, 1996. 354–58. Print.

Walcott, Rinaldo. *Black Like Who: Writing Black Canada*. Toronto: Insomniac Press, 2003. Print.

– "Disgraceful: Intellectual Dishonesty, White Anxieties, and Multicultural Critique Thirty-Six Years Later." *Home and Native Land: Unsettling Multiculturalism in Canada*. Ed. May Chazan, et al. Toronto: Between The Lines, 2012. 15–30. Print.

– "The Desire to Belong: The Politics of Texts and Their Politics of Nation." *Floating the Border*. Ed. Nurjehan Aziz. Toronto: TSAR, 1999. 61–79. Print.

Wallace, Michelle. "A Black Feminist's Search for Sisterhood" *All the Women Are White, All the Blacks Are Men, but Some of Us Are Brave*. Ed. Gloria T. Hull, Patricia Bell Scott, and Barbara Smith. New York: The Feminist Press, 1982. 5–12. Print.

Ward, Frederick. "*Dialogue #1, Mama.*" Clarke 18–19. Print.

Ware, Tracy. "The Unmaking of Modern Poetry in Canada." Rev. of *Bolder Flights: Essays on the Canadian Long Poem*, Ed. Frank M. Tierney and Angela Robbeson. *Canadian Poetry* 46. Web. 10 July 2009.

West, Cornel. *Race Matters*. Boston: Beacon Press, 1993. Print.

"What Judge Dunlop Told the Jury." *Contrast* [Toronto] 21 Nov 1980: 8. Print.

White, Evelyn C. "'Soul Survivors' Rev. of *What We All Long For* by Dionne Brand." *Canadian Literature* 188 (Spring 2006): 183–4. Print.

Wiens, Jason. "'Language Seemed to Split in Two': National Ambivalence(s) and Dionne Brand's 'No Language Is Neutral'." *Essays on Canadian Writing* 70 (2000): 81–102. Print.

Woodsworth, J.S. *Strangers within Our Gates*. Toronto: Doreen Stephen Books, 1909. Print.

Wyile, Herb. *Speaking in the Past Tense: Canadian Novelists on Writing Historical Fiction*. Waterloo, ON: Wilfrid Laurier Press, 2007. Print.

Wynter, Sylvia. "Unsettling the Coloniality of Being/Power/Truth/Freedom: Towards the Human, after Man, Its Overrepresentation – An Argument." *The New Centennial Review* 3.3 (Fall 2003): 257–337. Print.

– "Towards the Sociogenic Principle: Fanon, Identity, the Puzzle of Conscious Experience." *National Identities and Socio-Political Changes in Latin America*. Ed. Mercedes F. Durán-Cogan and Antonio Gómez-Moriana. New York: Routledge, 2001: 30–6. Print.

– "The Pope Must Be Drunk, the King of Castile a Madman: Culture as Actuality and the Caribbean Rethinking of Modernity." *Reordering of Culture: Latin America, the Caribbean and Canada in the 'Hood*. Ed. Alvina Ruprecht and Cecilia Taiana. Ottawa: Carleton University Press, 1995: 17–41. Print.

xtheWitnessx. "My Advice to the Racist Brampton Girl – Kyla Pawis." *Youtube.* Web. 1 Aug. 2012.

Yalden, Maxwell. "Invited Address: Multiculturalism – An Anniversary Celebration." *Canadian Ethnic Studies/ Études ethniques au Canada*. 43.1–2 (2011): 5–15. Print.

Index

www.ingramcontent.com/pod-product-compliance
Lightning Source LLC
LaVergne TN
LVHW090807070826
844660LV00022B/1104

* 9 7 8 1 4 4 2 6 1 5 7 6 2 *